T0341356

CONSPIRACY THEORY IN LATIN LITERATURE

Ashley and Peter Larkin Series in Greek and Roman Culture

CONSPIRACY THEORY
in LATIN LITERATURE

VICTORIA EMMA PAGÁN

FOREWORD BY MARK FENSTER

UNIVERSITY OF TEXAS PRESS
Austin

Copyright © 2012 by the University of Texas Press
All rights reserved
Printed in the United States of America
First edition, 2012

Requests for permission to reproduce material from this work should be sent to:
Permissions
University of Texas Press
P.O. Box 7819
Austin, TX 78713-7819
www.utpress.utexas.edu/index.php/rp-form

♾ The paper used in this book meets the minimum requirements of
ANSI/NISO Z39.48-1992 (R1997) (Permanence of Paper).

LIBRARY OF CONGRESS CATALOGING-IN-PUBLICATION DATA
Pagán, Victoria Emma, 1965–
Conspiracy theory in Latin literature / by Victoria Emma Pagán.
pages.   cm. — (Ashley and Peter Larkin series in Greek and Roman culture)
ISBN 978-0-292-75680-9
1. Conspiracy theories—Rome.   2. Rome—History.   3. Conspiracy in literature.
4. Juvenal—Criticism and interpretation.   5. Tacitus, Cornelius—Criticism and
interpretation.   6. Suetonius, ca. 69–ca. 122—Criticism and interpretation.
I. Title.   II. Series: Ashley and Peter Larkin series in Greek and Roman culture.
DG211.P343   2012
870.9′3556—dc23
2012016119
doi: 10.7560/739727

First paperback edition, 2013

For Andy
AEI

. . . solum insidiarum remedium esse sensit, si non intellegerentur.

She figured the only way to avoid the plot was to seem unaware of it.

———

TACITUS, *Annales* 14.6.1

CONTENTS

FOREWORD

On occasion, a harried reporter contacts me to ask what I think about some present conspiracy theory infecting the republic. Explain this craziness to us, Professor. Is the United States a nation of nutcases, or what? Dinner party conversation often transpires similarly when a new acquaintance learns that I've written a book about conspiracy theory. How interesting, the companion states, before he or she declares with confidence that those crazy believers (who, not coincidentally, believe something opposite to the speaker) are unique to our time, our culture, our nation.

This lay impulse neatly tracks a more ambitious intellectual and academic perspective that understands what it sees as conspiracy theorists' paranoia as a functional but irrational response to stimuli extant in the political air—stimuli from which elites are curiously immune, despite their own willingness to view theorists' political organization itself as something of a conspiracy. Some of the academic work on conspiracy theory thus frames the object of its research as merely the product of particular conditions unique to the time period and culture under consideration, one that can simply be diagnosed as a dysfunction and pathology produced by and contingent on present events.

The error in these assumptions is obvious to historians and comparativists—or, really, to anyone with a memory or who has traveled. It ignores that previous periods and other popular and political cultures harbor groups and individuals who view the world around them as orchestrated by powerful characters who operate off stage. Viewing the current political leadership as criminally illegitimate; the moneyed elite as holding excessive and unchecked control; a foreign power as holding too much influence over domestic events, or a racial, ethnic, or religious Other as an existential threat to the nation—none of these is a new phenomenon. Indeed, such beliefs seem quite common if not endemic to modern democracies. (Allow me to defer for the moment the question of whether such views may on occasion be accurate.) Conspiracy

---

MARK FENSTER

theory serves as a rhetorical tool commonly used to persuade, build political organizations, and mobilize populations. To dismiss the fear of conspiracy as a unique expression of a presumptively irrational time and place is to miss the continuity of such fears across time and culture.

An opposite, equally ahistorical error in studies of conspiracy theory assumes that the fear of conspiracy is an *inevitable* element and failing of human thought. Some schools of social science and those who would dress their prejudices in a universalist cloak dismiss conspiracy theory as the paranoid ravings of lunatics or as a necessary and singular product of a particular type of political order, whether democracy or authoritarianism or primitive societies. Conspiracism, in this view, is the inexorable crutch on which the poor, benighted people lean when they find themselves frustrated or confused. But to dismiss the fear of conspiracy as an essential cognitive and social phenomenon is to miss the specific ways in which such fears manifest themselves in popular and political cultures.

These, then, constitute the dangers that any effort to describe and analyze conspiracy theories, whether as a general phenomenon or in a particular manifestation, must avoid: one should neither essentialize conspiracy theory, because doing so fails to view the important context from which it emerges and the role it plays in solidifying or disrupting the political order, nor view conspiracy theory as an idiosyncratic expression of a particular subculture or isolated individual, because doing so fails to view the broader cultural and social forms and patterns that such theories tend to share across time. Neither of these warnings seems unduly complicated, particularly for those working within humanistic, interpretive traditions wary of essentialism and vigilant about history and context. And yet, there's something about conspiracy theory, whether found in the past or present, that seems to cause commentators to lose their bearings. It leads writers to project a simplified narrative—conspiracy theorists are pathological!—upon precisely those they accuse of building their theories on simplistic misunderstandings of the present and past. It leads analysts also to overlook or deny inequities in the distribution of power, willful political machinations, and, occasionally, actual conspiracies (albeit in narrower forms).

Ironically, conspiracy theory spawns two intellectual communities: the conspiracy theorists who engage in their hermetic practice of (over-) interpretation to find conspiracies that threaten the republic by causing everything of consequence; and those who seek to condemn conspiracy theory in the broadest possible manner, who engage in an accusatory practice of finding conspiracy theorists who threaten the republic by roiling the margins. Every conspiracy theory is at once similar and distinct. It tells a particular story about the teller and the world he describes, but in doing so it appropriates a narrative structure and mode of interpretation that conspiracy theories before and after it have also used.

Although I am not a classicist, my pleasure in Victoria Pagán's *Conspiracy Theory in Latin Literature* comes precisely from her ability to make the ancient world's anxiety about secret power and plots both familiar and strange. She identifies how Roman elites, poets, and historians utilized conspiracy as a trope and storytelling device, a rhetorical means to call listeners to action, and a strategy both to supplement the unknown with the known and to replace uncertain causes with real actors—all in ways not too dissimilar from contemporary deployments of conspiracy narratives. But also like modern versions, Roman conspiracy rhetoric did not serve simply as an instrumental means to achieve political goals. It arose from and thrived in mystery, filling gaps to support conjectures in the face either of inexplicable events or of informational asymmetry, when those who know the truth about certain suspect events refuse to disclose it.

Pagán leads us to the courtroom and the stage and through oratory, poetry, and history so that we might see how speakers and authors explicitly or implicitly used the specter of conspiracy to persuade and educate. In doing so, she does not attempt to show, in didactic, History Network style, how Romans were conspiracy theorists in ways that we can comfortably recognize. Rather, she illustrates how these are distinctively Roman conspiracy theories that work within distinctively Roman genres and respond to specific circumstances and historic events. As merely one example that in broad outline seems to resemble modern day Jeremiads, Juvenal's *Satires* offers a deeply xenophobic and paranoid vision of the events and circumstances they describe. As Pagán shows, however, the texts are ambiguous as to the author's relationship to its characters; invoking conspiracy (among other things) within a complex genre, the *Satires* multiply the possible meanings and cloud the intent of Juvenal's speech act. Pagán pays careful attention to the distance at which she must work when she discusses such texts; she recognizes the dangers of anachronistic argument and of projecting onto the past either our current understanding of conspiracy or our anxieties about those who believe in it.

In so doing, Pagán offers a snapshot of Roman culture and society with its many fissures, habitual violence, and code of honor; its complex politics, social hierarchies, and difficult relationships with foreigners and slaves; and above all, the deep-seated suspicions and outright paranoia of its leaders and subjects. Invited to view conspiracy theory anew, the reader might well return to her own age suspicious of conspiracy theory; if she does, having read of the emperors whom the Roman texts describe and the people they rule, she will also harbor a sense that there may well be someone out to get her (and us), and that they're using our own fears to do so.

ACKNOWLEDGMENTS

This book stems from my participation in the conference "Dark Powers: Conspiracy Theory in History and Fiction" at the University of Konstanz in May 2006. I am grateful to Eva Horn and Anson Rabinbach for the invitation, for the travel support, and for editing the proceedings that appeared in the *New German Critique*. Parts of chapters of this book were presented at the meetings of the American Philological Association (Chicago 2008), the Classical Association of the Middle West and South (Tucson 2008), the University of North Carolina–Greensboro (2008), Washington University in St. Louis (2011), and the Classical Association of the Canadian West (Winnipeg 2009), where I was honored to be the keynote speaker. On each occasion I benefited from the audiences' keen insights.

Research for this project was made possible by two generous Humanities Enhancement Grants from the University of Florida College of Liberal Arts and Sciences in the summers of 2006 and 2009. Timely completion was ensured by the intervening support of the Department of Classical Studies in the spring of 2007 and by the award of the Waldo W. Neikirk Term Professorship in the College of Liberal Arts and Sciences for 2008–2009.

It remains a singular pleasure to work with Jim Burr, humanities editor; Nancy Moore, copy editor; and the production staff at the University of Texas Press. Two anonymous referees gave thoughtful comments, suggestions, and corrections that caused me to rethink the shape of the book and its outcomes. For reading drafts at various stages along the way, I thank Rhiannon Ash, Susanna Braund, Shawn Daniels, Mary Ann Eaverly, Mark Fenster, Sharon James, Wayne Losano, Eleni Manolaraki, Carole Newlands, Marjorie Pagán, Joseph Roisman, and Andy Wolpert. Blake Landor and Christopher McHale of the Smathers Libraries at the University of Florida were always, within minutes, at my assistance. I am especially grateful to Robert Wagman, Allan Burns, David Pharies, and Paul D'Anieri for the steadfast leadership that granted me the peace of mind to write this book.

Abraham Ricardo and Natalie Eleutheria Wolpert deserve special mention for their maturity, goodwill, and sweetness; I love them dearly. I acknowledge once again the extended families of Pagáns and Wolperts for their continued encouragement of my endeavors as a professor and mother. My deepest gratitude is reserved for my husband, Andy, who helps me in more ways than I can enumerate, who makes every minute count, and to whom I dedicate yet another book on conspiracy—for reasons best left to conjecture.

CONSPIRACY THEORY IN LATIN LITERATURE

From CONSPIRACY to
CONSPIRACY THEORY

"Why do many bad things happen to good people?"[1] To this perennial question Seneca's *De Providentia* is a reasoned response constructed according to
the precepts of Stoic philosophy: fortune is fickle, capricious, and unstable;
fate is steadfast and irrevocable; evil cannot befall a good person, since oppo-
sites do not admit each other. In fact, Seneca argues, apparent evils are actually occasions for virtue: "Disaster is virtue's opportunity."[2] Seneca harnesses
fortune's caprice in service of fate's purpose. Only those who triumph over
calamity can prove their virtue. Therefore, the good person willingly accepts
fate because the creator has endowed him with the capacity to endure whatever comes his way. The Stoic *sapiens* is thus supposed to believe not that bad
things happen to good people but that divine Providence sends trials the good
person ought to welcome so as to prove his virtue. Tribulation is necessary and
good, and if life's trials become too much to bear, Providence gives the wise
person the option of suicide. Seneca provides a list of famous men who em-
braced their misfortunes as opportunities to display their prowess: Decimus
Mucius, Fabricius, Rutilius, Regulus, Socrates, and, above all, Cato. These
are exceptional men with an exceptional answer to a very ordinary question.

What about the average (less-ideal, less-virtuous) person's answer to the
perplexing question of why bad things happen to good people? The norma-
tive is more likely to be found in texts selected from across Latin literature
that reflect a wide range of temporal, social, and literary registers: comedy,
oratory, satire, history, and biography. Literary characters make radical conjectures about people of certain social standing to explain why bad things
happen to good people. Social stereotypes explain the otherwise unproven—
and often unprovable—causes of misfortune. Without solid evidence, average people ascribe blame and can be disposed toward the seemingly irresist-
ible "temptation of conspiracy theory"—in the seminal formulation of Dieter
Groh.[3] Scapegoats are easy enough to find in Roman literature; women,
slaves, and foreigners make easy targets. The social equality of the senatorial

elite, on the other hand, complicates the efficacy of conjecture, while the extraordinary status of emperors renders it a necessary defense mechanism. Yet the social dynamics of conjecture are more complex than would appear at first glance, with residual effects that tell us much about Roman attitudes toward uncertainty.

Conjecture is made necessary by a lack of knowledge; it attempts to explain an event and attribute causes to a particular agent. Conjecture offers an explanation — right or wrong — in spite of uncertainty. It is based on appearances or indications that in and of themselves are inadequate but that can achieve the status of fact when supported by a series of irrefutable examples. Yet conjecture also serves a useful purpose. Unproven but not apparently contradicted, it allows for the quick circumvention of an epistemological impasse. It is an everyday mechanism that facilitates progress beyond (or at least around) the brink of uncertainty. Assumptions and small conjectures allow us to get on with our lives. At the polar ends of the ethical spectrum, conjecture either repairs (when exercised cautiously) or damages (when exercised rashly) social bonds; therefore, it must be exercised responsibly. Who can be trusted to conjecture? Who is reckoned so untrustworthy as to invite it and on what grounds?

Conspiracy theory accounts for the epistemological, social, and ethical concerns at the heart of this investigation. Furthermore, a sophisticated body of scholarship on conspiracy theory has emerged in the last twenty years, making it a viable and valuable critical tool and one that is only now making its mark on the study of classical antiquity. Roman literature radiates a sense of conspiracy theory because the Romans did not shy away from conjecture, even if they were not always conscious of its effects, both constitutive and corrosive, on their society.

In this introduction I describe the salient features of conspiracy theory, defend its usefulness as a critical lens, situate my contribution within the growing scholarship on the more general phenomenon of conspiracy in antiquity, and outline the contents of the remaining chapters.

THE POWER OF CONSPIRACY THEORY

According to philosopher Charles Pigden, "A conspiracy is a secret plan on the part of a group to influence events partly by covert action."[4] This neutral definition situates conspiracy squarely in the realm of social intercourse, thereby keeping the social aspect at the forefront of attention at all times. In the words of David Coady, "It is impossible to conspire alone."[5] When two conspire, they necessarily plot against a third party. Examples of betrayed conspiracies in Roman political history include the well-known Catilinarian conspiracy of 63 B.C.E. and the Pisonian conspiracy of 65 C.E. The assassination of Julius Caesar in 44 B.C.E. is the paradigmatic successful conspiracy. Historians composed narratives of these secretive events that posited a chain of causality from beginning to end. The historians sought to contain fear of such internal threats and to deter future attempts at conspiracy.[6] To distance the grim events from the more celebratory and uplifting achievements of the Romans, the conspiracies and their explanations were presented as exceptional.[7]

Most people have a rough idea of conspiracy theory based on a set of preconceived (and traditionally negative) assumptions; however, Brian Keeley offers a somewhat neutral definition as a useful starting point:

A conspiracy theory is a proposed explanation of some historical event (or events) in terms of the significant causal agency of a relatively small group of persons—the conspirators—acting in secret. . . . It proffers an *explanation* of the event in question. It proposes reasons why the event occurred.[8]

Conspiracy theory is a secondary phenomenon that arises in the wake of events; it is not a causal agent in and of itself but rather a response to an event. The key component of conspiracy theory is conjecture, the attempt at explanation. As a crisis of epistemology, conspiracy theory is not negligible; it tells us a great deal about the range of responses to *aporia* ("doubt"), knowledge, and the shadowy zone between fact and fabrication. It rushes in, so to speak, to fill the vacuum left by a lack of knowledge about an event, its causes, and the motivation of its agents.

Inherent in the notion of conspiracy theory is a belief that some covert but influential agency is responsible for an unexplained event. Thus, *conspiracism*, a recently coined word that entered the on-line version of the *Oxford English Dictionary* in draft form only in June 2005, is a belief that major historical and political events are brought about as the result of a conspiracy between interested parties. Conspiracism and conspiracy theory can be used synonymously because the conspiracy theorist believes that hidden forces are at work, machinating plots known to only the powerful.

Belief also contributes to the success of a conspiracy. In increasingly colorful terms, Pigden asserts that conspirators

must believe that there are other people who believe (or can be made to believe) that they face a problem with the same solution. (This last belief must be true, or the conspiracy will never get off the ground.) They must believe that these other people can be relied on not to blab (otherwise the conspiracy will leak like a sieve).[9]

Pigden's spirited diction ("get off the ground," "not to blab," and "leak like a sieve") suggests to me a nagging discomfort with the duplicity of belief. As conspirators are bound to each other by belief in a common goal, so conspiracy theorists believe that hidden forces are the causes of misfortune. Yet the double-edged sword cuts far more deeply. Because minority groups partake of different beliefs that are separate and distinct from the majority, they invite fear that generates hostility until at last this hostility becomes a collective force that shapes a society and its models of the self, and hence we have scapegoats.

In his provocative and influential discussion of "conspiracy mentality," social psychologist Serge Moscovici defines conspiracy theory, which resides at the "figurative or imaginary core of a social representation" and "forms a group of beliefs, practices, and languages that make a whole. It depends on collective adherence and leaves its mark on the personality of those who share in it."[10] Whether intentionally or not, conspiracy theory does more than attempt to develop a plausible chain of causality. By laying blame on certain groups, conspiracy theory creates and sustains individual identity as well as societal values. As it divides society against some members along lines of belief, it unites others in opposition.

Moscovici summarizes the psychological reasoning behind conspiracy theory that gives rise to the scapegoat: "Whoever feels deprived of something instinctively looks for a cause of the deprivation. More precisely, they look for who deprived them. To be even more precise, they look for a guilty party whom they can deprive in turn, on whom they can act out their aggressions."[11] An example of this pattern in Roman imperial history is the Great Fire of 64 C.E. Without sufficient proof as to its cause, conspiracy theories arose, and some blamed Nero for the disaster. As a sensible and trustworthy historian, Tacitus distanced himself from the controversy: "A disaster ensued, although it is uncertain whether by chance or by the treachery of the emperor (for historians hand down both versions of the story)."[12] Into the epistemological vacuum flooded competing popular explanations, including the belief that Nero ordered the fire.[13] To deflect these beliefs, Nero in turn blamed the Christians, who because of their alternative religious tenets were credible scapegoats. The Christians were persecuted not so much for the crime of arson as for an alleged "hatred of mankind" (*odio humani generis*).[14]

Although conspiracy and conspiracy theory are often difficult to disentangle, they differ in appreciable ways. Conspiracy is a historical phenomenon that influences political, social, or economic events. For example, certain persons may form a secret band to assassinate a dictator. The conspirators plot their actions so as to bring about this desired result. Two outcomes are possible. Either the conspirators succeed and the assassination is perpetrated or they are detected (and punished) and the goal is thwarted. While the conspiracy is afoot, the event approaches the zero-degree of revelation, the point where it is either successful or halted. Explanations that arise in relation to these kinds of conspiracies attempt to connect every step in the chain of causality, from the secret inception of the plot to its public revelation, brought about either by its success or by its apprehension and punishment: "a conspirator succeeds or dies."[15] The conspiracy becomes part of the historical record, and the theories put forth about it are the creation of the so-called "refining historians."[16] Historical explanations are given for the chain of causality that leads to the successful fulfillment of the conspirators' goal. Should the conspiracy fail, however, explanations are also offered for the chain of causality that leads to the betrayal and punishment of the conspirators.[17]

Conspiracy theory, on the other hand, is embedded more deeply within society. In an attempt to cope with the destruction wrought by an event, people blame unknown causes on those united by a bond of identity that is construed by the conspiracy theorists as secretive and sinister. Periods of large-scale social unrest tend to generate conspiracy theories that attribute blame to minority groups.[18] The ascription of blame is unfounded because the causes of the destructive event lie in an epistemological gap. Conspiracy theory meets the challenge of the lack of knowledge with a preponderance of explanation. At best, it holds out a hope of understanding, but conspiracy theory can also beget hatred and prejudice in response to resentment and misunderstanding.

Conspiracy surfaces as a response to a particular historical moment, while conspiracy theory is the manifestation of the frustration caused by the lack of knowledge at the core of any conspiracy. A conspiracy may reveal underlying socioeconomic tensions, but conspiracy theory sustains those tensions. Conspirators may eventually abandon a plot, but the conspiracy theory abides and eventually shapes society and its self-perception. In more concrete terms, a coup d'état or assassination points to social unrest, economic disparity, or political corruption. Conspiracy theory, on the other hand, can sustain lasting prejudices that justify and maintain unequal relations of power. In his analysis of the prevalence of conspiracy theories in nineteenth-century Europe, Raoul Girardet explains that conspiracy is a symptom of collective fear or distress:

Mais définie et développée à partir d'un obscur sentiment de menace, témoignage d'incertitude ou de panique, la mythologie de la Conspiration

---

tend en même temps à apparaître comme la projection négative d'aspirations tacites, l'expression inversée de souhaits plus ou moins conscients, mais toujours inassouvis ("But defined and developed out of an obscure sense of threat, evidence of uncertainty or panic, the mythology of the conspiracy tends at the same time to appear as the negative projection of tacit aspirations, the inverted expression of wishes more or less conscious, but still unfulfilled").

The "mythology of conspiracy" turns the tables: the power that conspirators are accused of amassing and are imagined to hold is in direct proportion to the power that conspiracy theorists desire for themselves. In the face of conspirators and in the service of their own cause, conspiracy theorists claim a complete mastery of events and thus a capacity for social control.[19]

To explain the way the discourse of conspiracy theory can exert social control and construct social forms, I rely on Bruce Lincoln's anthropological analysis of the relationship between history and myth. In his three-dimensional configuration, history and myth are plotted along axes of credibility, claims to truth, and authority.[20] Conspiracy theory can also be located along these coordinates. Conspiracy theory is a kind of story telling that makes claims to credibility and truth. In this sense it is much like history; however, history authorizes its claims with evidence and testimony. Because in conspiracy theory evidence and testimony are either compromised or lacking altogether, claims to credibility and truth are insubstantial. The authority upon which research and narrative rest is fundamentally different; unlike conspiracy theory, history derives its authority from evidence. Evidence for the conspiracy theorist, on the other hand, tantalizes—always within reach yet slipping through the grasp. Unable to make successful claims for the status of truth, the conspiracy theorist ends up constructing only a blueprint onto which truth can be mapped but always in part and with flaws. Should the evidence ever present itself, the conspiracy theory would materialize into history; in this way Mark Felt enters the history books as Watergate's secret informant "Deep Throat."[21] Thus, conspiracy theorists (aspiring historians) cannot completely usurp the function and power of the historian, but they can manipulate that function and power.

According to Lincoln, credibility and truth claims alone are not catalysts for social construction; rather, a change in authority initiates social change: "A narrative possessed of authority is one for which successful claims are made not only to the status of truth, but what is more, to the status of *paradigmatic* truth." The shift renders a narrative that does more than just convey information; the narrative becomes "a discursive act through which actors evoke the sentiments out of which society is actively constructed."[22] Lincoln's anthropological model is useful because it allows for an understanding of different kinds of political myths, depending on the various mutations of authority. For my purposes, conspiracy theory is a particular kind of political myth in which authority is mutated by the absence of positive evidence.[23]

Conspiracy theory posits credibility and truth but with shifted, indeed vanishing authority, so that it becomes an imperative to action:[24] punish the conspirators, protect against them, root them out, be vigilant, keep them in their place. Unlike history that supports its claims of causality, the very lack of plausibility means that the producers and consumers of conspiracy theory cannot afford to be inert. Conspiracy theory abhors complacency and demands action. According to Lincoln, in response to such a political myth, a society can reconstruct accustomed social forms, construct novel social forms, or change its nature altogether.[25] Attention to conspiracy theory in ancient Rome will afford a glimpse of one type of political mythology and its effect upon society.

Any attempt at an objective and unbiased definition of conspiracy theory is at the mercy of a vocabulary whose semantics is largely pejorative. No doubt, in the main, conspiracy is polemical; it is attributed to one's enemies. It need not have substance to achieve the desired effect; to hurl the accusation of conspiracy against another is a powerful way of discrediting one's opponent. Those who claim the act of conspiracy for themselves, on the other hand, commit an act of resistance; admitting conspiracy is a desperate act. As Carl Graumann puts it, "Conspiracy as well as *Verschwörung* were never meant to be descriptive but to denounce adversaries and their activities."[26] The problem is likewise found in the Latin vocabulary of conspiracy.[27] Etymologically, the word *coniuratio* is neutral; it refers simply to the act of taking an oath or joining in league with others for a common purpose. Historically, the word referred to the soldiers' oath of allegiance, taken in times of extreme and sudden danger. Thus, initially it was a legitimate measure taken by law-abiding citizens dedicated to defending the Republic; neither wholly positive nor negative, *coniuratio* was necessary. After Cicero's denunciation of Catiline, however, the word is rarely employed without inescapable negative connotations and is practically synonymous with *tumultus, seditio,* and *insidiae,* for example, words that denote upheaval, unrest, and treachery.[28]

Furthermore, the very term *conspiracy theory* embodies a certain irony. To operate, a conspiracy must attempt to leave no trace of evidence. In a conspiracy, evidence, with its root in the Latin verb *videre* meaning "to see," is *in*visible. These evidential blind spots stymie the historian, whose etymology is derived from the Greek *historia,* a learning or knowing by inquiry. In turn, *historia* is rooted in the Greek verb *horao,* "I see." The perfect tense, *oida,* from which *historia* derives, thus means, "I have seen—and therefore I know."

Evidence of a conspiracy denies and defies visual verification. On the other hand, theory, rooted in the Greek *theorema*, meaning "sight," is a hypothesis that has been confirmed by observation and is propounded as accounting for known facts. It starts with a set of assumptions and then makes a statement about a phenomenon that is supported by evidence. Furthermore, if the function of theory is to simplify and to explain, conspiracy theory complicates and fails to explain.[29] The result is a palpable tension between a theory—intended to clarify and predicated on evidence—and a conspiracy—intended to obscure and predicated on the absence of evidence.[30] Inherent in conspiracy theory is a dialectic between the seen and the unseen, the explainable and the inexplicable. With its every use, the term recreates and renegotiates the disparity, giving conspiracy theory its allure—and frustration. Conspiracy theory bespeaks the very epistemological rupture it attempts to mend.

CONSPIRACY THEORY AS A CRITICAL LENS

Conspiracy theory is a distinctly modern sociological phenomenon for which there is no lexical equivalent in Latin or Greek. Yet recent debates about the value of conspiracy theory prove that it can have a profound impact on our understanding of antiquity; however, certain preconceived notions need to be systematically dismantled.

The term *conspiracy theory* usually evokes the petty cobwebs spun by a paranoid kook who thinks that there are evil, unseen forces at work; that powerful groups control events for their own purposes; and that the individual is impotent before these dark powers. The conspiracy theorist proves the existence of these dark forces by hunting down clues, which he is far more perceptive in apprehending than the average individual. Conspiracy theory appears to be the antithesis of formal, rigorous, scientific inquiry. Not only is the conspiracy theorist skeptical of rational explanations, he in turn invites skepticism. Thus, the conspiracy theorist is marginalized by virtue of the skepticism he practices and provokes. Unable or unwilling to admit a fundamental ignorance, he concocts far-fetched explanations that blame covert agents for the disasters that befall him and his society. Much of this perception (perpetuated in Hollywood film and popular media) derives from the frequently cited essay by Richard Hofstadter, who identifies the so-called "paranoid style" of American politics and candidly brands it as decidedly pejorative. The conspiracy theorist, according to Hofstadter, is suspicious of a vast and sinister conspiracy; he is a militant leader whose enemy is clearly delineated. He relies on overwhelming, yet pedantic evidence that although rooted in verifiable facts, is nevertheless marred by leaps of imagination at critical junctures.[31]

Yet the pejorative label "conspiracy theorist," flung at an enemy, dismisses the possibility that he may be on to something.[32] It is precisely this potential for unwanted, uncontrolled exposure that makes it so important to shut down conspiracy theory and shut up the conspiracy theorist.[33] Such a contemptuous stance ought to be rejected on the grounds that it is uncritical[34] and hinders the quest for transparency. Even if such a static perception of conspiracy theory were accurate, it does not explain why it is so prevalent and persistent. According to Lee Basham, we live in a Golden Age of conspiratorial thinking.[35] Why do people produce and consume conspiracy theories?[36] What is the appeal of this seemingly irrational mode of thought? Why can't we ignore conspiracy theory?

By taking such questions as their starting point, Mark Fenster (1999, revised 2008), Peter Knight, and Timothy Melley (whose books appeared concurrently in 2000) justify conspiracy theory as a useful approach to understanding modern contemporary culture; each contributes a useful facet to the composite approach that I take to conjecture and to social status in Latin literature. Rather than dismiss conspiracy theory as the domain of the paranoid, they seek to bring it into the light, into discussions of contemporary politics and social intercourse. So for Fenster, conspiracy theory is a kind of political resistance; although unsuccessful at accomplishing any permanent change, nevertheless it calls the existing power structures into question and forces a reconsideration of facts and explanations for historical events. To regard conspiracy theory as paranoia, or even a paranoid style, is not productive; Fenster seeks to engage with conspiracism as a valid mode of discourse in its own right. If conspiracy theorists, forced to occupy the fringes of society, are marginalized persons seeking a voice, then perhaps in the spirit of open dialogue it is worth listening to what they have to say, even if they are wrong. In the end, however, Fenster must admit that "conspiracy theory ultimately fails as a political and cultural practice."[37]

Knight nuances his contribution as a study of conspiracy culture; only an understanding of the popular appeal of conspiracy will allow us to curb "its worst excesses (or even its creative ironies)."[38] Rather than seek a mechanism by which conspiracy theory operates, Knight observes the ways the phenomenon shapes contemporary American culture. Although he predictably uses as his case studies the conspiracy theories surrounding the assassination of President John F. Kennedy and the popularity of the 1990s American television series, *The X Files*, Knight contributes more substantively in the chapters analyzing the conspiracy theories that attend feminism and racism in the United States. The rhetoric of feminism is suffused with hints of conspiracies, either of women or against women; likewise, the prominence of conspiracy theories in African American communities reveals anxiety over institutionalized racism. The existence of conspiracies by women or African Americans is not the point. Rather, the capacity for conspiracy theory to speak to the unequal relations of power attests its ability to permeate society deeply. Conspiracy theory raises the hope of an explanation for otherwise incomprehensible (or embarrassing or uncomfortable) attitudes and behaviors.

Melley attempts to demonstrate that the tendency toward conspiracy theory in the United States is a distinctly post–World War II phenomenon driven by a sense of individual autonomy in decline. The rise of conspiracy and paranoia "is connected to changing social and technological conditions and to new conceptions of human subjectivity."[39] Melley coins the term *agency panic* to refer to the anxiety about an apparent loss of autonomy or self-control that is mapped onto explanations of events as the result of a conspiracy—something out of one's control. Conspiratorial interpretations restore a sense of freedom and control in the quest for predictability.[40]

All three contributions force us to consider the usefulness of conspiracy theory to society and its usefulness as a critical perspective. Fenster is the first to contend that any society that imagines itself as originating from—or aspiring to—a liberal position must at least acknowledge the existence of conspiracy theory within the parameters of its discourse.[41] Knight's interpretations politicize the inequalities of race and gender. Melley's agency panic explains the way conspiracy theory mediates the relationship between the individual and society.

Conspiracy theory may thus serve a positive purpose. At the least, it can articulate alternative points of view, and in this sense conspiracy theory is a vehicle for debate and self-examination. Pigden argues that a universal presumption against conspiracy theories is itself a superstition: "Where the evidence suggests a conspiracy, we are quite at liberty to believe in it."[42] That is to say, conspiracy theory has its merits, and Coady emerges as one of its more vocal proponents. The conspiracy theorist has a special role in society; his job is "to investigate officialdom."[43] Coady defends conspiracy theorists from charges of irrationality, and though he admits that sometimes the unfavorable label is warranted, he seeks to disentangle the morality of rationality that others so readily lump together. The conspiracy theorist performs an important task on behalf of the community, but with moral and epistemic risks; however, those prone to excessive belief in conspiracies harm only themselves, while those prone to summary dismissal of conspiracies potentially allow universal harm to come to all members of the community.[44] Arguing against the primacy of radically socialized knowledge proposed by Neil Levy (which I discuss below), Coady asserts that intellectually autonomous people do not deserve to be called conspiracy theorists in a pejorative sense simply because they reject the "information cascade," or *ad populum* arguments based on common sense or received tradition.[45] The conspiracy theorist's skepticism is vital to the health and welfare of a social and political community. So, for example, in his study of the rhetoric of conspiracy in democratic Athens, Joseph Roisman discerns "positive plotting" and argues that "it was thanks to the belief in plots and the plot detectors that faith in the validity of basic values and the existing system could be reaffirmed."[46] Who engages in conspiracy theorizing, when, where, and why are important factors in the legitimization of conspiracy theory.[47]

Conspiracy theory has its opponents. In his conservative attack, Levy argues that engaging in conspiracy theory is bad because the conspiracy theorist willfully disengages from society and, in so doing, from the ability to engage in genuine enquiry, including the enquiry needed to evaluate a conspiracy theory properly. For Levy, "a conspiracy theory that conflicts with the official story, where the official story is the explanation offered by the (relevant) *epistemic authorities*, is *prima facie* unwarranted."[48] Such epistemic authorities are constituted on the model of science; they achieve knowledge based on a socially distributed network of trained inquirers.[49] The conspiracy theorist overestimates his individual ability to explain; he rejects the socially embedded network of knowledge and thereby isolates himself. Yet in the event of a failure of epistemic authority, the conspiracy theorist should not cut himself off "from the very resources one needs to correct one's beliefs," a move that "requires a measure of epistemic humility that is far greater than we are accustomed to, or accustomed to counting as a virtue."[50] Levy's expressed need for humility implies that the conspiracy theorist is egotistical, ready to trust his own knowledge base over received tradition, common sense, or a body of knowledge systematically generated by epistemic authorities. Levy's thesis hinges on his untenable definition of "epistemic authorities," which Coady sufficiently dismantles: no structure or science satisfactorily lives up to the criteria that Levy proposes.[51] There are grounds for a partially pejorative sense of conspiracy theory, but not for a completely pejorative sense.

According to Steve Clarke, conspiracy theorists fail because they "are typically victims of a form of cognitive failure."[52] They are overwhelmed by a "degenerating research program" in which, contrary to a progressive research program, "successful novel predictions and retrodictions are not made. Instead, auxiliary hypotheses and initial conditions are successively modified in light of new evidence, to protect the original theory from apparent disconfirmation."[53] In other words, the conspiracy theorist will modify or even reject evidence so as to leave a preconceived explanation intact. The conspiracy theorist does this by subscribing to what social scientists call the "fundamental attribution error." When seeking to understand unknown causes, the overestimation of a dispositional explanation to the exclusion of a situational one is a widespread and frequent mistake. For example, one might believe that U.S. military leaders are conspiring to keep the public unaware of contact with alien species by appealing to the disposition toward conspiratorial paternalistic behavior.[54] Such conspiracy theories are flawed because they are highly dispositional. To abandon a conspiracy theory is to disregard a (highly appealing) dispositional reason in favor of a (more rational) situational one.[55] The persistence of conspiracy theory is a result of the fundamental attribution error that overemphasizes dispositional explanations that depend on character traits (e.g., the government is disposed to conceal information) and correspondingly underemphasizes situational explanations that depend on extenuating circumstances (nothing happened in Roswell, New Mexico).

Pigden rejects Clarke outright. He decries the fundamental attribution error as "simply absurd" and insists upon the value of dispositional evidence.[56] Coady is less strident. He argues that disposition and situation cannot and do not operate in isolation, but rather both are present and often complementary.[57] Revising his thesis, Clarke concedes that "plausible explanations of behavior should appeal to a combination of situation and dispositions. . . . Behavior is the joint product of dispositions and situations, but the scope of the majority of dispositions is determined by situations."[58] Pigden is intent upon legitimizing conspiracy theory, and Coady considers Clarke together with Keeley and Basham as "being (no doubt inadvertently) enemies of the open society, because they discourage an activity that is essential to its survival, conspiracy theorizing."[59] My purpose is not nearly so polemical, and given my emphasis on conjecture, attention to the dispositional and situational explanations (one, or the other, or both) proffered by our ancient authors is, as I hope to show, an extremely productive way of looking at these texts.

Thus, the debate over the politics and epistemics rages, evidence that the study of conspiracy theory has moved well beyond the so-called "paranoid style." But it is also interesting to note that nearly every scholar who undertakes the subject includes a clear statement of position. Fenster is an unequivocal traveler: "Let me declare my own position clearly: There *are* elements of secret treachery in the contemporary political and economic order."[60] In contrast, Melley denies actively generating any conspiracy theory: "I want to make it clear that my intention here is not to weigh in on the validity of particular conspiracy theories."[61] Likewise Roisman, in his study of the rhetoric of conspiracy in the Attic orators, tries to resist: "Where proper or possible, I have tried to test the probability and substance of the orators' allegations, occasionally using the conspirator's analytical tools for this purpose, although with the hope of not falling into the enticing trap of conspiratorial logic."[62] In an attempt to take a social-anthropological approach to the study of conspiracy theory, the scholar armed with methodology and theoretical frameworks necessarily distances himself from the conspiracy theorists who, although they are the subject of study, appear to be the scholar's mirror image. The study of conspiracy theory is built on the twin pillars of self-reference and detachment, both of which serve to reinforce a distinction between "us," the rational scholars, and "them," the conspiracy theorists under scrutiny. When a scholar of conspiracy theory situates himself vis-à-vis the conspiracy theorist, he or she recapitulates the intellectual presumption against conspiracy as if to say, "You can trust me; I am a sensible scholar who declines to participate in conspiracy theory." The study of conspiracy theory always begins with a line in the sand.

This is in part because of the tendency for readers to assimilate the subject matter to the scholar, and nobody wants to be perceived as a conspiracy theorist. Coady presents an alternative:

> We could continue to talk about conspiracy theorists but without the negative connotations, and particularly without the connotations of irrationality, that currently go along with such talk. This approach is implied by my definition of a conspiracy theorist as a person who is unusually willing to investigate conspiracy. This definition, if accepted, should lead to conspiracy theorists being viewed as valued members of the community who undertake a morally and epistemically dangerous task that most of us don't have the stomach for.[63]

Scholars have a duty toward the morally and epistemically dangerous task, and in what follows I would rather risk the charge of being overly eager than overly reluctant to perceive conspiracy in the Roman literary imagination. Historians of women and slaves in antiquity know full well that a subject's systematic absence from the sources is not sufficient cause for willful neglect. A conspiratorial mindset attends a fair amount of Latin literature, yet because of the stigma attached to the notion of conspiracy, it has received little scholarly comment. This reticence is due in part to the nature of conspiracy; since it demands concealment, it will not be obvious in the sources and therefore in the scholarship. This concealment, however, has also served to naturalize the phenomenon. Thus, where conspiracy theory is not explicit, where it does not venture above the surface to announce its ideological purpose, it conveys its meaning unquestioned. It is my goal to question this latent conspiracism in Latin literature and to interrogate its possible ramifications.

In the last twenty years, social-psychological (Graumann and Moscovici), philosophical (Pigden, Keeley, Clarke, Basham, and Coady), and cultural (Fenster, Knight, and Melley) studies have advanced our understanding of conspiracy as a meaningful mode of critical thinking. In 2007, Coady edited a special issue of *Episteme: A Journal of Social Epistemology* on the theme "Conspiracy Theories," with contributions from eight philosophers, including Keeley, Clarke, and Pigden, whose groundbreaking work in 1999 and the early years of this decade have defined — and defended — the epistemology of conspiracy theory. The 2008 winter issue of the *New German Critique* contains the proceedings from the international conference "Dark Powers: Conspiracies in History and Fiction," held at the University of Konstanz in May 2006. The editors, Eva Horn and Anson Rabinbach, begin with the premise that "conspiracy theories have to be taken seriously as a mode and a model of critical political thinking."[64] Amid this steadily mounting attention across disciplines in the social sciences and humanities, conspiracy is at last recognized as a fruitful avenue of inquiry in the ancient Mediterranean world.

In his 2001 doctoral dissertation, Walter Spencer outlined a narrative structure in accounts of conspiracy and identified a "rhetoric of conspiracy" evident in Cicero and the historians. He began with an investigation into the notions of intrigue and subversion that suffuse Cicero's Verrine orations to demonstrate a "high degree of thematic stability" and "a vocabulary common to conspiracy stories."[65] He then turned to Livy's Bacchanalian affair, Tacitus' account of the Pisonian conspiracy, and Cicero's Catilinarian orations, to identify similar patterns in their story telling. Attention to diction reveals that the Romans had a distinct concept of conspiracy and consistent expressions of its morality.

My first book, *Conspiracy Narratives in Roman History* (2004), treated the narrative strategies that five prominent historians used to disclose events that had been deliberately shrouded in secrecy and silence. It compared how Sallust, Livy, and Tacitus constructed their accounts of the betrayed Catilinarian, Bacchanalian, and Pisonian conspiracies and revealed how a historical account of a secret event depends upon the transmittal of sensitive information from a private setting to the public sphere and why women and slaves often proved to be ideal transmitters of secrets. The analysis of Josephus' and Appian's accounts of the assassinations of Caligula and Julius Caesar showed how the two historians maintained suspense throughout their narratives despite a reader's prior knowledge of the outcomes. To narrate conspiracy, historians disconnect the possibilities of alternative narrative outcomes by assigning causality, even where it is tenuous. Above all, the book was concerned with the *writing* of conspiracy and with identifying the epistemic difficulties that a historian faces when embarking on a narrative of a conspiracy.

Roisman (2006) is the first to analyze the rhetoric of conspiracy in ancient Athens. He mines the corpus of Attic orators for evidence of a conspiratorial mindset and examines how such a worldview contributed to the maintenance of the Athenian democracy. He begins with the rhetoric of conspiracy as evidenced in cases of homicide and inheritance and in cases in which litigants attempt to entrap their opponent. He then moves to the rhetoric of conspiracy in the public sphere, with chapters devoted to the charges of conspiracy in speeches that deal with the internal politics of Athens, especially in the wake of the Thirty Tyrants. The last two chapters take up the rhetoric of conspiracy as it is employed in instances of foreign and international policy.

According to Roisman, the rhetoric of conspiracy is dynamic and fluid, a strategy useful in a wide variety of forensic and deliberative situations. Adapted by prosecutors and defendants, the rhetoric of conspiracy is deployed always to strengthen the litigant's case and to discredit his opponent's. In disputes over inheritance, the rhetoric of conspiracy compensates for a weak argument.[66] When a litigant claims entrapment, the rhetoric of conspiracy reminds jurors of the opponent's attempt to divert them from their obligation to justice.[67] Speakers who claim that the democracy is the target of a conspiracy sustain democratic ideology. By virtue of its "elasticity,"[68] the rhetoric of conspiracy can also apply to foreign policy. The ubiquity of the rhetoric of conspiracy therefore points to the receptiveness of the audience to this kind of thinking. Its prevalence derives from its efficacy.

From the rhetoric of conspiracy, Roisman draws conclusions about a conspiratorial mindset in ancient Athens. Amply attested across the board, the rhetoric of conspiracy was produced and consumed by the masses and by the elite, and it suggests an Athenian anxiety about conspiracy. With a suspicious worldview, the conspiracy "spoiler" had the ability to police Athenian society; in this sense, the rhetoric of conspiracy reminded fellow Athenians that their behavior was always under scrutiny and their attempts at conspiracy were detectable. Finally, Roisman collates the similarities between ancient and modern conspiracy theory: both design for themselves a perfect logic born of fantastic tales that explain hidden agendas. Both are born of a state of crisis in which scapegoats are blamed for the misfortunes of others. The major difference, according to Roisman, is that modern conspiracy theory will lay blame on nameless, impersonal groups, whereas in ancient Athens, "the notion of a single conspirator, a semantic oxymoron, posed no difficulties for the Athenians."[69]

While the rhetoric of conspiracy occupies Spencer and Roisman, Stephen Hinds (2007) formulates a "poetic of conspiracy," by which Ovid's poems convey an "excess of interpretive possibility." Hinds reviews the "history of Ovidian conspiracy theory" that attends the mystery of Ovid's exile, and, after presenting the evidence, he traces the explanations that have been given over the centuries. He argues that

> there is no fundamental difference in kind between the raving of the con-spiracy theorist who finds an Ovidian affair with the Elder Julia in the pseudonymity of Corinna . . . and . . . the investigative work of supposedly respectable Latinists like myself who find subtexts, and sub-subtexts. . . . We are all abnormal readers placing extraordinary pressure upon these poems to answer our questions on something . . . which just seems too important not to be answered.[70]

The poetry of Ovid makes conspiracy theorists of every reader.

Two articles on the reception of the Catilinarian conspiracy in European literature explore the relationship between the ancient conspiracy narratives of Sallust and Cicero and modern retellings. In George Chapman's early modern tragedy *The Conspiracy and Tragedy of Charles, Duke of Byron* (1608), a carpet is spread on which is depicted the Catilinarian conspiracy. But as Christine Sukic argues, the ecphrasis (description in verse of an object of art) is a stylistic device that replaces the narrative elements it should have contained. Both ecphrasis and conspiracy narrative are "unnarratable."[71] Michèle Lowrie takes up a nineteenth-century rendition of the Catilinarian conspiracy by Prosper Mérimée to examine the way he reduplicates the job of the "ancient 'detectives'" and "his awareness of the epistemological re-gress."[72] Her conclusions account for both "historiography and sovereignty." Conspiracy confounds the former because of the epistemological crisis that hampers narration, the latter because of the dissolved distinction between sovereign and citizen body.[73]

Spencer discerns patterns for narrating historical and political conspira-cies. Roisman identifies the rhetoric of conspiracy that speakers use to achieve their goals in court. Hinds deploys conspiracy theory as a mode of critical reading. Sukic and Lowrie explore the reception of ancient conspiracy narra-tive in modern literature. In spite of the growing body of scholarship, there is no study of conspiracy theory as a social construct and its expression in Latin literature.

This book attempts to excavate the ways Romans explained misfortunes to themselves by blaming others and how these latent, often negligible, seem-ingly harmless explanations can exert social control and construct social forms. A synchronic approach compensates for the scarcity of comprehen-sive sources that address a particular subject such as conspiracy, a plight typical of the study of the ancient Mediterranean world.[74] The extant sources register an elite bias, and care must be taken to avoid reinscribing the elite perspective. While it is easy enough to ascertain moments when marginalized groups are passively suspected of conspiracy, it is nearly impossible to detect the suspicions that such marginalized groups actively held. We would need the testimony *of* women, slaves, and other outsiders of this highly stratified society, not elite testimony *about* them.[75] By no means do I posit a static view of either conjecture or social status in ancient Rome; in the material from which I draw, the political, social, and economic structures of Rome underwent significant change. Rather, a heuristic approach reveals a general pattern of conspiracy theory that emerges from the dialectic between the constant and the variable factors of particular examples. Literary influence, allusivity, and intertextuality indicate the prevalence of intrinsic expressions of conspiracy from one author and age to the next, though the progression is not always linear. Questions of origin and development defer to contexts of literary production; prescription defers to description.

When we ask why bad things happen to good people, there is an unspoken assumption as to what constitutes a bad thing and who can be judged a good person: morality is at stake. In her innovative study of the politics of immorality, Catharine Edwards demonstrates that the Roman preoccupations with morality deflect attention from the socioeconomic disparity that defines Roman society. The sources for conspiracy and conspiracy theory carry such moral valences, and the conjectures posed by characters raise grave ethical concerns. Yet modern moral schemes should not be mapped onto the Romans. What is distasteful to us may not be a problem for the average Roman writer. Slavery was a condition of the ancient way of life. Rape violated not only the victim but, more importantly, the victim's guardian, whose integrity as a male citizen was at stake. Furthermore, genre complicates our ability to discern clear-cut expressions of morality. Comedy exaggerates and stylizes; satire distorts and disorients. In these genres it is difficult to sort out active misogyny, xenophobia, or homophobia from critiques of misogyny, xenophobia, or homophobia. Not only poetic texts but, as Edwards points out, "texts generally classified as 'history' are equally problematic." Morality or, more often, acts of immorality attributed to a historical figure may be hurled metahistorically against a contemporary political figure. Anecdotes, our main source for the suspicion of emperors, are notoriously untrustworthy. Edwards is correct in asserting that "whether these incidents actually happened or not is impossible to ascertain and considerably less important . . . than the fact that people told the stories and their reasons for doing so."[76] Therefore, given the several limitations that confront the study of conspiracy theory in ancient Rome, it is prudent to cast the net as widely as possible.

Conspiracism permeated the habits of thought of those who wrote virtually all the texts that today constitute the principal remains of Roman culture, and an appreciation of the dynamics of Roman conspiracism is intended to set the scene for the permutations effected in the works of Juvenal, Tacitus, and Suetonius, three contemporary writers of what I should like to call "the Golden Age of conspiracy theory in ancient Rome."

Chapter 1 catalogues various ways that conspiracy theory makes dubious claims to truth and credibility. First, there is Cicero's masterful deployment of the rhetoric of conspiracy in his prosecution of Verres, governor of Sicily, for provincial maladministration. Cicero alleges that Verres mishandled and even concocted slave conspiracies for his own benefit. Although never delivered, the speeches against Verres (and *In Verrem* 2.5.1–15 in particular) are primary evidence that suggests the susceptibility of audiences to believing claims of conspiracy. Second, by removing a conspiracy from its historical context, a Roman writer can inflate its potential to instill fear or broadcast inherent prejudice. Dramatic performance flirts with the unnerving possibility that make-believe can spill over into real life, and so the stage is yet another venue for the performance of conspiracy theory. Terence's *Hecyra* ("The Mother-in-Law") is a comedy steeped in conspiracy thinking, from its opening salvo against women as conspirators, to its metatheatrical asides, to its dubious recognition scene. The last two sections consider what happens when truth and credibility are so straightforward that obvious conspiracy can be quelled or averted. Rather than impose a taxonomy or typology, the survey demonstrates the manifold iterations of conspiracy in areas relating to almost every facet of Roman life.[77]

The rest of the book focuses on the manifestations of conspiracy in three contemporaries: Juvenal (c. 55–127), Tacitus (c. 56–117), and Suetonius (c. 69 or 70–128). Born before the death of Nero, all three lived through the Year of the Four Emperors. Young adulthood was shaped by Flavian politics and the tyranny and assassination of Domitian. As writers, they flourished "in that rare happiness of the times, when you could think what you wish and say what you think"[78]—a sentiment best taken with a grain of salt, for although the days of Trajan and Hadrian promised a free and open society, the memory of Domitian was still fresh.[79] In spite of Juvenal's violent anger, Tacitus' seething indictments, and Suetonius' scathing anecdotes, these authors did not produce literature filled with as much mutilation, dismemberment, or sexual perversion as characterizes Neronians such as Lucan, Perseus, or Petronius or Flavians such as Statius or Martial. In post-Domitianic literature, a different kind of decorum prevails, less physically violent and more psychologically virulent.

According to Ronald Syme, "Tacitus and Juvenal could be regarded as parallel and coeval phenomena. Style, tone, and sentiment are comparable. Juvenal has point and concentration, command of rapid narrative and of pictorial evocation—and a dramatic power supremely manifested in scenes like the fall of Seianus."[80] Catherine Keane attributes the parallelism to a shared literary culture between Tacitus and Juvenal: "In the senatorial historian and the muckraking poet we can see treatment of some of the same material, a certain affinity of viewpoints, and a similar penchant for epigrammatic wit— parallels that reflect the two authors' shared literary culture."[81] This makes it difficult if not impossible to trace tangled lines of influence and to argue that one borrowed directly from the other. Instead, what we observe is a nexus of conspiratorial thinking that percolates even through the biographies of the slightly younger Suetonius.

Chapter 2 is a study of Juvenal that reaches several conclusions: (1) Because of its inherent duplicity and secrecy, conspiracy finds a ready home in the ironic world of satire. (2) The xenophobic tirades against those of foreign extraction do not reflect a historical reality; the Rome of Juvenal's day was a polyglot cosmopolis in which various ethnic groups coexisted. The satirist does not outright accuse foreigners of conspiring against Rome; instead, he is a man trapped on all sides, as troubled by the prevalent threat of conspiracy from within his society as he is by the constant fear of foreign contagion from without. (3) Juvenal denigrates conspirators and foreigners in similar ways; however, conspirators are by definition insiders, while foreigners should be outsiders. Indeed, the two confound the regular configuration of insider/outsider, much to the speaker's dismay. (4) At any given moment, the speaker is able to represent only *part* of the condition of either conspirator or foreigner and never the entire condition of both. Insofar as the speaker is not comprehensive, his images of conspirators and foreigners are only partial; however, the reader is distracted from this selectivity by the larger argument at hand. The images of foreigners and conspirators can be associated, albeit tenuously, without direction from the speaker. Such synecdoche is at work in Juvenal 15, the most explicitly xenophobic of the poems.

Chapter 3 takes as its starting point the difficulty of punishing conspirators. In his version of the popular Greek tragedy *Thyestes*, Seneca articulates a hauntingly familiar sentiment that illustrates the dilemma: "It is too late to take caution when in the midst of evils."[82] In his speech to the senate advocating the death of the Catilinarians, Cato based his argument on the simultaneity of punishment and prevention: "You can punish other crimes when they have been committed; but with this, unless you take measures to prevent its being committed, it is too late: once it has been done, it is useless to appeal to legal proceedings."[83] Perhaps this is why the Roman senate met the threat of conspiracy with a *senatus consultum ultimum* ("a final decree of the senate"), a mechanism based on custom (*mos*) rather than statute (*lex*) that ignored strict legality. Under the *senatus consultum ultimum*, the safety of the Republic was entrusted to the consuls to take any measure necessary to counter a violent threat to public security. Yet the definition of the *senatus consultum ultimum* occludes the paradox that conspiracy per se can be punished only if it is aborted.[84] Even when the punishment of conspirators is justified, it is still problematic, for the intended crime has not yet been committed.

The strident debate in Sallust's *Bellum Catilinae* (51–52) between Cato and Caesar over the execution of the Catilinarian conspirators as deterrence to further civil unrest articulates (but does not solve, to be sure) the problem of punishing senators. From agents of conspiracy, we turn to Pedanius Secundus, victim of a conspiracy. Because he was murdered by one of his own slaves, every slave in his possession would have been put to death, but the number (400) was so extraordinary that the citizens protested the severity of the punishment. The conservative senator Cassius Longinus spoke in favor of summary execution. His speech, recounted by Tacitus, *Annales* 14.43–44, makes several arguments that reveal deep-seated assumptions about how senators thought of themselves. Conspiracy theory is thus implicated in senatorial self-fashioning. While these historical examples show punishment in practice, Cicero's *De Officiis* (especially 1.88–89) and Seneca's *De Ira* (Book 1) and *De Clementia* (Book 1) approach punishment theoretically. In addition to the allusions to Sallust in Tacitus, the two historians are in dialogue with the philosophers. An ongoing dialectic emerges between theory and practice; Sallust and Cicero, Tacitus and Seneca continually reevaluate the critical dispute over the punishment of conspirators in concrete and abstract terms.

Chapter 4 arrives at last at the bustling crossroad of conspiracy theory and suspicion, twin acts of mind that are social and epistemic at their core. Both are predicated on a lack of evidence; both rely on dispositional and circumstantial explanations as their proof; both destabilize authority by casting doubt on intentions and motives that cannot be proven; both can be taken to harmful extremes. According to Melley, paranoia is "an interpretive disorder that revolves around questions of control and manipulation," traditionally defined as "a condition in which one has delusions of grandeur or an unfounded feeling of persecution, or both."[85] Melley contextualizes paranoia in a postwar crisis of human action and agency, in which there is an increasing sense "that individuals are no longer as autonomous or unique as they once seemed."[86] This crisis fairly describes the changed relationship between senate and emperor in the development of the principate under the Julio-Claudian and Flavian regimes, as described by Tacitus and Suetonius. The suspicion that some emperors exhibit (or that all emperors exhibit at some point) is the result of an excessive willingness to believe that hidden forces are at work, preparing to destroy them. This excessive willingness is a moral vice that leads them to avoid responsibility for their own actions.[87] Kept in check, suspicion can be healthy. If an emperor, tired of fearing for his life, decides to act upon his suspicions and eliminate potential assassins, is he not ensuring the security and stability of the state? For if he waits for conspirators to succeed, he will no longer be in a position to punish them. Yet it is a fine line between protecting oneself from potential conspiracy and succumbing to paranoia. Such is the dilemma of Domitian, who "used to say that the lot of emperors was most wretched, because they were not believed about a proven conspiracy unless they were killed."[88]

Suspicion is a recurring theme in Suetonius' *De Vita Caesarum*. From Julius Caesar to Domitian, it is inextricably woven into the fabric of the biographies, individually and as a whole. Suspicion was a condition of rule, but different emperors responded differently to the threats to their power. Emperors are objects of suspicion by virtue of their autocracy; wiser emperors understand this and even take steps to avoid it. Emperors also exercise suspicion, as numerous examples attest. Repeated stories of the suspicion of emperors are perhaps the clearest indication of the prevalence of conspiracy theory not only in the political sphere but in the received and transmitted traditions about Rome's rulers. Some may have good reason for distrust, but others take it too far. Judicious suspicion extends an emperor's life; excessive suspicion can lead to his eventual demise. From judicious mistrust, to dysfunctional suspicion, to unbridled and deadly paranoia, a spectrum emerges that is visible only when the twelve biographies are considered as a complete unit; hence my contention that suspicion is a narrative framework for Suetonius' entire enterprise, with conclusions that bear upon our understanding of the Hadrianic context of production.

As a culturally embedded mechanism for explaining why bad things happen to good people, conspiracy theory harnesses the power of an epistemological crisis for a variety of purposes, but, at the same time, it also generates side effects, welcome or not. To subscribe wholesale to conspiracy theory is as foolhardy as to reject it outright as a mode of critical inquiry; to accept untenable explanations is as dangerous as to condemn to silence the potential for truth. This is what fascinates me most about conspiracy theory: its resolute unsolvability persistently challenges morality. To walk away from the challenge is to forego a good deal of otherwise unharvested information about the Romans and ultimately about ourselves.

CHAPTER I

CONSPIRACY THEORY *in* ACTION

Conspiracy theory is naturalized in the sources so as to convey an implicit ideology; in this it is no different from other types of stories that make social, economic, or political inequality palatable, although its prevalence in the public forum and the private home testifies to a widespread recognition of its power. Women and slaves emerge as obvious conspirators; however, if we resist the temptation offered by the sources to assign natural justifications to what are in fact historical intentions, then in the examples of conspiracy and conspiracy theory gathered in this chapter, we begin to see how complexity is replaced by simplicity, ambiguity by clarity, mystery by fact. When bad things happen to good people, the complexity, ambiguity, and mystery of the situation are resolved by a substitution that purports to convey a clear-cut explanation that is scarcely more verifiable than the conspiracy itself. Yet the process of replacement demonstrates the strength of conspiracy theory to articulate robust attitudes without much fanfare.

In the first section of this chapter, I demonstrate Cicero's active deployment of conspiracy theory in his prosecution of Verres. From there, the discussion turns to allusions to conspiracies and the consequences of removing them from their original temporal and spatial context, leading to an in-depth discussion of staging conspiracy in the third section. The last two sections treat the ways the Romans either crushed or averted conspiracy. Because conspiracy theories, though ubiquitous, belong to a historical context, an analysis that preserves specificity promises better results than an artificially imposed classification.[1]

MASTERMINDING CONSPIRACY

Against Gaius Verres, governor of Sicily from 73 to 71, the people of Sicily brought a charge of extortion, and in 70 B.C.E. the Roman senate prosecuted him.[2] It was Cicero's debut as a prosecutor, and he defeated Quintus Hortensius Hortalus, the best orator in town.[3] The trial began on the afternoon of August 5 (*Ver.* 1.31). Dispensing with a long introduction and sacrificing the apparatus of *eloquentia* in the interest of time, Cicero delivered the short but incisive *In Verrem actio prima* in which he exposed the defense strategies for delay; explained his need for haste; and put his trust in his witnesses, the facts, and the justice of his cause. He examined witnesses for nine days (*Ver.* 2.1.156); however, by the third day Verres' confidence was exhausted. He was absent from the courtroom on an excuse of illness, and before the verdict was rendered, he took himself into voluntary exile.[4] Because the second part of the trial never took place, the five parts of the *actio secunda* were never delivered. Thomas Frazel argues convincingly, however, that Cicero composed the *actio secunda* before Verres went into exile as part of pretrial preparations, so that he was able to publish the *Verrines* as soon as possible after the trial.[5] By publishing the speeches, Cicero could justify constitutional reform while enhancing his reputation.[6] Whatever the reasons for publication of the undelivered *actio secunda*, the speeches were widely read. Quotations in Pliny and Quintilian presume familiarity.[7] The *actio secunda* must contain what Cicero perceived would be a convincing set of arguments. Thus, the intimations of conspiracy theory at the beginning of *In Verrem* 2.5 (also transmitted under the title *De Suppliciis*)[8] take on added significance.

Cicero begins the *De Suppliciis* by anticipating Hortensius' defense argument: that the exceptional courage and vigilance of Verres protected Sicily from the dangers posed by the recent uprising led by Spartacus. Indeed, a precedent was set for an acquittal on just such grounds. In 98, Aquilius, the former governor of Sicily, was tried for extortion. His defense attorney graphically reminded the jurors that this man had in fact soundly quelled a rebellion of slaves (*Ver.* 2.5.3). Cicero thus implies that the fear of slave revolts mattered more to the jury than the injustice of provincial extortion. Of course the difference is that Aquilius really did crush the slaves in Sicily, whereas Verres can make no such claim; the troubles with Spartacus were confined to the peninsula. Furthermore, Cicero argues that if Crassus and Pompey had barely acknowledged each other's claim to glory for defeating Spartacus, then these two powerful men would surely not share credit with Verres.[9]

To strengthen his attack on Verres, Cicero discounts that Sicily is exceptional: "Why should that infection of a slave war be mentioned by you more than by all those who govern our other provinces?"[10] The attitude that slave revolts are a fact of life in the provinces colors all that follows. After Aquilius, slaves never disturbed Sicily again. Thus, Cicero uses the recent events in Sicily (the defeat of the slave rebellions and the extreme punitive measures to deter any further unrest) to thwart the possible defense that Verres, like Aquilius, may deserve acquittal on the basis of his military achievements.

From these arguments based on historical fact, Cicero then turns to conjecture. Although no reports of slave conspiracies during Verres' governorship were brought to the senate, "still I suspect that in some places in Sicily the slaves began to rise up. And I know this not so much from fact as from the deeds and decisions of that man."[11] How simple is the diction of conspiracy theory, how unmistakable: *suspicor,* "I suspect," *non tam ex re,* "not so much from fact." So unmistakable, that Cicero must pause to regain the confidence of his audience: "I am not driven by enmity but by the facts." Cicero has six examples of Verres' suspicious involvement in slave conspiracies across the island.

At Triocala (a place once occupied by rebels), the slaves of a Sicilian named Leonidas were convicted of conspiracy and sentenced to capital punishment. Cicero teases the audience to imagine what happened next, though "I will surpass the expectation of all. Men convicted of the crime of conspiracy, handed over for execution, tied to the stake, were suddenly before many thousands of onlookers freed and returned to their master, the man from Triocala."[12] There is no explanation for such an unbelievable act that defies all sensibility, except that Verres must have had a secret hand in their release. Cicero conditions his audience to accept this theory with a rhetorical question—albeit ironic: "Who can doubt (*quis dubitet*) that he oppressed the daring of slaves with the greatest fear, when they saw the praetor was so easygoing that the executioner himself was the agent who purchased from him the lives of those slaves convicted of the crime of conspiracy?"[13]

Any such doubts are put to rest by two further occasions when Verres behaved in the same way: in spite of sudden evidence of armed conspiracy, the slaves of Aristodamus of Apollonia and Leon of Imachara were released, presumably because Verres took a bribe.[14] Apparently, Verres had stumbled upon a money-making plan: for saving the property of wealthy men, he was paid handsomely. Leonidas, Aristodamus, and Leon were able to keep their slaves, in spite of the convictions on charges of conspiracy, and Verres was able to line his pockets.

Lest Cicero seem to rely too heavily on conjecture, he brings witnesses to substantiate his next two examples. Since Verres could find no more convicted conspirators to sell back to their owners, he trumped up charges of conspiracy against the *vilicus,* the overseer, of Eumenides of Halicyae, a man of distinction and wealth. Verres charged Eumenides sixty thousand sesterces for the return of the innocent *vilicus.* Moreover, Verres extorted sixty thousand sesterces from the equestrian Gaius Matrinius, whose *vilici* and shepherds were brought under suspicion. In both cases Cicero has sworn testimony that Verres concocted a conspiracy for his own profit.[15]

The sixth and most outrageous is the case of Apollonius of Panormus, and Cicero's rhetoric rises to the occasion. By quoting the gossip of anonymous witnesses, Cicero lends not only an air of suspicion but an element of suspense to the story: "At once, men about town began talking like this: 'I was wondering (*mirabar*) how a wealthy man like Apollonius had managed to remain unscathed by that Verres for so long; he has thought up some scheme or other, he has got hold of something. Surely a well-to-do man is not summoned by Verres without good cause.'"[16] Verres accused a slave of Apollonius of conspiracy and ordered the slave to be produced, but when Apollonius said he had no such slave, Verres imprisoned Apollonius. At this point Cicero cleverly harnesses the power of conspiracy theory for his own rhetorical purpose: "Amid the fears of a slave rising, he inflicted upon slaveowners who had *not* been found guilty the penalties from which he exempted slaves who *had*."[17] Apollonius was imprisoned for eighteen months (*Ver*. 2.5.21) before he was finally set free, presumably having paid Verres the bribe. Why, asks Cicero, was Apollonius suddenly released from prison? "I will affirm that the suspicion in this charge is so great that I may now allow the jurors themselves, without my arguments, to make their own conjecture (*coniecturam*)."[18] Cicero gives the jury enough circumstantial evidence to draw their own conclusions.

Let us attempt to peel back the layers of conspiracy theory that hold this part of the prosecution together. In the wake of the revolt of Spartacus, Verres first conspires to release slaves convicted of conspiracy. Then, he falsely accuses slaves of conspiracy. Finally, he imprisons an innocent man because he does not produce a (nonexistent) slave charged with conspiracy. Why would Verres do these things? Cicero's job as prosecutor is to explain it—with only inference and circumstantial evidence. In the absence of proof, Cicero in turn spins a conspiracy theory of his own, one that attributes all this behavior to a dispositional explanation: Verres' greed.

Cicero weaves together all the circumstantial evidence in a summary paragraph that, thanks to the strategic use of directional adverbs such as *primum*, *deinde*, and *postremo*, appears to move toward a logical conclusion.

I would have you first (*primum*) consider briefly the number and the magnitude of the several features in the man's ill-treatment of Apollonius, and then to reckon up their value in terms of money. Next (*deinde*), we have the accusation brought by no prosecutor, the verdict pronounced by no court, the condemnation preceded by no defense. Lastly (*postremo*) there is the darkness, the chains, the prison, the tortures of being shut up. . . . I cannot assess [the evils] in terms of money (*Ver.* 2.5.23).

Cicero thus ties together seemingly unrelated events to expose the well-guarded secrets of a well-known public figure, whose true intentions are nefarious.

Later in the speech Cicero alleges that pirates secretly bribed Verres. "Conjecture, you say? No one can be a good judge who is not moved by convincing circumstantial evidence" (*coniectura est. iudex esse bonus nemo potest qui suspicione certa non movetur*, 2.5.65). The oxymoron *suspicione certa* ("convincing circumstantial evidence" or, more literally, "a sure doubt") is subordinate to the appeal to moral obligation by which Cicero implicates the jury in his theorizing. The risk of playing conspiracy theorist pays well, for Hortensius (whether he spoke or not) would have had to uproot the image of Verres the conspirator that was planted in the jurors' imaginations, and as Roisman points out, the allegation of conspiracy is "more easily made than refuted."[19] Furthermore, by painting Verres as a conspirator, Cicero wins points for saving the general public from a hidden danger. It is a political strategy to which he would return triumphantly seven years later.

DE-HISTORICIZING CONSPIRACY

In defense of those accused of *vis* (violence against the *res publica*),[20] Cicero routinely invoked the tumultuous Catilinarian conspiracy for a variety of purposes. In the *Pro Sulla*, delivered in the immediate aftermath, Cicero denies the claim that he is presently abusing his power, since he did not abuse his power during his consulship: "Will you say that then, in such command and such power, I was not a king, but now as a private citizen I am?"[21] In the *Pro Caelio* (delivered in 56, after his return from exile) an oblique reference strengthens the force of the *lex* under consideration: "a law which, after the flame that raged in my consulship had been allayed, extinguished the smoking relics of the conspiracy."[22] In the *Pro Sestio* (delivered the same year), Cicero bolsters Sestius' character by reminding the jury that his client helped crush the conspiracy: "Wherefore even then, that assembly at Capua (which because their city's security was vouchsafed during my consulship, they adopted me as sole patron) returned the greatest thanks to this Publius Sestius at my home."[23] Each changing context, however, involves its own historical specificity and erodes the original sense of the conspiracy, including the questionable legality of the execution of citizens without a trial before the people (a variation of the charge of *vis*). Divorced from their immediate circumstances to fulfill different needs, references to the suppression of Catiline were especially valuable for their potential to bury the traces of a particular situation (citizens were executed) under a self-evident and unquestionable verity (Rome was saved). Much of the outrage and indignation that flavors the speeches of Cicero derives in part from the easy replacement of historical specificity with utilitarian generality.

A similar de-historicizing strategy is at work in Livy's account of 195 B.C.E. He records the senatorial debate over the repeal of the *lex Oppia* that restricted women's ownership of gold, expensive clothing, and use of horse-drawn vehicles. In characteristically staunch opposition to the repeal, Cato the Elder alludes to the women of Lemnos:

> Certainly, I used to reckon that it was a made-up story that an entire race of men on a certain island was destroyed root and branch by a conspiracy of women (*coniuratione muliebri*), but no race is free from utmost peril, if you allow women their gatherings, councils, and secret deliberations.[24]

Because they neglected the rights of Aphrodite, the women of the island of Lemnos were punished with a foul smell that drove their husbands to the arms of their Thracian slaves. The Lemnian women conspired to kill their husbands for their infidelity.[25] As a result, only women inhabited the island until the arrival of Jason and the Argonauts, whom the Lemnian women eventually married. Cato inoculates the bizarre story with a shot of common sense: "Certainly, I used to reckon that it was a made-up story. . . ." Admitting the outlandishness of the mythological exemplum protects against the risk of dismissing an otherwise distasteful or irrelevant statement and renders the rest of the *oratio obliqua* (indirect discourse) legible: ". . . that an entire race of men on a certain island was destroyed root and branch by a conspiracy of women."[26] Such an admission of fiction clears the ground for the statement of fact: "No race is free from utmost peril." Cato cashes in on what Groh describes as "the explosiveness, the social and political extent, and unbroken relevance of conspiracy theories" that result from "their being ubiquitous and timeless, in their being easily spread 'from above' due to the fact that they were always believed, and passed on 'below,' apparently relevant in every stratum."[27] Conspiracy theory makes it easy for Cato to elide the boundary between mythology and real life. The comparison of the treacherous women of mythological Lemnos to the extravagant women of Republican Rome slips effortlessly into a timeless indictment of women as conspirators not only in mythology but in real life.

Juvenal effects a similar, albeit more exaggerated, slip from myth to present circumstance. He concludes poem 6, the bombastic tirade against marriage, with a comparison to women on stage:

> Every morning you'll run into a granddaughter of Belus and an Eriphyle many times over. There's no street without its Clytemnestra. The only difference is this. The daughter of Tyndareus wielded a stupid and clumsy double-headed axe with both her hands, but these days the matter is accomplished with the tiny lung of a toad. Yet she'll use steel too, if her Atrides has taken the cautionary measure of dosing himself with the Pontic antidotes of the three times conquered king.[28]

The granddaughters of Belus are the Danaids, the fifty maidens who (with one exception) killed their husbands on their wedding night. Eriphyle persuaded her husband Amphiaraus to take part in the fatal expedition against Thebes. Clytemnestra, the daughter of Tyndaraeus, in vengeance for the sacrifice of Iphigeneia killed her husband Agamemnon on his return from Troy. The women of Juvenal's day simply poison their husbands, unless the men have immunized themselves against poison, as did Mithridates VI, king of Pontus; only then do wives resort to bloodshed. In the easy substitution of the modern-day Clytemnestra for the vengeful Clytemnestra of old lurks the persistent attitude identified by Amy Richlin, namely, a longstanding tradition of invective that reinforces aggressive behavior toward women.[29]

But there is more. As with Livy's temporal elision of myth and reality, so in a seamless transition from the tragic stage to the streets of Rome, Juvenal's accusation is limited neither by time nor by space. The boundary between representation and reality is effaced, signaling the unnerving possibility that make-believe can spill over into real life. Perhaps nowhere is this anxiety more evident than on the stage, and Plato indicts comedy as readily as tragedy because it too muddles the distinction between imitation and truth.[30] The complicity of women, couched in traditional invective that casts them as wicked conspirators with problems of their own making, has as its counterpart the complicity of an audience that cannot discern rhetoric from reality. As allusion de-historicizes conspiracy by substituting general for specific contexts, so performance hypostatizes conspiracy by substituting appearance for reality. As a result, conspiracy is atemporal, omnipresent, and all the more worrisome.

STAGING CONSPIRACY

Terence's *Hecyra* ("The Mother-in-Law") produced in 160 B.C.E. leaves an unmistakable residue of moral ambiguity that can be understood, in part, by recourse to conspiracy theory. In its open indictment of women as conspirators, its metatheatrical asides, and its unusual *anagnoresis* ("recognition scene"), the *Hecyra* perpetuates (to the point of implicating the audience) rather than arrests the force of conspiracy that gives the plot its forward momentum and its disturbing resolution.

The play is set in Athens. The main character, Pamphilus, kept a courtesan named Bacchis until his father Laches prevailed upon him to take a wife. Pamphilus married the girl next door (named Philumena; she never appears on stage),[31] but he continued his liaison with Bacchis. Eventually the courtesan, tired of dealing with a married man, ended the relationship, and Pamphilus came to love his wife. He was sent to Imbros on a family errand, and in his absence, his wife, for reasons unknown, returned to live with her parents. The slave Parmeno relates all this to the audience in Act I, in a sidewalk conversation with a courtesan Philotis and the older, retired courtesan Syra (76–197).[32]

Thus, the play begins with the problem of the broken marriage and Laches' conjecture that his wife Sostrata, the girl's mother-in-law (hence the title of the play), caused the rift.[33] He enters the stage, and his first words of Act II, a misogynistic tirade,[34] set the tone for the rest of the play:

> On the honor of gods and men, what a race this is, what a conspiracy (*coniuratio*) this is! How all women are eager for and do not want all the same things equally, nor would you ever find a one differing in any way from the mentality of the others! And so to such an extent, unanimously, do all mothers-in-law hate their daughters-in-law. They share this equal desire, this similar stubbornness, that they oppose their husbands, and they all seem to me to have been trained for wickedness in the same school. Indeed, if there is such a school, sure enough I know that *this* woman is headmistress.[35]

Sostrata pleads innocence and hopes that her son will exonerate her. Upon his return in Act III, Pamphilus finds his wife has left him; he is told that she is mortally ill. Standing before her parents' house, he hears her screaming in agony (316–317). He rushes into the house, only to find that she is in the throes of childbirth (361–414). Myrrina, *his* mother-in-law (now adding a second layer of meaning to the play's title), explains that Philumena left his house because she had been raped before their marriage and wanted to hide the resulting pregnancy from him. Myrrina had promised to expose the unwanted child and begged Pamphilus to keep the birth secret from everyone; no one need ever know the girl's condition (400). In this, William Anderson recognizes a conspiracy, for "Myrrina has already conspired to end the crisis by lying to her husband," while Sostrata is "still another victim of this conspiracy."[36]

Pamphilus is torn. When pressed by his father Laches (whose chief interest is a stable and fertile marriage for his son) and by his father-in-law Phidippus as well, Pamphilus blames the rift in his marriage on the hatred between mother- and daughter-in-law; he cannot take Philumena back because of Sostrata (451–515).

In Act IV, Phidippus then learns of the birth of the grandchild and, assuming the child is Pamphilus', accuses Myrrina of plotting to keep a secret—justly, it would seem, for she did attempt to conspire with Pamphilus (516–576). Meanwhile, to remove any obstacle to her son's successful marriage (577–622), Sostrata vows to leave Athens and live with Laches in the country. Laches gladly reports to Phidippus that the meddlesome mother-in-law problem has been solved. Phidippus retorts that Sostrata was not the problem; rather, Myrrina was the troublesome mother-in-law because she hid Philumena's pregnancy and birth of their grandchild. The old men are delighted with their new status as grandparents; with Sostrata removed to the country and Myrrina's secret revealed, it would seem that Pamphilus has no grounds for refusing his wife. Yet he knows that he cannot possibly be the father; allowing the mother-in-law to take the blame, he adamantly rejects his wife. The old men conclude that he must still be involved with Bacchis (623–726).

In Act V, Laches finds Bacchis, who is willing to help. She promises to end her relationship with Pamphilus and agrees to speak to Philumena. Bacchis reports that during her visit, Myrrina recognized her ring: it is in fact her daughter's, stolen from Philumena by her rapist—the father of her child.

So Bacchis orders the slave to summon Pamphilus: "Tell him Myrrina has recognized that the ring he once gave me is her daughter's" (830). As it happens, one night, about nine months ago, Pamphilus visited Bacchis soon after dark, alone, rather drunk, clutching this very ring. He was reluctant to tell Bacchis what was the matter but finally confessed to having raped a girl—Philumena (816–840).

In the final scene, when one would expect the true state of affairs to be revealed to both families before the audience, Bacchis and Pamphilus instead conspire to keep his identity as the rapist a secret:

PAMPHILUS: Tell me, you haven't already told any of this to Dad, have you?
BACCHIS: Not a word.
PAMPHILUS: Nor is there need for so much as a whisper. It's so tedious, when over and over again in comedies, everyone gets wise to everything. Those who are suited to know, know; but those not equal to the knowing don't know, nor will they know.[37]

The hero, such as he is, is free to take back his beloved wife and the child he in fact fathered, with no repercussions for his past actions, in a resolution that may be mechanically complete but is far from morally satisfying. Revelation of the rape to the characters would probably not have changed anything; in Roman comedy, marriage is the solution to rape,[38] yet in the *Hecyra* the problem is solved from the outset because Pamphilus and Philumena were already married.[39] Revelation of the rape to the audience, however, has an impact on the interpretation of the play.

Two critical readings of the play take the rape of Philumena as their central concerns. For Niall Slater, "The real and potentially tragic story of rape and rejection disappears behind a narrative in which the women are to blame for all the problems."[40] He argues that male authority, that is, patriarchy, is preserved by the suppression of truth. In her feminist reading of the play, Sharon James outlines the way this play depicts the range of Roman manhood from *adulescens* ("youth") to *senex* ("old man") and the role of rape in this development.[41] Slater and James put the play in its social context so as to glimpse the inner workings of the Roman social structures of gender and status and are good starting points for my own interpretation of the *Hecyra* as a veritable hotbed of conspiracy theory.

Many have noted a disturbing moral ambiguity in this play,[42] namely, that by means of shifting arguments, Pamphilus manipulates his mistress, his wife, his mother, his father, his mother-in-law, his father-in-law, and even his slave to achieve his own personal level of social comfort. David Konstan recognized the play's metatheatrical *anagnoresis* (865–868) as a conspiracy: "The air of secrecy, of conspiracy, at the resolution of the play is an emblem of its dubious propriety."[43] I would like to situate this conspiratorial *anagnoresis* within the larger framework of the play. By the time we get to the point where Bacchis and Pamphilus promise to keep a secret from everyone else, the audience has been steeped in conspiracism.

Ignorance is the catalyst of the *Hecyra*; nobody knows why Philumena left her husband. In the absence of knowledge, two explanations are offered: the one situational and the other dispositional. The first attributes her departure to a mortal illness; she does not wish to subject her husband to the pain she will cause. In other words, her departure is caused by a particular situation. The second attributes her departure to a general disposition that obtains among in-laws; she and her mother-in-law hate each other so much that she is forced to leave.[44] Thematically, the play's dual explanations may be aesthetically pleasing (as a substitute for the dual love plots);[45] when viewed ethically, however, such duality pilots the ethics of this play into troubled waters.

Parmeno lays out both of these causes in the opening scene (a dialogue that replaces New Comedy's more customary prologue that provides background for the plot). First he says that Philumena hated Sostrata, although he is unable to provide any evidence for this discord: "There weren't quarrels between them, never a complaint."[46] Then he reports that although Philumena was summoned, she did not return, on the pretense of illness.[47] Thus, in the first act of the play, the slave who is in no position to judge or even to sway opinion lays before the audience both the dispositional and the situational explanations. The former is unsubstantiated; the latter is undercut, at this point, by pretense (although later Philumena's cries will lend credibility to the charge of illness). It is up to the characters, and to the audience, to choose for themselves why they believe the marriage came to ruin.

Laches, of course, makes the mistake of overestimating the importance of the dispositional argument while simultaneously underestimating the force of the situational; hence, conspiracy theory prevails. Operating under the assumption that the women must be in league together, Laches is driven by an agency imperative: he spends the entire play trying to get other people to do something about this broken marriage. When Pamphilus returns from Imbros, Laches makes Phidippus confess to having sent for his daughter with the intention of returning her. He all but puts words in Phidippus' mouth:

LACHES: Yesterday he ordered Philumena to come to him. Say you ordered it.

PHIDIPPUS: Don't jab me. I ordered it.

LACHES: But now he will return her.

PHIDIPPUS: Of course.[48]

By this time, of course, Pamphilus knows the truth, so that this little ruse and his father's imperatives to Phidippus are wasted on him. In desperation, Laches bullies his wife and by the end of the play gives his son a direct command: "Take back your wife and do not contradict me."[49] Laches is driven throughout the play by his acceptance of the dispositional explanation for the breakdown of his son's marriage, and laboring under this false reasoning, he is taken in by conspiracy theory. The more his imperatives are disobeyed, the more he is convinced of a conspiracy.

On the other hand, because Pamphilus does not make an irrevocable choice between the dispositional and the situational explanations, his epistemic flexibility yields ethically equivocal results. When he returns from Imbros to find his wife inexplicably gone, he is uncertain as to the cause of her departure, and he reserves judgment about whom to blame: "Then I guess that I will find either my mother or my wife at fault."[50] When Pamphilus hears Philumena's cries (physical evidence for her departure), he pursues a situational explanation: "What is this disease? . . . Has no one summoned a doctor?"[51] Driven by this evidence, he enters the house to discover the truth.

———

Truth rarely suits a protagonist, and in the *Hecyra* the truth does not suit Pamphilus at all. Therefore, he spends the rest of the play manipulating the perceptions of others. To his mother he offers the situational explanation. When she asks the very same question, "What is this disease?" (*quid morbi est?*), he replies "a fever" (*febris*, 357). With his father he reinforces the dispositional explanation; he blames Philumena's departure on the hatred that obtains between mother and daughter-in-law. Pamphilus preys upon and thereby reinforces Laches' flawed tendency toward the erroneous, dispositional explanation:

> But since she thinks that it is beneath her to yield to my mother and to endure her ways with modesty, and since it is not possible to restore favor among them by any means, it's either my mother or Philumena: one of them has got to go. And my sense of duty bids me pursue my mother's convenience first.[52]

The irony is thick, for clearly Pamphilus is driven by a desire to pursue his own convenience above all. Furthermore, his plan backfires.

According to Sander Goldberg, "Though Sostrata and Myrrina are among the most finely drawn women in Roman comedy and though their difficulties are credible and dramatic, there is still something wrong with *Hecyra*."[53] The root of the problem lies in the response to the dilemma of the situational versus dispositional explanation: the mothers-in-law are unwittingly made to support the stereotype.[54] Because Myrrina is privy to the truth, she cannot be fooled that her daughter is ill, nor is she susceptible to the rhetoric of the mother-in-law conspiracy theory. Furthermore, she cannot wield either explanation in her own defense; she is caught having lied about her daughter's pregnancy, thereby reinforcing suspicion against her.

With so many characters swayed by the dispositional explanation and with her own son invoking this cause, it is no wonder that Sostrata herself finally gives in. Although in the beginning of the play she vehemently denies her guilt (274–280, esp. 278, *haud pol mequidem*, "but not me, by god"), in the end she concedes—although to be sure she does not confess to having quarreled with her daughter-in-law. She allows the men in the play to have their stereotype of the evil mother-in-law. All she asks is that she be allowed to withdraw: "Please, let me avoid this charge with which all women are reproached."[55]

Locked in their ignorance of the rape, the characters in this play either subscribe to an explanation for themselves or impose an explanation on others. Although Laches and Phidippus seek to restore the marriage, and Pamphilus and (to an extent) Bacchis seek to dissolve it, the effect is the same. This play exhibits all the features of conspiracy theory, whereby women are blamed for all the problems[56] whose causes are otherwise unexplained. Then, when these causes ought to be explained, yet another conspiracy takes place before the audience's eyes. Indeed, just by calling the play "The Mother-in-Law," Terence prepares the audience to adopt the dispositional outlook conducive to conspiracy theory. As Terence conditions the audience with the title, so he implicates the audience in the conspiracy that brings the play to a close.

Let us consider the qualities of Pamphilus and Bacchis, the two conspirators. It would be difficult to redeem the character of Pamphilus.[57] One could point to his noble qualities, as reported by the slave Parmeno in the opening scene. The boy married Philumena out of filial duty (120–122), and once married, he actually came to value his wife's respectability over his courtesan's disrepute (161–170). Yet it is important to remember that this is only the testimony to Pamphilus' behavior before his life became complicated by the disappearance of his wife and the birth of a child. One could also argue, *ex silentio*, that he wanted to keep his wife's rape a secret to spare concerned parties the grief such knowledge would cause. Yet in the text as we have it, Pamphilus is motivated solely by his own happiness; the glee of *hahahae, tun mihi istuc?* ("hahaha! are you saying that to me?") (862) is almost sinister. Pamphilus' egotism may be obvious and simple, but Terence crafts it with subtlety and complexity.

Less obvious and more complex, however, is Bacchis' motivation for participating in this concluding conspiracy, for she is privy to the secret only because Laches suborned her first. Laches approaches Bacchis on the assumption that she will do his bidding, precisely because women of her sort lack integrity and can be manipulated. He assumes she is the kind of woman who would say or do anything, regardless of the ethics that the situation demands. By agreeing to present herself to Philumena (who is, after all the legitimate wife of the man with whom she had for some time been conducting an illicit affair), Bacchis does what no "respectable" courtesan would do. Furthermore, she betrays her profession not for her own purpose but to oblige Laches. Bacchis is the worst kind of woman: she collaborates with the father to maintain the patriarchy, and then, as if to go from bad to worse, she conspires with the son. Bacchis is, however, the best kind of courtesan, for in her ability to walk both sides of the street, as it were, she follows the very advice that the old and experienced Syra gave to the young and inexperienced Philotis in the opening scene of the play: take down your enemy by the very same method he would use against you (72–73).[58] A more moderate reading of Bacchis, however, would admit that the vulnerable courtesan must do what she can to protect herself. Laches and Phidippus effectively threaten her with physical harm, against which she has no recourse. Complicity is a matter of survival, and a courtesan must above all look after her own interests, as Syra had told Philotis.

To think of the *Hecyra* in terms of conspiracy theory allows us to come a bit closer to understanding why the play is so disturbing, for, as we have seen, the morality is by no means clear cut. Where it would seem that Pamphilus conspires to keep everyone in ignorance to protect them from an awful truth, he stands to gain too much to make his motives innocent. Laches and Phidippus subscribe to an explanation that blames women for the state of affairs; Myrrina attempts, unsuccessfully, to perpetrate a lie to save her daughter's reputation; Sostrata simply concedes her status as scapegoat (in fact, she goes so far as to drive herself from the city); Pamphilus and Bacchis perpetrate the ultimate, successful conspiracy. There is something very wrong with the way this play is "resolved," for one conspiracy (to hide a rape and pregnancy) is replaced by another (to keep the identity of the rapist a secret). To a certain extent, the first can be seen as a good; the conspirators seek to reconcile the marriage and protect family members from painful information. The second, however, is more difficult to swallow.

Anderson argues that the unusual, metatheatrical *anagnoresis* of the *Hecyra* raises "serious ethical questions about any character who sought this privilege" of limiting access to the truth.[59] The *anagnoresis* of the *Hecyra* is further constrained because it lacks the final step of reconciliation that accompanies and completes the process: husband and wife are not reunited on stage.[60] The ethical imperatives of the *Hecyra* are compromised not only in its troublesome conclusion but at every moment throughout the play because of the conspiracism that drives the plot and the unwitting complicity of women that lends it credence.

CRUSHING CONSPIRACY

So far we have been looking at what Roisman would identify as the rhetoric of conspiracy theory, so encompassing as to be useful in a variety of contexts and genres. To see conspiracy theory in action, we turn our attention to intrigues and blunders involving slave rebellions that either did or did not get off the ground.

According to Livy (32.26), in 198 B.C.E., a slave conspiracy took place quite close to Rome.[61] At Setia, a town off of the Appian Way south of Rome, Carthaginian hostages were held, along with their slaves. In addition, the people of Setia had purchased a large number of prisoners of war, adding to the number of slaves in the town. The slaves "formed a conspiracy" (*cum coniurationem fecissent*, 32.26.7) and sent messengers to stir up the slaves in neighboring Norba and Cerceii. The plan was to attack while the people were distracted by the games at Setia. The slaves were successful and captured Setia, but they failed at Norba and Cerceii. News was sent to Rome. Two slaves approached Lucius Cornelius Lentulus, the urban praetor, and told him what had already happened and what else was planned. He put the informants under house arrest and brought the matter to the senate. He was "ordered to investigate and suppress the conspiracy" (*ad eam coniurationem quaerendam atque opprimendam iussus*, 32.26.10) and set out with five junior officers. He quickly raised a force of about 2,000 men and took Setia by surprise. He arrested the ringleaders and sent troops to pursue the fugitives. He returned to Rome and rewarded the informants. Remnants of the conspiracy were found at Praeneste and executed, and Rome was put under heavy surveillance as a precaution against further slave unrest.

Two years later another slave conspiracy occurred in Etruria. Livy's account (33.36), much more abbreviated than the first, is marred by a lacuna. As praetor with jurisdiction over foreigners, Manius Acilius Glabrio was sent with two city legions to investigate; he succeeded in cutting off the conspirators, killing and capturing many. He crucified the ringleaders (*principes coniurationis*, 33.36.3) and returned the rest to their masters.

In the aftermath of the Bacchanalian *coniuratio* in 186,[62] Roman officials continued to investigate and repress conspiracies of slaves and herdsmen; the notices are brief. According to Livy (39.29.8–10), the praetor Lucius Postumius (who was assigned the province of Tarentum) conducted ruthless (*severe*) judicial inquiries into a conspiracy of herdsmen (*de pastorum coniuratione*, 39.29.9) who were menacing roads and common pasturelands by their acts of banditry. He condemned some seven thousand men; some escaped, some were executed. The next year, Postumius repressed large-scale conspiracies of herdsmen (*magnas pastorum coniurationes vindicavit*, 39.41.6). In 182 B.C.E., the praetor Lucius Duronius was still weeding out the remnants of the Bacchanalian troublemakers hiding in Apulia (40.19.9–11). Thus, we find in Livy the record of slave *coniurationes* of various sizes and potential threats in mainland Italy, spread over a period of sixteen years: the immediate wake of the Second Punic War.

The First Sicilian Slave War began in 135 B.C.E.,[63] some ten years after the Third Punic War. It was thoroughly recorded in an ample monograph by Caecilius of Caleacte, the first-century B.C.E. rhetor and historian; unfortunately, all that remains is the single testimonium of Athenaeus.[64] Instead, we are at the mercy of the summaries of Diodorous Siculus, muddled in their chronology yet tantalizing in their level of detail.[65]

According to Diodorus, the cause of the revolt was the rapid accumulation of large numbers of slaves and the arrogant and harsh treatment of the newly acquired chattel. Given the least possible food and clothing, the slaves were forced to banditry to provide for themselves.⁶⁶ The Roman governors were hampered in their efforts to punish the slaves because of the influence of the landowning masters, *equites*, who also served as jurors in cases of provincial maladministration and so were not likely to favor the governors' cause (34/35.2.1–3). The situation grew critical until the slaves formed a conspiracy: "Gathering together as opportunities arose, they discussed revolt, until they brought their plan to action" (συνιόντες οὖν ἀλλήλοις κατὰ τὰς εὐκαιρίας συνελάλουν περὶ ἀποστάσεως, ἕως εἰς ἔργον τὴν βουλὴν ἤγαγον, 34/35.2.4). They found a ringleader in a Syrian slave named Eunus, a magician, wonder-worker, and charlatan who claimed the ability to communicate with the gods and predict the future. He was told in a dream that he was to become king and repeated the story at a banquet. Some guests mocked him; others gave him gifts to curry his favor in case he should become king (34/35.2.5–9).

In Enna a wealthy citizen by the name of Damophilus treated his slaves so poorly that "reduced by the insults to the level of beasts, they conspired to revolt and murder their masters" (ἐξ ὧν ἀποθηριωθέντες οἱ προπηλακιζόμενοι συνέθεντο πρὸς ἀλλήλους ὑπὲρ ἀποστάσεως καὶ φόνου τῶν κυρίων, 34/35.2.10).⁶⁷ These slaves approached Eunus and asked him to consult the gods about a plan to revolt. Eunus confirmed divine support and led the band of slaves in an assault on Enna. The slaves went after Damophilus and his equally cruel wife but spared their daughter, proving that their cause was not simply madness but revenge for harsh treatment. Damophilus was captured and brutally murdered. Eunus was chosen king. He murdered his masters, appointed a royal council, armed six thousand men, and joined battle with Roman field commanders (34/35.2.10–16).

This success in Sicily provoked smaller revolts in Rome, Attica, and Delos, where they were suppressed. In Sicily, however, the slaves remained firm, until at last the consul Publius Rupilius was dispatched in 132 B.C.E. He besieged the town of Tauromenium on the coast, where the rebels were forced to cannibalism before they were betrayed. Once Tauromenium capitulated, Rupilius marched on Enna. Eunus escaped with four companions and took to caves in the nearby mountains, but Rupilius flushed him out. Eunus died in prison (34/35.2.20–23).

It is tempting to suggest that the origins of the slave revolts narrated by Livy and Diodorus Siculus lie in the aftermath of the large-scale social, economic, and political upheavals wrought by the Second and Third Punic Wars; however, a generation after Rupilius' consulship, yet another slave revolt broke out in Sicily. Again, our main source for the Second Sicilian Slave Revolt is Diodorus Siculus (in epitome).⁶⁸

News of the slave uprising in Sicily was brought to Rome in 104; yet even before this, Italy was subject to three short-lived and minor revolts: (1) thirty conspirators (τριάκοντα οἰκετῶν συνωμοσίαν ποιησαμένων, 36.2.1)[69] at Nuceria were quickly punished; (2) two hundred slaves were quashed at Capua; (3) a Roman knight armed his own slaves in response to a dispute over a debt and plotted against his lenders (ἐπιβουλεύει, 36.2.3).[70] In Sicily, thirty slaves led by a man named Varius banded together, murdered their masters, and summoned others to freedom: "in one night more than one hundred twenty gathered together" (καὶ ἐν αὐτῇ τῇ νυκτὶ συνέδραμον πλείους τῶν ἑκατὸν εἴκοσι, 36.3.4). They held a position so strong that, rather than attempt it by force, the governor enlisted loyal slaves to betray the rebels (36.3.4–6). In the meantime, another rebellion was forming, and the praetor failed to respond forcefully enough before the number of armed slaves reached two thousand. The slaves achieved victory against Roman forces in pitched battle. They held an assembly and chose Salvius as their king; he besieged Morgantina (36.4.5). Meanwhile, at Segesta and Lilybaeum, slaves revolted under the leadership of Athenion, a Cilician (36.5). Thus, Sicily became a veritable *Iliad* of troubles (εἶχε δὲ τὴν Σικελίαν πᾶσαν σύγχυσις καὶ κακῶν Ἰλιάς, "turmoil and an *Iliad* of troubles held all Sicily," 36.6).

To oppose this widespread turmoil, the senate sent Lucius Licinius Lucullus as propraetor with an army of 17,000, but he accomplished nothing.[71] The next year (102) they sent Gaius Servilius, who likewise achieved nothing of note; both were condemned and sent into exile (36.9). Not until 101 when the consul Gaius Aquilius received command was victory in Sicily obtained (36.10).

The last and largest slave revolt of Roman antiquity was led by the Thracian Spartacus, who led a band of conspirators in escape from their gladiatorial training school at Capua in 73.[72] They took refuge at Mount Vesuvius, where the praetor Gaius Claudius Glaber, sent from Rome with three thousand soldiers, assumed that the gladiators could not descend unnoticed; the rebels, however, outwitted the Romans and put them to flight. That same year a second praetor, Publius Varinius, and his co-commander Lucius Cossinius were also unable to match the speed and agility of Spartacus' forces, which were rapidly increasing. During Varinius' command the geographical scope of the rebellion broadened such that the next year the senate sent both consuls, and their army achieved momentary success but could not subdue the rebel forces of now 70,000. Recalled to Rome in disgrace, they were replaced by Marcus Licinius Crassus who was given extraordinary command and ten legions.[73] By the spring of 71, after six months, the war was finally over, but not before Spartacus and his men had traversed the lower reaches of the peninsula in defiance and rebellion.

———

CONSPIRACY THEORY *in* ACTION

Perhaps the slave revolts were the exceptional result of a particular time and place in Roman history.[74] The unusual accretion of revolts in Sicily and southern Italy in 140–70 is easily attributed to the effects of the Second and Third Punic Wars; such is the thesis of Arnold Toynbee:

> The cause of this sinister local development was the rapid extension into Peninsular Italy and Sicily, after the Hannibalic War, of the nomadic animal husbandry and the plantation agriculture. . . . Considering the inhumanity with which these hordes of imported slaves were treated in Italy and Sicily by their purchasers and exploiters, it is not surprising that they took up arms against the established order whenever they found the opportunities.[75]

In more general terms, we might attribute the revolts to the rapid growth of empire in the third and second centuries and an inability to manage newly acquired property and wealth; the revolts were fostered by the concentration and neglect of the newly enslaved.[76] Géza Alföldy suggests that no major slave revolt is recorded after 70 because the Romans learned from experience to treat their slaves better and to make conditions livable, so that they would not revolt again: "The fact that there were no great slave revolts in the last 40 years of the Republic . . . indicates how the position of the slaves slowly improved after the rebellion of Spartacus."[77] On the other hand, the condition of chattel slavery, a "social death" in the words of Orlando Patterson,[78] means that the time was always ripe for slave revolt. Keith Bradley is definitive: "Resistance had a structural, and elemental, place in the history of slavery at Rome."[79] Thus, the latent potential for slave revolts necessitated the oppressive violence of the slave regime.[80] As we shall see, however, the Romans did not rely on institutionalized violence alone.

AVERTING CONSPIRACY

Slaves lived in constant fear of the master's abuse and violence, but the master also had to fear the possibility of slaves' secret plots. With their persistent alterity, their silent omnipresence, and their ambiguous humanity, slaves were conspirators — operatives acting in secret — by their very existence. Slaves were privy to everything the master did and said; they could keep or betray secrets. They could also operate behind the master's back, keeping and betraying secrets among themselves. So troublesome was the slaves' unique status that the Romans feared to distinguish them as a group. When a proposal was once made in the senate to distinguish slaves from free by their dress, "it then became apparent how great a danger threatened, if our slaves began to count our number" (Sen. *Clem.* 1.24.1).[81]

The well-known case of Larcius Macedo vividly illustrates the potential for slaves to conspire against the master. In a letter to Acilius (3.14) written in 103 C.E., Pliny the Younger recounts that Larcius Macedo was attacked by his slaves in the bath and left for dead. Although some loyal slaves rescued and attempted to revive Macedo, he died, but not before he saw to it that all the slaves of the household, the *familia*, were summarily executed. Pliny is explicit: "You see with how many dangers, insults, and ridicules we are surrounded; no one can be safe if he is lax and lenient; for masters are not murdered rationally but criminally."[82] According to Kathryn Williams, Pliny consistently paints the slaves in a negative light. He impugns the assistance of those who attempted to rescue Macedo, calls their loyalty into question, and approves without hesitation of their summary execution.[83]

Slaves who came from the same place posed a special threat. To minimize the danger, Varro advises the Roman farmer to take preventative measures:

Avoid acquiring too many slaves from the same place of origin, since this is the most usual cause of domestic quarrels. The foremen are to be made more zealous by rewards, and care must be taken that they have a bit of property of their own, and mates from among their fellow-slaves to bear them children; for by this means they are made more reliable and more attached to the place.[84]

Although such advice shows that the Romans were at least aware of the benefits of ameliorating slave conditions, the thesis founders when we compare this passage of Tacitus:

The slaves' ingenuity was an object of suspicion among our ancestors, even when they were born in their own fields or homes and they immediately conceived an affection for their masters from the start. But now that we have foreigners among our *familiae*, whose religious rites are different, or foreign, or nonexistent, you will not keep that rabble in check but by fear.[85]

Context, of course, can account for the different approaches to managing slaves. Varro, writing in 37 B.C.E., refers to slaves on a farm, and the speaker is the agronomist Scrofa; Tacitus, writing more than one hundred years later, refers to slaves in a household, and the speaker is the jurist Cassius Longinus. Yet they both attest a general anxiety and the range of possible responses, from (positive) incentive to (negative) fear.

As slaves could conspire, so they could betray; the Romans were occasionally indebted to loyalty from unexpected quarters. In 66 B.C.E., Oppicianus charged Cluentius with murdering his father. Cicero conducted the defense. In the *Pro Cluentio*, we learn that years ago Oppicianus with the help of a certain Fabricius attempted to poison Cluentius. At the time, Cluentius was in poor health and under the care of a trusted physician named Cleophantus. Cleophantus had a slave named Diogenes, whom Fabricius suborned to administer the poison. But the slave Diogenes was honest and upright (*frugi atque integer*), and he reported the plot to Cleophantus, who in turn told his master Cluentius, who purchased Diogenes. The bribe and the poison were found in the possession of Scamander, a freedman of Fabricius. Thus, a loyal slave betrayed the plot and rescued Cluentius from poison.[86]

Livy tells a tale of slave loyalty that saved Rome from treacherous poisoners. In 331 B.C.E., Rome was suffering a terrible affliction of unknown cause; leading citizens were succumbing to a common illness and practically all of them were dying. An unnamed *ancilla* (slave woman) approached the curule aedile, Quintus Fabius Maximus, and offered testimony if granted immunity (Liv. 8.18.4). He immediately took the matter to the consuls and the senate, who assented, and she led the authorities to the women who were preparing poisons. The concoctions, along with approximately twenty women, were brought to the forum. Two of the women, Cornelia and Sergia, asserted that the drugs were salutary. The *ancilla* challenged them to drink the cups, and after deliberating among the others, the women openly, in the sight of all,[87] drank the poison and died (8.18.5–9). The slaves of other women betrayed their mistresses; in all, one hundred and seventy were found guilty (8.18.10). According to Livy, this was the first time that a case of poisoning had ever been brought forth in Rome. The entire affair struck the Romans as quite unusual, and they attributed the matter to madness rather than criminal intent (8.18.11). Based on a precedent from the olden times of the secession of the plebs, the people decided to elect a dictator to perform the apotropaic ritual of driving in a nail (*claui figendi causa*, 8.18.12). Once Gnaeus Quinctius[88] performed this ritual, he resigned the office (8.18.13).

Livy begins the episode with an overdetermined disclaimer that points to his anxiety over recounting such a lurid story: "One thing, however, I should be glad to believe had been falsely handed down—and indeed not all historians mention it—namely, that those whose deaths made the year notorious for plague were in reality destroyed by poison; still I must set down the story as it comes to us, so that I may not deprive any writer of his credit."[89] To a certain extent, the sentiments expressed are rather commonplace.[90] Elsewhere, Livy wishes that the tale he is about to tell were not true (9.18.4, 10.18.7); elsewhere he employs variations on the formula of dissent, *nec omnes auctores sunt* (8.6.3, 10.25.12); elsewhere, he regards it his duty to report what he has found in his sources (7.10.5). But the collocation of these three ordinary expressions introducing a story of intrigue by women demands closer scrutiny. Livy disavows responsibility for the damaging story of upper-class women poisoners, yet he continues to narrate the conspiracy.[91] The wording is curious, for the disclaimer is counterintuitive. He wishes that the story were false, not true; he points to the disagreement, not the agreement, of his sources. He elaborates with litotes that it would be *ir*responsible *not* to report the tale. Finally, the disclaimer, framed in negative terms, strengthens his authority by deflecting the blame onto other, unnamed historians.[92] Why, when the women are found guilty and convicted of poisoning citizens, does Livy exhibit such trepidation? What is it about this story that begins with unexplained deaths and ends with the just punishment of the perpetrators that bothers the historian so much?

The questions raised by the prologue to the story echo in its epilogue. The punishment of the conspirators was perceived as insufficient; to ensure the safety of the citizens, the bygone ritual of driving in a nail that had its origin in extreme social conflict (the plebian secession) was invoked.[93] The need to appoint a *dictator claui figendi causa* betrays the insufficiency of the punishment of the women conspirators in ending the plague. What if the women were not the cause of the plague after all? What if their acts of poisoning were independent of the plague, and the revelation of their plot was completely fortuitous?

In his account of 419 B.C.E., Livy records:

The following year was remarkable due to the good fortune of the Roman people rather than because of the enormous danger that threatened. The slaves conspired (*servitia . . . coniurarunt*) to burn the city in different places and, while the people were intent on bringing help from every quarter to the buildings, to take arms and seize the citadel and the Capitolium. Jupiter averted the unthinkable plans, and the guilty, arrested on the information of two, were executed. For the informants there was a reward of ten thousand coins valued at the oldest standard from the public treasury (which at that time was considered quite a sum) as well as their freedom.[94]

It is a simple story, simply told. Slaves conspired to burn Rome, but Rome was saved by divine intervention.[95] The slaves were betrayed from within; the guilty were punished, informants rewarded.[96] The offhandedness suggests that such an event was so commonplace as to require scant embellishment. Of course, in a work as comprehensive as Livy's, detail is reserved for exceptional cases such as the women poisoners of 331 B.C.E. However, the prominence of the good fortune of the Roman people (*felicitate populi Romani*) deflects attention from the facts that contributed to the outcome, namely, the betrayal of two slaves (*indicioque duorum*). Luck overshadows loyalty.

Compare this paragraph from the *Annales* of Tacitus:

> During the same season [24 C.E.], luck checked the seeds of a slave revolt scattered throughout Italy. The leader of the uprising, Titus Curtisius, once a soldier of the praetorian cohort, at first with secret meetings at Brundisium and outlying towns, then soon with pamphlets openly distributed, began to call to freedom the defiant field slaves throughout the remote pastureland, when, just as if a gift from the gods, three biremes moored to meet the needs of those crossing that sea. And there was in that region Cutius Lupus the quaestor, to whom the pasture lands had fallen as his responsibility according to the ancient custom; with the marines arrayed, he disbanded the conspiracy just when it was beginning. Staius the tribune was hastily sent by Caesar with a strong force, and he dragged the leader himself and those next in daring to the city that was already worried because of the great number of household slaves (*familia*) who continued to increase immeasurably as the freeborn population diminished daily.[97]

Again we see that fortune and the favorable disposition of the gods keep a conspiracy from gaining ground; however, unlike Livy, who attributes the repression of the slaves to divine agency first and the informants second, Tacitus credits Cutius Lupus (who was by chance at hand) and his marines and the tribune Staius—or rather Tiberius, who was quick enough to send a tribune—with arresting the conspirators. Still, the competence of the Romans is prefaced by *fors* ("luck"). The best defense against slave conspiracies, it would seem from both Livy and Tacitus, is fortune, an irrefutable force impervious to contradiction; yet it is hollow comfort indeed to admit that the powder keg of contingencies is doused by something so intractable as luck.

Quelling a slave rebellion is scarcely worthy of praise in the historical record. Since it is a source of embarrassment to the ruling class, the revolt of lowly persons who have conspired in secret should never be allowed to happen in the first place. According to Edward Arthur Thompson in his discussion of peasant revolts in late Roman Gaul and Spain, "When it is dangerously threatened, a propertied class will often conceal (if it can), and even deny, the very existence of those who seek to overthrow it."[98] Yet because our Roman sources are unable to claim a world free of slave revolts, we may be witnessing an attempt to impose social order by warning the public of imminent disaster. The crafted insecurity is a cautionary tale, a sign of a fractured discourse that, once threatened, will work ceaselessly toward a single aim: to govern the shadowy territory between fact and fiction, innocence and guilt, slave and free, and in the process reconstitute its dominance. When the sources monopolize the history of the slave revolts, they also fail to tell the story of a Rome safe from threat.

Conspiracy theory operates by replacement and substitution. In crafting the prosecution of Verres, Cicero displaces the need for evidence with a preponderance of conjecture; as a result, he can wedge an elaborate conspiracy into the minds of the jurors such that Verres is more fully discredited. Allusions to a conspiracy lift the event from its original context and drop it into another; such historical relocation imparts a sense of alarming ubiquity and timelessness. Through evocations of Catiline, Cicero can ground the morality of his case in a complex set of temporal reverberations; what happened in the past carries into the present, signaling a constellation of conspiratorial themes that link continually to other times and places.

Theatrical performance captures other times and places in an imitation of the real world on stage; however, there is always the uncomfortable possibility that actions on stage will seep into the real world, for example, the implication of the audience in the conspiracy at the end of Terence's *Hecyra*. The rhetoric of conspiracy operates by means of subtle replacements that import subsidiary consequences. So while the Romans were continuously on guard against conspiracies of slaves, they averted peril by incentive, fear, violence, and occasionally loyalty. When luck comes to the rescue, moral superiority is reasserted; however, luck is a poor substitute for sure-footed certitude. In fact, the invocation of luck underscores its inadequacy as a safeguard. The next three chapters will demonstrate that by a process of replacement, conspiracy theory can convey habits of mind inconspicuously: when Juvenal, Tacitus, and Suetonius evoke conspiracy, they get more than they bargained for.

CHAPTER 2

JUVENAL *and* BLAME

Of the poet Juvenal we have fifteen complete satires and a fragment of a six-teenth, divided into five books that seem to follow in chronological order and offer a few fixable dates (for example, the murder of Domitian in 96 is mentioned at 4.153, while the consulship of Iuncus in 127 is mentioned at 15.27). Susanna Braund has been instrumental in helping us understand the progression of Juvenal's poetry from engaged anger to removed cynicism: Book 1 (*Satires* 1–5) treats traditional themes of indignation; Book 2 is comprised of a single, long diatribe on private life that targets women; Book 3 (*Satires* 7–9) shifts away from anger toward irony; Book 4 (*Satires* 10–12) represents an attempt at tranquility and detachment; Book 5 (*Satires* 13–15 and the fragment of 16), although unfinished, exhibits aloofness and "superiority over the whole of humanity."[1]

Replete with generalities, moral imperatives, and the preference for dispositional explanations, the *Satires* of Juvenal exhibit all the contours of a conspiracy mentality. As Jonathan Walters has shown, *Satire* 2 targets unmasculine sexuality to implicate the readership in the spectacle of deviancy: "This is a satire in which the theme of secrecy and disclosure, of looking at what is or should be hidden, is central." Hidden truth is brought to light even though these kinds of deviant males stick together.[2] According to Walters, "The implication is that there is a conspiracy under way, that these deviants are a danger to 'normal' society."[3] In *Satire* 3, Umbricius suspects that Persicus set fire to his own house to defraud his neighbors.[4] In 6.231–241, a mother-in-law conspires with her daughter, evidence that the troubles in Terence's *Hecyra* spring eternal. In *Satire* 14, a daughter acts as go-between for her mother and is accomplice to her adultery.[5] Conspiracism is pervasive in the *Satires*.

These poems have long been recognized as a particularly rich source for evidence of Roman xenophobic attitudes[6] that are often expressed by stereotype, a particularly efficient tool because it need be voiced in only one or two lines for its effect to resonate across the rest of the poem.[7] Thus, the prejudice against foreigners does not escape the reader's attention for long. Together with the manifold allusions to conspiracy throughout the satires emerge the implications of xenophobia, not so much its causes, which are presumed obvious, but its possible and implied effects. These themes are neatly telescoped at the beginning of *Satire* 10:

> In all the lands extending from Cadiz as far as Ganges and the Dawn, there are few people who can remove the fog of confusion and distinguish real benefits from their opposite. After all, what is rational about our fears and desires?[8]

The first two lines of the poem delineate the boundaries of the world, from an assimilated western terminus (Cadiz) to an eternally foreign eastern limit (the Ganges), beyond Rome's reach. Even when the fog of confusion is lifted and the true value of something is revealed, there still lurks the propensity to misjudge. If reason were to guide men (*ratione*), then there would be nothing to fear or want and no need for conspiracy theory. The speaker laments (or rather, is incensed), however, that reason is not the norm. Ironically, throughout the *Satires*, the speaker's relentless, vitriolic anger is devoid of reason;[9] conspiracy theory is one way to fill the vacuum.

Like comedy, satire may seem an unexpected source for conspiracy theory; however, as Braund points out, secrets are a major theme of satire.[10] As in comedy, the excess and exaggeration of satire diminish its credibility. As with comedy, care must be taken to avoid anachronistic morality; what offends the modern reader may not have offended the Roman reader. Because satire is written in the first person, it raises the question of whether the "I" is the actual historical poet (Juvenal) or a voice through which the poet speaks (a persona).[11] Are the events real or the creation of the poet's imagination? The satirist may reveal biographical details about his own life and express criticism so strident that it would make his character, if real, most irksome. Satire is riddled with contradictions; the satirist may partake of the very behavior he deplores, and while he begs to stand outside the society he criticizes, he never fully escapes participation. As for the audience, some may fully embrace the speaker's outlandish point of view, while others may vehemently reject it; however, the speaker's scornful derision must be believed by at least some to be effective. Irony, humor, anger, and hatred constantly undercut meaning in satire.[12]

The *Satires* contain a remarkable number of allusions to historical events, and here we may be on firmer interpretive ground, for whether one agrees with the speaker's slant on the event, its historicity is unassailable.[13] Toward the end of the first poem, the speaker announces the need for a satirist to steer clear of dangerous topics; for instance, epic is safe (1.162–164). If he must mention individuals, then he will speak only of the dead (1.170–171).[14] History in the *Satires* is thus born of necessity. Juvenal's lifetime was perhaps the golden age of conspiracy in ancient Rome. Born under Nero (in 55 or 60), Juvenal lived possibly as late as 127.[15] He thus grew up with stories of Julio-Claudians, his childhood marked by the Year of the Four Emperors,[16] his adulthood shaped by Flavian politics and the tyranny and assassination of Domitian, and his sunset days spent putting pen to paper in the company of Hadrian.[17] Beside him as he wrote were the works of Tacitus, who, although in prose form, addressed many of the same issues as the satirist with the same irony, humor, and anger (even if abjured, *sine ira et studio*, "without anger or eagerness," Tac. *Ann.* 1.1.3).[18]

In her recent monograph, *Nation, Empire, Decline: Studies in Rhetorical Continuity from the Romans to the Modern Era*, Nancy Shumate demonstrates the rhetorical interchangeability of the categories of ethnicity, gender, and class in the *Satires* of Juvenal. The negative attitudes about one group "expressed in one poem may be imported as subtext into another." Notions of viciousness, criminality, and contagion are substituted across categories. So, for example, "women are, in several senses, sex and gender deviants, as well as xenophiles and class traitors; male sex and gender deviants are 'female', as well as xenophiles and class traitors; and foreigners are also 'female', as well as sex and gender deviants and class transgressors."[19] Thus, Shumate shows us how to apply the lessons learned about representations of women and slaves in Juvenal to our understanding of foreigners as well.

In *Satire* 3, the poet's friend Umbricius explains why he is quitting Rome for Cumae: the city is overrun with foreigners and other degenerates; there is no room for a decent man such as himself. The attacks on foreigners are sustained and ferocious. Shumate remarks on the "essentially paranoid character of [Juvenal's] vision" in this poem, framed "in terms of conspiracy (ubiquitously suggested although never explicitly formulated as such)."[20] This essentially paranoid vision is in part the result of the accumulation of allusions to historical conspiracies scattered across the poems. This chapter attempts to enumerate these implicit, ubiquitous suggestions not only in *Satire* 3 but throughout the corpus that contribute to the essentially paranoid character of his vision: the hallmark of the conspiratorial mindset.

Throughout the sixteen satires, Juvenal alludes to historical conspiracies in a variety of ways, from veiled references to overt declarations. The speaker of *Satire* 1 announces the need to rely on historical, not contemporary, events for his subject matter (1.170–171); however, it is remarkable that so much of this historical material relates to conspiracy and imperial intrigue. If the speaker appears to be obsessed with secrecy and deception, it is because at nearly every turn he invokes a conspiracy of some sort to make his point. This kind of allusion, in contrast to literary allusion, has many advantages.[21] We need not question whether we are meant to recall a particular event, whether it is merely an accidental confluence of diction that brings the historical event to mind. Rather, in his historical allusions, Juvenal undoubtedly seeks to activate in the reader's mind all the connections that the event evokes. Verres, Catiline, Sejanus: just a name can evoke intrigue and conspiracy with arresting economy. Most frequent are allusions to plots and schemes in the courts of Claudius, Nero, and Domitian.[22]

From these historical conspiracies, the chapter moves to a reading of the xenophobic tirades that characterize the satires. At the same time that readers are pounded with imagery of conspiracy real and imagined, they are pounded with hard-core xenophobic rhetoric. With the constant and interchangeable collocation of the two, Juvenal leaves it to the reader to connect the dots. Rather than voice sincere testimony of conspiracy theory, Juvenal (like our other sources) creates room for diverse audiences to understand politics and society diversely. If we were to ask what it was like to live during this golden age of conspiracy, Juvenal has a comprehensive answer framed in an all-too-familiar rhetoric that lays blame for any misfortune caused by Rome's moral decline at the feet of anyone not like himself.

ALLUSIONS

Verres is mentioned by name in three poems.[23] Of course, Verres is not a conspirator; he is the infamously rapacious governor prosecuted for extortion. Walter Spencer has shown, however, that Cicero paradoxically portrays Verres as an open conspirator, the leader of a criminal *societas* bent on frustrating Cicero's prosecutorial efforts.[24] Furthermore, as we saw in the previous chapter, the *De Suppliciis* is shot through with conspiracy theory that implicates Verres in underhanded, but unsubstantiated, dealings. Verres first surfaces in *Satire* 2 in a tirade against hypocrisy elaborated by a catalogue of infamous criminals:

> Who could stand the Gracchi moaning about revolution? Who would not confuse sky and land, sea and sky, if Verres took exception to a thief or Milo to a murderer, if Clodius accused adulterers and Catiline Cethegus, if Sulla's three disciples criticized his hit list?[25]

Interchangeability is nature's outward manifestation of inward moral degeneration; hypocrisy turns the world upside down. Milo and Clodius are identified as murderers and adulterers, but the crime that Catiline would accuse Cethegus of need not be mentioned. Their conspiracy is so famous as to go unspoken. The ellipsed verb, the alliteration of the names, and the metrical position of the phrase contribute to the crescendo of criminality that is nevertheless the most economically expressed item in the catalogue.

In *Satire 3*, another indignant rhetorical question raises Verres as an example of the secrecy inherent in conspiracism:

> Is there anyone these days who inspires affection unless he's an accomplice, his mind boiling and seething with secrets that must never be told? If he's made you share some innocent secret, there's nothing he thinks he owes you and there's nothing he'll ever give you. Verres will be fond of the person who can bring an accusation against Verres whenever he likes.[26]

Umbricius is weary of the scoundrels who inhabit Rome, among them the *conscii*, men with a guilty conscience. Although he does not name conspirators, he provides a most accurate description; hidden secrets that must be kept silent bind conspirators together and give them sway over others. In a poem that is an overt attack on the pervasiveness of foreigners in the city, conspirators constitute their own category of undesirables. Verres best exemplifies the conspirator, not so much because of his secret plans as because of his guilt, evidenced by his coddling of anyone who might expose him. He must keep his friends close, but his enemies, closer. Thus, his "affection" (*diligitur*, 3.49) is not genuine but rather a necessary precaution. The criminal and his accomplice share in a symbiotic relationship based on mutual distrust. One could go so far as to sympathize with Verres, who is as vulnerable to conspiracy as his victims. Counterconspiracy confounds the subjectivity of suspicion.

After warning the reader of the consequences of success and wealth achieved through corruption, Umbricius launches into sixty-five lines of what Braund calls "an extravaganza of xenophobia directed chiefly against the Greeks of the eastern Mediterranean." By singling out conspirators as a distinct category of social degenerates, Juvenal preconditions the reader for the tirade against foreigners that follows. Braund also warns that this passage "should not be taken as evidence for Trajanic/Hadrianic Rome, in which Greeks were much better integrated than some other foreign groups whose arrival was more recent."[27] Rather, the passage is part of a worldview constructed by the speaker who draws boundaries between Roman and non-Roman with the broad strokes of satire.

Verres makes his final appearance in *Satire* 8, crowning a list of famous, rapacious governors convicted of provincial extortion:

From there, Dolabella, * * * Antonius, from there that villain Verres kept bringing home secret loot in their tall ships—more triumphs in peacetime than in war.[28]

The phrase "secret loot" (*occulta spolia*) is a resounding oxymoron. *Spolia* are the weapons and equipment stripped from the body of an enemy in battle. The *spolia opima* are the spoils taken by a Roman general from an enemy leader in single combat. *Spolia* are thus objects very much on public display.[29] Yet in hiding the *spolia*, obtained not according to the rules of combat but from the anarchy of piracy, Verres makes public symbols of foreign domination into private possessions of domestic conspiracy.

When Verres first appears at 2.24–28, Juvenal also mentions Catiline, who enjoys a fair amount of press throughout the *Satires*, in allusions both explicit and implicit. Less overtly, for instance, in *Satire* 6 Eppia is smitten with a gladiator whom she calls "Sergiolus," the endearing diminutive of Sergius, the conspirator's *gens*.[30] The metonymy whereby the *gens Sergia* stands for Catiline is established by Vergil in the breathtaking ship race in *Aeneid* 5, in which Sergestus wrecks his ship. Sergestus is the founder of the *gens Sergia* (5.121: *Sergestusque, domus tenet a quo Sergia nomen*, "And Sergestus, from whom the house of Sergius derives its name"). According to Kevin Muse, "Commentators since Servius have noted in their glosses on this passage the most infamous member of the *domus Sergia*, Lucius Sergius Catilina." Furthermore, "it has been suggested that Sergestus' mishap is an allusion to the failure of Catiline's conspiracy."[31] Muse argues convincingly that Vergil uses the shipwreck to adumbrate the future disaster that Catiline will pose to the Roman ship of state. With the rococo *Sergiolus*, Juvenal telescopes Vergil's elaborate metonymy into a diminutive that emphasizes the allusion all the more.

The fateful year 63 is brought to mind at 10.122, when the speaker quotes Cicero's most memorable hexameter, *o fortunatam natam me consule Romam* ("O Rome, you are fortunate, born in my consulate").[32] In addition to these allusions to the Catilinarian conspiracy, Catiline is twice more mentioned by name as metonymy for vice. At 10.286–288 he and Cethegus suffer a fate better than Pompey, for at least they were not decapitated, while at 14.41–42, Catiline's name is generic for a common criminal. These passages across the *Satires* attest the lasting hold that the Catilinarian conspiracy had on the Roman literary imagination and the way this particular conspiracy wrote itself into the Roman mindset. After 63, Catiline by metonymy signaled conspiracy.[33]

An apostrophe (a pointed, direct address) to Catiline brings conspiracy to the fore:

What ancestry could anyone find more exalted than yours, Catiline, or that of Cethegus? Yet you plotted to attack homes and temples at night and set them on fire, like the sons of trousered Gauls and descendants of the Senones, committing an outrage that could lawfully be punished by the "uncomfortable shirt." But the consul [Cicero] is vigilant and checks your banners. He—a nobody from Arpinum, low born and a town knight just arrived at Rome—posts a helmeted garrison on all sides for the terrified citizens and is busy on every hill.[34]

Three images are worth pursuing: the trousered foreigners, the "uncomfortable shirt," and Rome beset by a garrison.

Catiline and Cethegus are examples of blue-blooded Romans; Cicero is cast as the outsider. In these lines, however, conspiracy undermines pedigree. The high-born Catilinarian conspirators are compared to foreign rebels, Gauls in their customary pants and Senones, the tribe that sacked Rome in 390 B.C.E. Yet the Allobroges, a foreign tribe, saved Rome in 63: They betrayed the conspirators. With their cooperation, Cicero was able to seize evidence and arrest conspirators at the Mulvian Bridge.[35] Indeed, the Allobroges were even rewarded, proving themselves more devoted to Rome than the blue-blooded Catiline and Cethegus. The disapprobation of foreign affectation is undermined by the foreign intervention that saved Rome in 63.

The speaker then asserts that the crime deserves a dire punishment. *Tunica molesta* ("uncomfortable shirt," 8.235) is a euphemism for a garment smeared with pitch or wax so that when set on fire, it burned its victims alive; it was a common punishment for arson and an image Juvenal had already used. In the programmatic first satire, the speaker advises safe topics for poetry: "Describe Tigellinus, and you will shine on that fire where men stand and burn and smoke with transfixed throat" (1.155–156).[36] When Nero is suspected of having set fire to Rome in 64 C.E., he deflects blame onto the Christians, whom he punishes by burning alive. Tacitus' description is vivid:

As they perished, mockeries were added, so that, covered in the hides of wild beasts, they expired from mutilation by dogs or, fixed to crosses and made flammable, on the dwindling of daylight they were burned for use as nocturnal illumination.[37]

Juvenal's brevity at 8.235, *tunica molesta*, thus condenses his own earlier description of the punishment, while at the same time abridging the Tacitean imagery of the burning of the Christians. The allusion to the punishment of the Christians occurs in the middle of a summary of the Catilinarian conspiracy, defeated by the vigilant consul whose status as an outsider is made all the more conspicuous by his efforts from the inside, from the heart of the city.

The image of Rome besieged is interrupted by the description of Cicero as "a nobody from Arpinum." While Catiline's efforts to sack and burn the city are hidden and secret, Cicero's efforts to protect and save the city are open for all to see. In the speeches against Catiline, vigilance is a constant refrain by which Cicero reassures the people that he is in control of the situation.[38] Satire, however, reverses expectations. The affirmative value of vigilance is undercut by the recent arrival in Rome of a low-born knight who has provided the city with a garrison.

Beyond the overt allusion to the Catilinarian conspiracy, *Satire* 8 is haunted by a deeper sense of political intrigue. The speaker asks, "To whom do I direct these warnings? To you, Rubellius Blandus,"[39] who is taken by Duff to be "a type of noble birth and nothing more."[40] The name Rubellius Blandus, however, suggests a nexus of intrigue. Tiberius' son Drusus had a daughter Julia, who in 33 C.E. married C. Rubellius Blandus, a man who, according to Syme, "had slipped unscathed through the season of hazard and peril that opened with Agrippina and her eldest son consigned to imprisonment in 29, to culminate in the destruction of Aelius Seianus and the dreadful aftermath."[41] Rubellius Blandus appears three times in Tacitus' *Annales*. In 20, he proposed the punishment of Lepida, and in 22 he voted for a lesser penalty for Clutorius Priscus, the man put to death for writing a poem that anticipated the death of Drusus; thus, he is characterized as a respected senator caught in the intrigues of Tiberius' reign.[42] The final appearance of Rubellius Blandus is in the brief notice of Julia's marriage to him, embedded in Tacitus' account of the massacre of the detainees associated with the conspiracy of Sejanus (*Ann.* 6.27).

The marriage produced a son. C. Rubellius Plautus was the great-great-grandson of Augustus. As Tacitus points out, "By his maternal origins he was Nero's equal in his remove from the Divine Augustus."[43] This made him, as Syme succinctly puts it, "suspect and vulnerable."[44] According to Tacitus, Rubellius Plautus was accused in 55 of trading on his pedigree so as to marry Agrippina the Younger and thereby obtain rule and achieve a revolution.[45] Five years later the appearance of a comet gave people the chance to bandy about names of possible replacements for Nero; Rubellius Plautus was mentioned (*Ann.* 14.22.1), so Nero sends him a piece of friendly advice: To escape the rumors, why not retire with his wife Antistia to his family estates across Asia (*Ann.* 14.22.3)? Rubellius Plautus' compliant withdrawal from Rome bought him but two years. In 62, at the instigation of Tigellinus, Nero's dread praetorian prefect (cf. *Sat.* 1.155), Rubellius Plautus was marked for death on a pretext of fomenting revolution; his head was brought to Nero (*Ann.* 14.59). According to Courtney, the identity of the addressee of *Satire* 8 is "the otherwise unknown brother of Rubellius Plautus, executed by Nero in A.D. 62."[46] Syme follows, further noting the "strongly Neronian" tone of the poem; the addressee "may well be genuine. . . . Yet he might be only a plausible and malignant invention."[47] By addressing his poem to a Rubellius Blandus, Juvenal sets in motion for the reader a series of associations with family pedigree, imperial intrigue, and the deadly consequences of their intersection. In a poem obsessed with the contamination of pure blood by foreigners, the name Rubellius Blandus evokes a nexus of conspiracy from Tiberius to Nero.

As an example of the reversal of fortune, Juvenal adduces the fall of Sejanus, Tiberius' praetorian prefect. In 23 C.E. he concentrated the praetorian cohort for easier command; in 26 he induced Tiberius to retire to Capri; in 31 he attained the consulship with Tiberius and received the proconsular *imperium*.[48] He maintained his influence over Tiberius until Antonia, the emperor's sister-in-law, sent word to Tiberius that Sejanus was plotting against him.[49] In response, Tiberius enlisted Sutorius Macro to his cause and sent the *uerbosa et grandis epistula* ("long and wordy letter") of *Satire* 10.71 to Sejanus. While Sejanus read it, Macro had time to gather his forces. The senate convened at the Temple of Concord, the very ground on which Cicero denounced Catiline in 63.[50] The senate quickly passed sentence, and Sejanus was strangled before day's end. Macro succeeded him as Tiberius' right-hand man.

In a vivid and succinct vignette, the speaker of *Satire* 10 begins at the end of the story, so to speak. Statues were toppled and melted down and forged into common objects (10.58–64). The response of the crowd to the destruction of this powerful man is expressed in the imperative mood: "Hang a wreath on your door, sacrifice a bullock at the Capitolium; Sejanus is dragged by the hook, something to behold. Let everyone rejoice."[51] Popular opinion is fickle, as spectators deny ever having respected the man. "But what was his crime? Who was the informer, what information, what evidence sealed his fate? None of those; rather, a long and windy letter from Capri. Ah, well, say no more."[52] As with so much of Juvenal, the fall of Sejanus at 10.61–72 no doubt owes much to the (now lost) Tacitean rendition: adherence or departure, we cannot say.[53] When the tattered manuscript of Tacitus resumes, it reports a squabble between consuls in the wake of Sejanus' execution, the one accusing the other of participating in the conspiracy (*ut noxium coniu-*

rationis ad disquisitionem trahebat, "he was dragging him to trial as guilty of conspiracy," *Ann.* 5.11.1). Once again, Juvenal illustrates his point (the fickleness of fortune) with an example that imports notions of conspiracy.

In the *Satires* the historical conspiracies in the reigns of Claudius, Nero, and Domitian form such an indissoluble complex of allusions that the result is an impressionistic vision of conspiracy across time: uninterrupted, continuous, and pervasive.

Three times Messalina, wife of Claudius, is mentioned. At 6.114–132, the speaker describes in shocking detail her adulterous escapades. In *Satire* 10, the speaker describes how Messalina made herself the bride of Silius (10.329–336). Given Tacitus' lengthy account of the affair (beginning with Messalina's infatuation, Silius' bid for power, their mock wedding, the rapid response of the imperial freedmen, Claudius' order for her execution, and her last moments in the Gardens of Lucullus, *Ann.* 11.26–38), it is safe to assume that Juvenal was cashing in on a well-known event.[54] As further proof of the prevalence of the gossip surrounding Messalina's bigamy, *Satire* 14 closes with an allusion to the boundless wealth of Narcissus, Claudius' favorite; in contrast to the account of Tacitus, the speaker claims that Narcissus (not Claudius) ordered Messalina's death (14.328–331). Twice Juvenal alludes to the story that Agrippina, mother of Nero, poisoned her husband Claudius by serving him deadly mushrooms.[55]

Perhaps no other figure in the *Satires* of Juvenal is mentioned as often as Nero and so frequently in the context of conspiracy.[56] From his accession at the will of his conniving mother to his indecorous demise, Nero comes across the pages of Juvenal as paranoid, suspicious, vindictive, and finally helpless. Participants in the Pisonian conspiracy of 65 are mentioned specifically in *Satires* 6, 7, 8 and 10. In *Satire* 8 the speaker asks, "If the people were given a free vote, who would be so depraved as to hesitate about choosing Seneca over Nero?"[57] In *Satire* 10, the speaker describes how "in those times of terror, on Nero's orders, an entire cohort surrounded Longinus and the vast gardens belonging to Seneca the millionaire, and besieged the splendid house of the Laterani."[58] All three men were victims of Nero in the aftermath of the Pisonian conspiracy; Longinus was exiled, Seneca was forced to commit suicide, and Lateranus was executed.[59] In addition, the poet Lucan, driven to suicide, lies at rest in his garden cemetery (7.79); Petronius also perished in the aftermath of the Pisonian conspiracy.[60]

Barea Soranus aroused Nero's hostility, and in 66 he was prosecuted, *inter alia*, on the suspicion of plotting revolt. That same year saw the destruction of Thrasea Paetus (Tac. *Ann.* 16.21–35), a noble statesman, an ardent Stoic, and Nero's most outspoken critic. Juvenal does not miss the opportunity to bring their stories to bear in his *Satires*, and with their allusions he freights his poems with still more dread of Neronian paranoia.[61]

Naturally the fall of Nero and the rapid succession of Galba, Otho, and Vitellius fuel Juvenal's imagination. We have seen that Juvenal alludes to conspiracy for different rhetorical purposes: to emphasize a point, to undercut a premise, to illustrate his indignation. The theme of conspiracy is also privileged by its initial position in *Satire* 13; the addressee Calvinus was born in the consulship of Fonteius Capito (*Fonteio consule natus*, 13.17), that is, in 67 C.E. In 68, Fonteius Capito as legate of Germany joined a plot against Galba, who went so far as to style himself "Caesar."[62] Tacitus reports his death at the hands of Fabius Valens; however, some believed that Capito (although hardly of upstanding character) was innocent of revolution and that the charge was a pretext.[63] Tacitus briefly notes that Julius Paullus had been executed by Fonteius Capito on a false charge of rebellion.[64] Juvenal's allusion thus raises the specter of Fonteius Capito as subject and object of conspiracy and counterconspiracy.[65]

The final allusion to Nero returns us to *Satire* 10, the poem that contains the greatest number of allusions to conspiracy. The poem opens with a question of the role of reason in controlling fear (4) and closes with an allusion to the murder of Messalina (329–345). Lines 61–72 describe the fall of Sejanus; 122–123 and 288 allude to the Catilinarian conspiracy. Just after the overt allusion to Longinus, Seneca, and Lateranus, members of the Pisonian conspiracy (15–18), the speaker describes the paranoia of night travelers:

When you set out on a journey at night, although you may carry only a few goblets of plain silver, you will fear the sword and the pike, you will tremble at the shadow of a reed astir under the moon.[66]

Lucan draws a similar picture of the flight of Pompey from the battlefield of Pharsalus: "He dreads the sound of the trees astir in the wind, and those of his companions who fall back to join him arouse his terror and fear for his position."[67] A literary *topos* emerges that I suggest may also be found in historical anecdote. After Galba was hailed as emperor, when all hope was lost, Nero fled Rome for refuge at his freedman's villa outside the city. Although he had cloaked himself and covered his face, he was recognized. Dio recounts Nero's flight:

He turned aside from the road and hid himself in a place full of reeds. There he waited till daylight, lying flat on the ground so as to run the least risk of being seen. Everyone who passed he suspected had come for him;

he started at every voice, thinking it to be that of someone searching for him; if a dog barked anywhere or a bird chirped, or a bush or branch was shaken by the breeze, he was greatly excited.[68]

The literary commonplace thus takes on added significance after Nero's death, when anecdotes of his last hours may have circulated.[69] Juvenal follows Nero's cruel destruction of Longinus, Seneca, and Lateranus with an image that recalls the tyrant's own demise.[70]

Satire is nothing if not farcical, and in one stroke Juvenal mocks both Nero and Domitian. In the ridiculous poem on the deliberations of Domitian's advisors over what to do with the gift of a gigantic turbot, the speaker invokes the muse in mock-epic fashion, and then sets the stage: "When the last Flavian was tormenting the world half to death and Rome was slave to a bald Nero."[71] Juvenal capitalizes on Domitian's own association of his imperial identity with Nero's.[72] Both emperors were suspicious and paranoid, subjects and objects of conspiracy.[73] When the shore swarms with *agents provocateurs*, who would dare buy or sell such an exceptional fish?[74] Such an extraordinary catch must be presented to the emperor. Humorous and yet sinister, *Satire* 4 draws for the reader a picture of cruelty and fear—the stuff of tyranny[75]—especially in the catalogue of the members of Domitian's cabinet (4.72–118). Of the eleven councilors who survived the dangers of court life, two are of particular note. Pompeius is described as a *delator* (a malicious informer) who could slit one's throat with just a whisper.[76] Rubrius Gallus survived the year 69 by changing allegiance as often as necessary and by allegedly seducing Domitian's wife while she was pregnant (4.104–106).[77] The poem ends with an allusion to Domitian's execution of Lucius Aelius Lamia Aelianus on the pretext of "ancient and harmless jokes."[78] From beginning to end, *Satire* 4 is a caricature of imperial conspiracy.

In the same satire, the speaker describes one of the advisors whose poor son was unable to escape exile and execution. It did him no good to humiliate himself in the amphitheater, and his cleverness was useless. The speaker asks, "Is there anyone who'd be amazed at that old-time cunning of yours, Brutus?" (*quis priscum illud miratur acumen, / Brute, tuum?*, 4.102–103). The question is addressed to Lucius Junius Brutus, the traditional founder and first consul of the Republic, who in 509 B.C.E. expelled Tarquinius Superbus, the last of the Etruscan kings. A more overt reference to the tyrant occurs in a passage toward the end of *Satire* 8, where the speaker recounts the conspiracy to reinstate Tarquinius Superbus:

The last of our good kings to earn the cloak, the crown of Quirinus, and the fasces, was born of a slave woman. The sons of the consul, on the other hand, intended to open the gates that had been betrayed to exiled tyrants; these were boys who should have done something great for periled liberty, something that Mucius or Cocles or the girl who swam the Tiber, the limit of empire, would admire. Rather, a slave (whom the matrons should mourn for a year) betrayed the secret crimes to the senators, while those traitors got their just rewards: flogging and the first legally sanctioned axe.[79]

The legendary conspiracy makes a suitable finale for a poem saturated in conspiracy. Within the appeal to Ponticus on the value of a pedigree is a panel addressed to Rubellius Blandus (8.39–70). The poem alludes to Verres' corrupt governorship (8.105–106), the Catilinarian conspiracy (8.231–244), the Pisonian conspiracy (8.212), and the punishment of the "uncomfortable shirt" such as the Christians suffered (8.235). Livy narrates at length (including the name of the slave informant, Vindicius) the conspiracy to recall Tarquin (2.3–6); Juvenal abbreviates for his own purposes.[80] It should be clear by now that Shumate's sense of Juvenal's essentially paranoid character of vision, of threats framed in terms of conspiracy "ubiquitously suggested although never explicitly formulated as such,"[81] derives from Juvenal's repeated and continuous allusions to historical conspiracies—not only in *Satire* 3 but throughout the corpus. This is not to say that Juvenal is a conspiracy theorist. Rather, he is a poet for whom conspiracy was a historical reality that shaped his perception of his society, a perception distilled, distorted, and disseminated through that most Roman of genres: satire.

XENOPHOBIA

Satire 15 is the obvious place to begin a discussion of xenophobia in Juvenal. This strange and disturbing poem of cannibalism in Egypt perhaps more than any other conveys a deep-seated and frightened, virtually paranoid xenophobia, in spite of the historical reality that Egypt by Juvenal's day was an integral part of the Roman empire politically, economically, and socially.

In the first part of the poem, the speaker begins by sharing amazement with his addressee Volusius (otherwise unknown) at the strange religious practices of the Egyptians; they abstain from certain vegetables and animals, but they are allowed to feed on human flesh (15.1–13). Odysseus told incredible fables of cannibalism, but he had no witnesses: "For the Ithacan alone recited these things without any witness" (*solus enim haec Ithacus nullo sub teste canebat*, 15.26). The speaker, on the other hand, can attest firsthand the tale he is about to tell. Between the neighboring tribes of Ombi and Tentyra there was a longstanding feud over religious worship. When one tribe celebrated its festival, the other looked on with hatred and loathing. Insults escalated to punches, until everyone was embroiled in the brawl. A full-scale riot ensued. As the Ombites chased their enemy in retreat, a Tentyran slipped and fell:

> He's immediately chopped into hundreds of chunks and morsels—to get enough portions from one dead man—and completely devoured by the victorious mob, even gnawing his bones.[82]

Although Juvenal's hexameters draw a gruesome picture, the substance of these lines may not be entirely of his own devising. Suetonius records of Nero's atrocities: "It is even believed that it was his wish to throw living men to be torn to pieces and devoured by a *polyphagus* of the Egyptian race, who would crunch raw flesh and anything else given him."[83] *Polyphagus* occurs only here in classical Latin, and its meaning has been debated; Littman suggests "crocodile," which Baldwin rejects in favor of "glutton."[84] The word must denote a person who devours many (outlandish) things. More curious is the shared diction between Juvenal and Suetonius. Suetonius' phrase *crudem carnam* is evident a few lines later in the *Satire*:

> They were content with raw (*crudo*) corpse. . . . But people who could bring themselves to chew on a corpse never ate anything more willingly than this flesh (*carne*).[85]

If Baldwin is correct to assert "the existence of a human glutton in the time of Nero,"[86] then perhaps Juvenal alludes to this infamous freak of nature. In light of my observations about *Satire* 10.19–21 and the description of Nero's last hours, we may be looking at the vestiges of pulp tabloid about the reign of Nero that derive from a lost source at Juvenal's disposal.[87]

In the second half of the poem, the speaker tries to make sense of this ghastly incident. He recalls a historical example when cannibalism was necessitated by crisis, but that was a different situation (*sed res diversa*, 15.94). He simply cannot understand what drove the Ombites to consume the flesh of their enemy. In lines 15.120–131, the offending tribe is not named. The speaker's revulsion appears to be directed at both tribes indiscriminately, even though one was clearly guilty of the crime of cannibalism. He falls into a generalization: "You won't devise any punishment for the crime or provide retribution suitable for these peoples who assimilate and identify anger and hunger" (*nec poenam sceleri invenies nec digna parabis / supplicia his populis, in quorum mente pares sunt / et similes ira atque fames*, 15.129–131). Just as the speaker condemns these people, *his populis*, for not being able to distinguish between anger and hunger, so with the phrase *his populis* he fails to distinguish between the Ombites and Tentyrans. Generalization is the prerogative of the speaker.

Differentiation continues to be a major theme of the poem,[88] and it concludes with a philosophical reflection on the difference between animals and humans. For Juvenal's speaker, tears distinguish men from beasts:

> This is what separates us from the herd of dumb creatures. . . . We are the only ones to derive a sensibility sent down from the height of heaven, something missing from the four-footed creatures that face towards the earth (*prona*). To them, at the beginning of the world, our common creator granted only the breath of life. To us he gave souls (*animum*) as well.[89]

The passage is reminiscent of the opening line of the moralizing preface of Sallust's *Bellum Catilinae*:

> All men who are eager to outstrip other creatures ought to depend on their best asset so as not to spend life in silence like the beasts that nature makes prostrate (*prona*) and beholden to the belly. Our strength lies in both body and soul (*animo*).[90]

In *Satire* 15 and in the *Bellum Catilinae*, degenerating morality has caused a huge mess, and it is up to the speaker and the historian to sort out the good from the bad. Both attempt to mop up the problem by retreating to the creation of humankind when its most recognizable feature was still discernable. Neither is successful. After Catiline's last stand, the survivors at Pistoria who venture onto the battlefield to collect the dead are unable to distinguish friend from enemy, relative from rival. Even their emotions are inseparable: "Thus in various ways the entire army experienced happiness and sadness, grief and joy" (*ita uarie per omnem exercitum laetitia maeror, luctus atque gaudia agitabantur, Cat.* 61.9). In the chiastic flourish, *laetitia maeror, luctus atque gaudia*, Sallust exerts an artificial rhetorical control that highlights the chaos that lies at the feet of the survivors. For the speaker of *Satire* 15, nature (once again) has been turned on its head: "But these days, there is more harmony among snakes" (*sed iam serpentum maior concordia*, 15.159).[91]

The poem closes with a question, not an answer: "What, then, would Pythagoras say? Wouldn't he run off, anywhere, if now he saw these horrors? Pythagoras was the one who abstained from eating all living things as if they were human and who didn't treat his belly to every kind of bean."[92] Indeed, if anything, Pythagoras overcompensated by refusing to eat *any* flesh or even beans. With his well-ordered universe, Pythagoras stands in stark opposition to the chaos of cannibalism, and yet he is left speechless (*quid diceret ergo,* 15.171).[93]

The Roman association of cannibalism with Egypt is evident in a passage of Dio. Under Marcus Aurelius, Egyptian herdsmen revolted against the Romans. They struck down a Roman centurion, then "sacrificed his companion, and after swearing an oath over his entrails, they devoured them" (Dio 72.4.1). Yet as Harrill amply demonstrates, "Anthropophagy functioned in ancient polemics to brand an opponent or faction in terms of the Other who overturned not only the state but also the norms of language itself."[94] Cannibalism is an invective regularly hurled against factionalism; it is linked with *stasis, bellum civile,* and *coniuratio.* For instance, Catiline compels the conspirators to swear allegiance, and he is rumored to have sealed the conspiratorial oath with human blood (Sal. *Cat.* 22). The story is recounted by Dio: "Catiline imposed the obligation of taking a monstrous oath. For he sacrificed a boy, and after administering the oath over his vitals, he ate these in company with the others" (37.30.3).

Even in our satire, cannibalism is born of civil strife between the Ombites and Tentyrans. Cannibalism lurks on the margins of *stasis* narratives; for Juvenal, however, it takes center stage. He is less interested in the internal politics that evoked the act and more interested in the opportunity the act provides to lambast Egyptians. As Braund remarks, "Juvenal is reflecting and reinforcing the Roman attitude which regarded the Egyptians as weird, despicable, and even sub-human creatures."[95] Egyptian contributions in the areas of medicine, philosophy, and architecture did not go unnoticed or unappreciated. Rather, attitudes oscillated between fear and awe. *Satire* 15, however, is an unequivocal condemnation of the Egyptian people as a whole that erases any complexity inherent in the Greco-Roman Egypt of 127 c.e.[96] Juvenal's speaker allows one incident to represent an entire culture in an artful (to the point of deceitful) synecdoche that attempts to deflect moral degeneracy away from all things Roman.[97] In his outrage the speaker appears to have forgotten what Egypt meant to Hadrian.[98]

Egyptians are targeted throughout the *Satires,* and they are not the only foreigners to come under fire. The first satire opens with an attack on the ethnicity of Domitian's courtier Crispinus; he is Egyptian (1.26–28).[99] Later the speaker complains that foreigners with brash excuses edge out decent Romans at the daily *salutatio*: "I was here first! Why should I fear or hesitate to defend my position in line, even if I was born out East on the Euphrates, a fact which the effeminate windows in my ear would prove, although I personally would deny it."[100] The disgruntled speaker then follows his patron to the forum, where "some Egyptian mogul has dared to put his inscriptions" (*inter quas ausus habere / nescio quis titulos Aegyptius*, 1.129–130).[101] In the tirade against marriage, the speaker describes a superstitious wife who will make a pilgrimage to Egypt to fetch water for the Temple of Isis (6.527–530). Such a wife believes that the goddess herself summoned her in conversation — at night (*nocte*, 6.531). In addition to Isis, the speaker scorns the gods Anubis and Osiris (6.532–541). Once she has finished with her Egyptian practices, the wicked wife will turn to a fortune-telling Jew (6.542–547). Although a woman practices Etruscan haruspicy, Armenians and Syrians have contaminated it (6.548–552); Chaldaean astrologers inspire more confidence (6.553). In short, the speaker's revulsion at the wife's superstitious belief is consistently and repeatedly connected to her association with foreigners of all sorts. Memorable is the attack on Greeks at 6.185–199: What could be more repulsive (*rancidius*, 185) than a woman who thinks she is not beautiful unless her cosmetics are Greek? Women speak Greek when they are angry, happy, worried, when they are divulging secrets ("in this language they pour out all the secrets of the soul," *hoc cuncta effundunt animi secreta*, 6.190) — even when they are making love. Thus, the speaker intimately implicates fear of women's capacity for secrecy with fear of foreign, specifically Greek, influence.

Greeks and easterners come under attack in Umbricius' farewell to Rome, just after he complains that the city is too crowded with conspirators (3.49–54). "Fellow citizens, I cannot stand this Greek Rome" (*non possum ferre, Quirites, / Graecam Vrbem*, 3.60–61). Umbricius laments that both language and customs (*linguam et mores*, 3.63) have become polluted, as though the Tiber were polluted by eastern waters. Rome is infested with Macedonians and Greeks who crowd out the native-born son: "Does it count for nothing at all that my infancy was spent under Aventine skies and fed on Sabine olives?" (3.84–85). With this, the speaker makes a clear distinction between the native and the foreigner. Next, the speaker conflates the prejudice against foreigners with the longstanding prejudice against actors.[102] The display of one's body ran counter to the Roman value of *dignitas*, as Walters points out in his discussion of effeminate males in *Satire* 2.[103] Thus, the condemnation of showmanship in the contexts of foreigners and effeminate males demonstrates the mix-and-match interchangeability of stereotypes that Shumate identified.

Actors were among the most legally restricted professionals in ancient Rome, sharing status comparable to gladiators and prostitutes. They had no protection from corporal punishment, they could not lodge accusations in court, they could not serve as magistrates or as soldiers in the army, and they were not counted as members of tribal assemblies.[104] Socially and legally, actors constituted a separate subjectivity; their separateness suggested a disposition inclined toward secrecy. So Umbricius slips from a tirade against actors on the stage (3.93–99) to a sweeping generalization: "Greece is a nation of comic actors" (*natio comoeda est*, 3.100). With their skill at flattery, Greeks are capable of seducing matrons, daughters, betrothed sons-in-law, chaste boys, and if none of these are available, they will even go after their friend's grandmother (*horum si nihil est, aviam resupinat amici*, 3.112).[105] Worst of all, a Greek can, with just a small drip of a poisonous word in a patron's ear, displace a Roman like Umbricius (3.122–124). Braund's "extravaganza of xenophobia"[106] (3.58–125) is thus characterized by notions of separatism and secrecy that lend the passage an air of conspiracism. This air of foreign conspiracism is present from the start of the poem, for the setting for Umbricius' speech is the grove of Egeria on the Appian Way. The speaker mourns that this site of sacred antiquity, where once Numa conversed with the nymph, has been overrun with Jews (3.13–14).[107]

Satire 11 offers what appears to be the most explicit indictment that foreign influence caused Rome's moral degeneration. The poem begins with reflections on extravagant dining, followed by an invitation to dinner. A man should know his place and dine within his means. The speaker contrasts the frugality of old (*tunc*, 11.100) with the extravagance of now (*at nunc*, 11.120). In the old days, men did not know how to marvel at Greek frippery (11.100). Troops ate from simple clay bowls; silver was reserved for armor (11.108–109). So too, statues of Jupiter were not yet gilded (11.116). "Those times saw tables that were homegrown (*domi natas*), made from our own trees";[108] the speaker emphasizes the value of native over foreign material. He blames foreign influence for devaluing Roman ways; in particular, he links this degeneration to military conquest. "In those days a soldier was a simple man with no appreciation of Greek art" (*tunc rudis et Graias mirari nescius artes*, 11.100); the line recalls a passage of Livy, who speaks of Roman appreciation of Greek art after the sack of Syracuse in 212 B.C.E.[109] Livy attributes the introduction of foreign luxuries at Rome to the soldiers of Manlius who triumphed over the Gauls in 187; his description includes the same kind of tables found in Juvenal's poem.[110]

When Juvenal and the historians blame Rome's moral decline on the importation of foreign luxuries, they implicate the generals who sack cities, the soldiers who bring home the goods, and the citizens who allow themselves to be smitten with these novel objects. Foreigners as well as Romans are criticized, the one for inventing luxuries, the other for pillaging and prizing them, and ultimately neither is held accountable. As a result, stories of moral decline due to foreign opulence leave agency in the balance, in an equilibrium that immobilizes the value of the story altogether. Cloaked as an etiology (cf. Livy's *primum initium*, 25.40.2), the story does not effectively explain the ori-

---

gin of Rome's moral decline. Rather, it crystallizes the love-hate relationship of the conqueror and conquered, *Graecia capta ferum uictorem cepit et artis / intulit ingresti Latio*, in the words of Horace, "Captured Greece took captive her wild conqueror and brought the arts to rustic Latium" (*Ep.* 2.1.156–157). Because captor and captive cannot be distinguished, agency is relinquished. Both parties can be blamed; neither party is responsible. Such indeterminacy is cold comfort.[111] Of course this indeterminacy may be preferred to moments when Juvenal does distinguish between captor and captive, as for example, at the end of *Satire* 2 (163–170), when an Armenian came to Rome as a hostage but returned to Artaxata as an experienced, passive homosexual partner. Juvenal is the master of having his cake and eating it too.[112] Perhaps this more than anything contributes to the paranoid character of Juvenal's vision: the satires shower blame indiscriminately. No one is safe from invective; everyone is suspect.

In the *Satires* Juvenal alludes to historical conspiracies in a variety of ways, from overt mention of a name (e.g., Catiline) to a more veiled reference to an event (e.g., the burning of the Christians), with effects such as we saw in Chapter 1: ubiquity and timelessness make conspiracy all the more troublesome. The speaker of *Satire* 1 announced the need to rely on historical, not contemporary, events for his subject matter; however, it is remarkable that he so often tells of conspiracy and imperial intrigue. If the speaker appears to be obsessed with secrecy, deception, and conspiracy, it is because at nearly every turn he invokes a conspiracy of some sort to make his point.

The xenophobic tirades against Egyptians, Jews, Greeks, and others of foreign extraction that punctuate the *Satires* do not reflect a historical reality; the Rome of Juvenal's day was a polyglot cosmopolis in which various ethnic groups coexisted. Although this xenophobic rhetoric is embedded in a conspiratorial context, Juvenal's speaker does not accuse foreigners of conspiring against Rome. He is not a conspiracy theorist. Instead, he is a man trapped on all sides, as troubled by the prevalent threat of conspiracy from within his society as he is by the constant fear of foreign contagion from without.

In the *Satires* conspirators and foreigners are omnipresent and unfettered by loyalties other than to themselves. Each is an enemy within, although conspirators are by definition insiders, while foreigners should be outsiders. Indeed, conspirators and foreigners confound the regular configuration of insider/outsider, much to the speaker's dismay. Furthermore, as conspirators may have legitimate motives, so foreigners, especially Greeks, may have worthwhile contributions to society.[113] In other words, both conspirators and foreigners give the speaker the rhetorical flexibility he needs to state his case.

Yet at any given moment the speaker is able to represent only a select *part* of the condition of either conspirator or foreigner and never the entire condition of both. To the extent that the speaker is not comprehensive, his images of conspirators and foreigners are only partial. The reader, however, is distracted from this selectivity by the larger argument that the speaker develops (e.g., the dissuasion from marriage in *Satire* 6 or the folly of human wishes in *Satire* 10). Because the images of foreigners and conspirators are at any given time partial and selective, they can be substituted, albeit tenuously, for one another without explicit direction from the speaker. Such synecdoche is at work in *Satire* 15, the most explicitly xenophobic of the poems.

This assimilation of conspirator and foreigner bears on the satirist's purpose. In Richlin's now classic formulation:

> The satirist writes against those who oppress him or those whom he feels he ought to be able to oppress, depicting himself worsted by plutocrat, general, or noble, or sneering at out-groups (foreigners, "pathic" homosexuals, women, freedmen, and so on). By expressing his hostility, the satirist asserts his own power, and makes himself and his like-minded audience feel better. At the same time, the performance of the satire reinforces the desired social norms.[114]

Juvenal may not be a conspiracy theorist, but where there is smoke, there is fire. In the performance that "reinforces desired social norms," the speaker of Juvenal's satires desires for himself the very power that he decries in his enemies.[115] He reasserts a comforting model of the self as he struggles for authority with the out-groups—a struggle that he must win at all costs. We can walk away from the *Satires* of Juvenal knowing that the speaker has left no stone unturned in his quest for victory over his "oppressors," and if he loses, he has no one to blame but himself.

CHAPTER 3

TACITUS *and* PUNISHMENT

In 61 C.E. the urban prefect Pedanius Secundus was murdered by one of his own slaves. According to the provisions of the *senatus consultum Silanianum*, the entire *familia* would have been executed, but because he had four hundred slaves, the people protested the severity of the punishment.[1] The conservative senator and famous jurist Gaius Cassius Longinus spoke in favor of the execution. His speech as recorded by Tacitus (*Ann.* 14.43–44) skillfully deploys the rhetoric of conspiracy, in which we learn as much about the arguments as we do about the audience receptive to such arguments. Moreover, we learn as much about the historian and his methods as we do about the speaker.

The legitimacy of deterrence depends upon persuasion. In Sallust's account of the debate over the execution of the Catilinarian conspirators in 63 B.C.E. (*Cat.* 51–52), Cato and Caesar argue for and against deterrent punishment. Sallustian tone, diction, and even content suffuse the Tacitean speech of Cassius; allusions to the famous debate on the Catilinarian conspirators are manifest.[2] Beyond literary indebtedness, however, I am interested in the way these two episodes betray an anxiety over the dilemma of punishing a crime that is epistemically intractable and the way the speakers deploy a rhetoric of conspiracy to bolster their arguments for deterrence. In both cases a *senatus consultum* addressed the immediate circumstances, but the ethical issues were far from resolved.

If conspiracy theory is latent in the sources, discussions of punishment are recurrent. Cicero speaks in practical and theoretical terms. In the *Pro Sulla*, a speech delivered in 62 in which Cicero defends Publius Sulla Cornelius (nephew of the dictator Lucius Sulla) for complicity in the Catilinarian conspiracy, Cicero justifies the execution of the Catilinarian conspirators.[3] In the *De Officiis*, a philosophical treatise composed at the end of his career, he considers punishment from a more theoretical standpoint.[4] Seneca likewise contemplates punishment in twin treatises, *De Ira* and *De Clementia*, that situate punishment in the context of emotions and political theory.[5] The *De Ira* was composed before 52, under Claudius; the *De Clementia*, between 55 and 56, at the beginning of Nero's reign.[6] The execution of the four hundred slaves of Pedanius Secundus in 61 no doubt challenged Seneca's view. Tacitus may have in part been motivated to embellish the episode to provide a concrete example of the abstracts Seneca could only theorize. Thus, Sallust's speech of Cato depicts deterrent punishment in action, while Cicero continues to offer retrospective considerations. Tacitus' speech of Cassius, which also depicts deterrent punishment in action, on the other hand, challenges Seneca's notions of punishment in retrospection. Taken together, the two episodes demonstrate the ongoing dialectic between theory and practice and the continual reevaluation of the critical dispute over the punishment of conspirators in concrete and abstract terms.

From the highest to the lowest reaches of Roman society, the executions of the senatorial conspirators and the four hundred slaves are discomfiting, but the dialogue between the historians and the philosophers—between Sallust and Cicero, Tacitus and Seneca—elucidates at best a desire for resolution, at least an abiding anxiety over the paradoxes of punishment. Never taken lightly, punishment is especially complicated in the case of conspiracy, a crime difficult if not impossible to prove. Across genres and across time, recourse to prevention supports arguments for punishing conspiracy. Cato and Cassius (as transmitted by Sallust and Tacitus) triumph by persuasion and demonstrate in practice what Cicero and Seneca could only approximate in theory.

PUNISHMENT

Plato delineates three types of punishment:[7] Reform serves primarily the interest of the individual (the wrongdoer). Retribution serves primarily the interest of justice. Deterrence serves primarily the interest of society. Each presents ethical dilemmas.

Reform can take the form of condition, therapy, or education and has as its primary aim the improvement of the individual. The assertion that punishment is a benefit depends on the extent to which the wrongdoer can be reformed. If he cannot be reformed, Plato advocates his ultimate removal from society. In the *De Ira*, Seneca addresses the necessity of punishment with a medical metaphor: A doctor attempts remedies incrementally so that

> no treatment seems harsh if its result is salutary. Similarly, it befits a guardian of the law; the ruler of the state ought to heal human nature by the use of words, and these of the milder sort, as long as he can, to the end

that he may persuade a man to do what he ought to do. . . . Let him pass to harsher language. . . . Lastly let him resort to punishment, yet making it light and not irrevocable. Extreme punishment let him appoint only to extreme crime, so that no man will lose his life unless it is to the benefit even of the loser.[8]

Incremental reform culminates in the ultimate removal of wrongdoers from society, which is a universal good because the wrongdoers, who were unwilling to reform while alive, serve the state in their death as a warning to all.[9] Furthermore, the execution of an incurable provides him a relief from his evil doing and is, therefore, a good.[10]

Seneca returns to incurables at *De Ira* 1.15.1: "Let them be removed from human society if they are bound to make worse all that they touch."[11] Again he advocates levels of punishment, first in private, then in public (*priumum secreta deinde publicata*, 1.16.2). Seneca thus follows Plato's mixed theory that combines humanitarian reform of the curable with the utilitarian exploitation of the incurable to deter others.[12] Reform and deterrence merge again in the *De Clementia*:

> In punishing these, the law has three aims, and so too should the emperor: either to reform the person punished, or to improve the rest by punishing him, or to allow the rest to live in greater safety by removing the wicked.[13]

In this later treatise, Seneca argues that less severe punishments are more effective correctives. Men are more responsive to *clementia*. Yet we should not fail to recognize the association in the ancient mind between reform and deterrence. The failure of reform that results in the ultimate removal of wrongdoers from society is deftly crafted into success at forestalling others.

Retribution seeks to redress a wrongdoing in proportion to the victim's loss. Its primary purpose is "to reaffirm the just state of affairs, threatened by an unjust act," so as "to denounce the crime and dissociate the society from complicity in it."[14] Because retribution seeks to compensate for a past wrong and restore those who have been harmed to their state before being injured, it is retrospective. Yet no punishment can negate the wrong that was done or its effects; the restitution brought about by a principle of equivalency (whereby the punishment fits the crime) is in many ways a fiction of substitution. Furthermore, in its retrospection, retribution subsumes attitudes of resentment and reprobation and if not tempered runs the risk of becoming vindictive and violent.

Retribution depends on a system of substitution that redirects anger into proper channels. The principle of "an eye for an eye" does not attempt to return the eye but to remove an equivalent. The substitution is intended to prevent further conflicts from erupting, restore harmony, and reinforce social order. The benefits of equivalence depend upon a cognitive lapse: that exact equivalence is achievable. The impossibility of exactitude must be mutually misunderstood or at least overlooked. The victim who is compensated must be willing to live with an approximation.

The viability of retribution as an institution depends on reconciling both victim and wrongdoer to the approximation on which the punishment is based. Retribution operates by a sort of differential calculus that resolves the infinitesimal difference between consecutive, continually varying approximations in which justice is the coefficient; justice closes the gap between the eye that was taken and the eye that is taken in return. Furthermore, justice separates retribution from mere retaliation.[15] For example, the federal execution of Timothy McVeigh was retribution for the bombing of the Alfred P. Murrah Building in Oklahoma City—an act that was retaliation for the Waco Siege.[16] Yet neither retribution (one state execution for the murder of 168) nor retaliation (the murder of 168 for the 76 who died in the fire at Mount Carmel) restored any of the lives that were lost in these American calamities.

Braund describes the *De Clementia* as above all a protreptic treatise, intended to turn the young Nero toward the pursuit of philosophy. Book 1 (which contains the bulk of references to punishment) "most closely resembles panegyric."[17] Thus, when Seneca speaks of *ultio*, "retribution," his remarks are directed toward the emperor with a view to encouragement as well as flattery. The emperor is too great to require compensation; his strength, too palpable to need confirmation. In essence, retribution is dismissed but not before Seneca links it to deterrence:

> Retribution normally brings two outcomes: either it provides compensation to the injured party or it provides immunity for the future.[18]

Thus, in a mixed theory that effaces the differences to arrive at one unified purpose, reform and retribution are credited with effecting deterrence.

Retribution probes the limits of justice, for it depends on two variables. First, how is it possible to measure what is deserved such that the crime and the punishment are commensurate? Second, can the issue of responsibility for the crime be adequately settled? A retributive theory of punishment declares that punishment is just and should be carried out when deserved; its moral imperative is independent of any benefit to the individual wrongdoer or to society at large. The violence that retribution implies is endemic to punishment in general.[19] Ultimately, retribution seeks to redress a wrong that has been committed, whether the injured party or the community as a whole is compensated. Successful conspirators, assassins, or terrorists (such as McVeigh) who leave death and destruction in their wake can pay retributive punishment; betrayed conspirators who have not had a chance to complete their plans, on the other hand, require a different kind of punishment. Or rather, given the recurrence of the mixed theory that links reform and retribution to deterrence, conspirators require *every* kind of punishment.

In contrast to retrospective retribution, deterrence is prospective, forward looking, and seeks to prevent future wrongs from being committed.[20] It is not based on a moral imperative but on a principle of benefit to society at large; for this reason, it is often referred to as utilitarian. Such punishment should deter wrongdoers, protect the innocent, and prevent future disturbances in society. Because deterrence operates through threat and example, it exploits the human fear of suffering. Its effectiveness depends in part upon its publicity and its uniform application. For a punishment to be effective, all those known to have committed a crime must be punished, and only those who have committed a crime must be punished.[21]

When it comes to conspiracy, however, the condition "all and only" is especially difficult to satisfy. As Alan Goldman points out, "There are, for example, moral wrongs whose detection is so unsure that their official prohibition would involve costs too great to be worthwhile."[22] The wrongs in question must be so grave that the social cost of interference does not exceed the benefit in terms of reducing (if not preventing) further commissions. Therefore, to punish the innocent or excessively to punish the guilty of a wrongdoing whose detection is not forthcoming must result in overwhelming social benefit. In theory, Goldman's position is sound; in practice, however, it would seem untenable without the aid of persuasion. As Danielle Allen points out, to initiate punishment, the punishers must be able to produce an actionable accusation or story of wrong suffered; the narrative must have sufficient force to convey the wrong. Those with the ability to validate claims about both factual and ethical knowledge will be most successful.[23]

Deterrence is deceptively simple: its goal is to maximize the benefit to society. To the extent that it conflicts with justice, however, it can fail to persuade. Mary Margaret Mackenzie illustrates the dilemma of deterring conspiracy. The principle of utility does not exclude the following possibility:

A has committed no crime at all. Nevertheless, it is thought that his punishment may have a deterrent effect, perhaps because others think that he has committed the crime. On strict utilitarian lines, therefore, the general good is to be served by his being punished, so he is punished.[24]

As we shall see in the episode from Tacitus, a speaker's ability to persuade a decision-making body (the senate) of the justice of deterrence can carry more weight than evidence (or lack thereof). The speaker tries to convince his audience to think that A has committed a crime (even if A has not), that punishment of A will deter others from committing the crime, and that society benefits from this punishment, even if A suffers unjustly. The rhetorical tropes needed to achieve this persuasion are as diverse as they are dangerous.

Deterrence raises the possibility that innocent victims may be punished for wrongs they did not commit but were only thought to have committed. On strict utilitarian lines, however, victimization may be justified if it can prevent widespread and grave violence. Its efficacy, however, depends on ignorance. Victimization will deter so long as those who are to be deterred do not know that the victim is innocent; otherwise, the authority of the punisher is compromised. Thus, the utilitarian should proceed carefully so as to "keep it dark."[25] Such deterrence sidesteps justice and so leaves residual moral feelings unresolved, thereby losing its persuasive force.[26] Obscurity and transparency, however, are the filters of conspiracy and punishment: shrouded in silence, conspiracy survives only in the shadows. Performed before the eyes of all, punishment is most effective in the public forum. Deterrence, however, must avoid public scrutiny. In its opacity, deterrence thus draws dangerously close to conspiracy. The murky crime and its filmy punishment are separated by a very thin veil.

In her study of punishment in ancient Athens, Allen contends that once completed, a punishment ought to establish, if only temporarily, a sense that the challenge to the values of the city has been effectively brought to a halt: "Punishment is a practice through which a community could construct the myth that it is possible to have a system of norms in which all citizens will acquiesce."[27] Deterrence, however, fails to restore a sense of peace, for in its insistence on preventing future wrongs, it depends on the threat of fear that is meant not to close or resolve but to unsettle and disquiet. The difference between punishment that is intended to bring resolution and deterrence that purposefully fosters disquietude generates a "robust skepticism" (to use David Cohen's phrase) evident in the ancient sources.[28]

Deterrence fails to persuade, risks punishing the innocent, and deliberately fosters unease. Furthermore, it cannot be meted out, eye for an eye; it can only escalate. Deterrence has prevention as its social goal, and its only limitation will be the prohibition of punishing the innocent. Yet to be effective, the punishment has to be greater than the crime committed; there is no room for the justice of retribution whereby the punishment fits the crime. To lessen the force of deterrent punishment implies to potential wrongdoers that they have little or nothing to lose by attempting further wrongs. Therefore, wrongs that are more difficult to prosecute call for more severe threats. As Caesar says in the *Bellum Catilinae*, however, once the consul draws his sword, who will impose limits on his severity?[29] How is deterrence limited?

Goldman posits three ways.[30] First, the more zealous the detection of wrongdoing, the stronger the threat of punishment; vigilance is the right arm of deterrence. The ancient Greeks and Romans policed themselves, and to a certain extent the safety of the community depended on their vigilance.[31] In the four speeches against Catiline, Cicero returns repeatedly to the theme of his vigilance for the safety of the city and watchfulness in general.[32] Potential conspirators are told that "in the first place, I myself am watchful for, at hand for, and provide for the republic."[33] Cicero warns that "if anyone stirs in the city, and if I detect not just an action, but any attempt or design against the fatherland, he shall feel that there are in this city vigilant consuls, eminent magistrates, a brave senate, arms and a prison."[34] "Always," says Cicero, "I was vigilant and I took steps in advance, fellow citizens, to see how we might be saved in the midst of so much hidden treachery."[35] So many repeated assurances of the vigilance of the consul strengthen the ultimate argument for the punishment of the conspirators, especially as a deterrent to potential conspirators.

Yet vigilance looks in two directions: not only must society be watchful of potential wrongdoing but the potential wrongdoers must likewise observe and so learn from the punishment of others. Examples from the speeches of Lysias in the period following the reign of the Thirty Tyrants are instructive, for even after the overthrow of the oligarchy, the Athenians feared future civil unrest.[36] In prosecuting Eratosthenes, the speaker of Lysias 12 ("Against Eratosthenes") warns the jury to be on the watch (ἐπιμεληθῆναι), for the defendants believe "that there will be a general indemnity alike for their past actions and for whatever they may want to do in the future, if you let slip from your grasp the authors of our direst misery."[37] For, continues the speaker, "these men, if they escape, will be able again to destroy the city."[38] In Lysias 26 ("The Scrutiny of Evandros"), the speaker reminds the jury that it is on trial as well; "the whole city is watching even now to see what view you will take."[39] Lysias 27 ("Against Epicrates") provides the richest example:

All who are in the administration of the State have come here, not to listen to us, but to know what view you will take of the guilty. Hence, if you acquit these men, they will think that there is nothing to fear from deceiving you and making a profit at your expense; but if you condemn them and sentence them to death, by the same vote you will make the rest more orderly than they are now, and you will have done justice upon these men.[40]

Many more examples could be given of what Adriaan Lanni refers to as the "consequentialist *topos*," clear evidence of the high regard the Athenians paid to accountability.[41] This *topos* forms the substance of Cicero's initial—and re-soundingly successful—foray into the courtroom against Verres. In the *actio prima* he declares, "Today the eyes of the world are upon us, waiting to see how far the conduct of each man among you will be marked by obedience to his conscience and by observance of the law."[42] My point in marshaling these examples is to show the two directions of vigilance. Those who seek to per-suade a decision-making body to pursue deterrent punishment remind their audience that indeed, potential wrongdoers are watching.

If vigilance is the right arm of deterrence, consistency is the left. A sec-ond way to curb the possibility of deterrent punishment that exceeds the limitation of equivalence (just desert) is to impose the penalties consistently and automatically without granting discretion to the enforcement officials. Objections to a universal, unrestrained punishment are patent, and the ex-treme disregard for accountability need not concern us here. Beyond vigi-lance and consistency, Goldman offers a third suggestion worth mention: "The final, most fundamental, and most promising alternative would be (not surprisingly) to attack the social and economic causes of crime by reducing the great inequalities in our society."[43] On the one hand, the suggestion is evasive, deflecting attention away from the issue of punishment onto social inequality. On the other hand, the suggestion simultaneously points to the degree to which punishment itself is an evasion of social inequality. It is easier to punish, even if unconvincingly, than to admit (much less rectify) the obvious.

Finally, deterrence runs the risk of performing an inherently evil act; be-cause punishment injures, it is not consistent with good.[44] It depends on the indivisibility of intention and fulfillment. Yet while fulfillment is the easiest state to prove (the consul's dead body is proof of the successful conspiracy), intention is the most difficult. Intention is established either by the criminal or by the punishing authority. Yet both sources of intention are fraught with difficulty. The criminal's confession of intent can be compromised by many factors. He may confess to reap a reward; implicate an enemy; avoid punish-ment for a greater crime; or halt the discomfort, whether physical, emotional, or psychological, imposed by the interrogator. With nothing left to lose, he may figure that his confession is meaningless and so confess untruthfully. In the absence of confession, the punishing authority makes hidden assump-tions to determine the intention of the criminal. The authority comes to a conclusion based on the disposition of the defendant. Furthermore, one can contemplate murder daily and even feel bad for thinking in detail about the perpetration, but that does not constitute evidence. A guilty conscience is not proof of guilt; the adjective does not substantiate the noun.[45]

Deterrence causes evil if, in the name of forestalling further violence, the punisher corrupts himself by applying a sanction that turns out to be unjust. In light of this, Gregory Kavka asks of the punisher, "Being rational, how can he dispose himself to do something that he knows he would have conclusive reasons not to do, when and if the time comes to do it?"[46] Such a punisher must be able to perform an injustice. Once he has convinced himself, he then distributes the injustice across a decision-making body. Those who contemplate deterrence are willing to risk their own (and others') moral integrity for the sake of forestalling violence.[47]

Proponents of deterrence argue that it protects the innocent and forestalls violence. They claim that vigilance and consistency are sufficient safeguards. Critics counter that it is more unjust to avenge a potential crime than to deny retribution to hypothetical victims. They claim that there are no sufficient safeguards to curb the violence of deterrence once unleashed. As retribution devolves into retaliation, so vigilance swiftly devolves into vigilantism. Both sides are at the mercy of an essential ignorance. It is impossible to know how to punish a crime that has not been committed. Proponents of deterrence craft this ignorance into a paralyzing fear; critics claim that ignorance causes damaging opacity. Both claim discord; neither achieves concord.

Given the three types of punishment and their different ends, is it possible to punish the act of conspiracy? If conspirators are apprehended before committing a wrong, it is not possible to demand retribution. The principle of equivalence cannot apply to a zero sum. Reform in its Platonic conception is intended for individuals and so is not readily applicable to conspirators who band together. The crime of conspiracy is magnified by the participation of several individuals; the threat posed to society by the alliance of many is so great that the reform of such deviance is not probable. If anything, conspirators are so degenerate as to be what Plato would regard as incurable, although the ultimate reform can easily become a deterrent. The only way to rehabilitate a conspirator is to convince him to turn traitor; however, such turncoats are not punished but rather rewarded. Deterrence would seem to be the only remedy for conspiracy; punish conspirators to prevent further civil unrest. Indeed, the ultimate punishment of conspirators (execution) is an unequivocal deterrent. To make the case for punishing conspirators (either those whose intended crime is not yet committed or those whose intention is insufficiently proven), one must rely on a preponderance of explanation, enough to generate sufficient fear of future violence to the community. The greater the preponderance of explanation, the more likely the speaker will persuade the use of deterrent punishment. Conspiracy theory is the substance of the rhetoric of deterrence.

PERSUASION

In early December 63, Cicero denounced Catiline, who fled the city to join his forces at the small town of Faesulae north of Rome; the Allobroges betrayed the conspiracy, and the ringleaders were arrested at the Mulvian Bridge. On December 5, the senate debated the punishment of the five conspirators in custody. Decimus Brutus (former consul in 62) proposed exile and confiscation of property. Julius Caesar (who was in 63 *pontifex maximus*, chief priest of Rome) argued forcefully that the five prisoners not be executed; however, convinced by Marcus Porcius Cato (a former quaestor and plebian tribune-elect), the senate consented to their immediate execution. Cicero himself escorted the conspirator Lentulus from the aedile's house on the Palatine hill, along the Via Sacra, across the forum, to the so-called Tullianum, the prison where four other conspirators had been brought.[48] The five were promptly dispatched, and the consequences would dog Cicero for the rest of his life, for neither the decree of the senate nor the declaration of Catiline as a public enemy justified the execution of those under arrest. Cicero's enemies never forgot this.[49]

In 61, Cicero gave damaging evidence against Clodius Pulcher, who was on trial for trespassing the Bona Dea festival, a ritual open only to women celebrants.[50] Clodius never forgot this, and in 58 he took revenge. As one of the plebian tribunes, he introduced legislation to banish anyone who executed a citizen without a trial. Cicero left Rome before he could be convicted. Clodius then passed a second law declaring Cicero an exile, and he destroyed Cicero's house on the Palatine Hill.[51] In 57, the people issued a law that recalled Cicero. In spite of his continued political activity, he never recovered his former standing. After the assassination of Caesar in 44, Cicero proclaimed openly that Antony should have been killed too. Cicero tried to have Antony declared a public enemy but to no avail. When Antony and Octavian joined forces in 43, Antony proscribed Cicero, and Octavian did not object.[52] Cicero was killed on December 7, 43, twenty years to the month after the execution of the Catilinarian conspirators.

In the shadow of these grisly events, Sallust wrote the *Bellum Catilinae* (43 or 42).[53] Hugh Last argues that the assassination of Caesar shaped the way Sallust wrote the monograph, in which Caesar is carefully distanced from association with Catiline. It is precisely this intuitive matrix of story time (the Catilinarian conspiracy) and historical time (the aftermath of the assassination of Julius Caesar) that gives conspiracy theory its compelling force.[54] Sallust reduces the debate to just two speakers: Caesar, who argues for leniency, and Cato, for capital punishment. Regardless of the degree of authorial intrusion, whether we read the hand of Sallust or hear the voices of Caesar and Cato,[55] the arguments composed in 43 or 42 are likely to echo the arguments that would have been marshaled in 63.

Cato argues for deterrence and appears to disarm his detractors by facing its paradox head on: "For you can prosecute other evil deeds once they have been committed; but this, unless you take care that it not happen, when it does happen you will implore your case in vain."[56] Later in the speech he embeds the same sentiment in a religious context: "When you surrender yourself to indolence and cowardice, you implore the gods in vain."[57] Both statements are universalizing, and yet both use the second-person singular, the effect of which is to convince the body of senators, one man at a time.

The appeal to the individual in the second-person singular is all the stronger because it is couched in exaggerations of the totality of the danger. Cato begins with the broad sweeping admonition that "our liberty and our lives hang in the balance."[58] Senate proceedings that deliberated about sumptuary laws or the extension of empire are meaningless when the very existence of the Roman people is at stake: "We are not debating about whether we should live moderately or lavishly, or how big or how great our empire should be, but whether these things, whatever sort they seem to be, will belong to us or to the enemy."[59]

Repeatedly Cato exploits the appeal of the one for the many, arguing that if the senate decides to save a few (five men), they will in fact destroy many: "While they spare a few criminals, they proceed to destroy all good men."[60] When Cato casts suspicion on Caesar, he relies on the logic of the one versus the many: "I wonder what's going on, if in the enormous fear of all men, he alone is not afraid"[61] For those who are not convinced that sparing a minority of conspirators puts the majority of citizens in danger, Cato ups the ante. The liberation of a few conspirators can motivate an entire army: "So when you decide about Lentulus and the rest, know full well that you are simultaneously deciding about the army of Catiline and about all of the conspirators."[62] Cato concludes this part of his speech with the consequentialist *topos* that puts responsibility squarely on the shoulders of the senate: "If they think you are relaxing even just a little, they all will become ferocious right on the spot."[63]

Finally, Cato brings forward his strongest arguments for deterrence, namely, the clear presence of impending danger: "Are you even now hesitating and doubting what you should do, when the enemy is arrested within the city walls?"[64] The senators should be able to see for themselves that they are under attack: "We are beset on all sides; Catiline with his army has his foot at our throats, some of the enemy are within our walls and even in the bosom of the city, nor can any of their preparations or designs lay hidden, so much the more must we hurry."[65] Immediate deterrence is obviously necessitated by the visible circumstances.

In his recommendation to the senate, therefore, Cato effects a bold substitution. Capital punishment is warranted based on the evidence of Volturcius and the Allobroges. They confessed that they had plotted murder, arson, and other foul and cruel crimes against the citizens and the state. Punishment should be exacted from those who have confessed *as if* from those caught red-handed in capital cases: *de confessis, sicuti de manufestis* ("from those who confessed as if from those caught red-handed," 52.36). Yet they were not caught red-handed. The substitution is accentuated by the consonance of *confessis* and *manufestis*. The entire sleight of hand is possible because, as Cato himself remarks earlier in the speech, in these desperate times, "we have lost the true meaning for things" (*nos uera uocabula rerum amisimus*, 52.11).

Against Cato, Caesar begins by evincing the risks of deterrence. First, the senators must take care lest anger and fear get the better of them and they diminish their dignity: "Likewise you must take care, fellow senators, that the crime of Lentulus and the rest not prevail among you more than your dignity, and you give more thought to your anger than to your reputation."[66] Indeed, this principle seems to underlie the many historical examples that constitute the bulk of Caesar's speech, for he summarizes the *exempla* by saying, "Our ancestors, fellow senators, never lacked wisdom or boldness; nor did pride keep them from imitating the institutions of others, provided those institutions were upright."[67] At stake is not only the constitutionality of the senate but its continued dignity, virtue, and wisdom.[68]

Perhaps Caesar's strongest argument against capital punishment is the simplest. Deterrence knows no bounds: "When with this precedent issued by a decree of the senate the consul draws his sword, who decides his limit or who will restrain him?"[69] Caesar is smart enough to know that any form of violence, even sanctioned violence, must be curbed, restrained, and harnessed. By all accounts, the conspirators' violence would be even less restrained and more comprehensive. Yet, for Caesar, the possible murder of citizens at the hands of unpunished conspirators is less of a worry than the actual execution of citizens at the hands of an unrestrained consul.

Cato carried the day and convinced the senate to execute the Catilinarian conspirators, much to Cicero's ruin. As D. H. Berry explains, "The execution of the conspirators was of questionable legality because it had never been satisfactorily established that either the passing of the S.C.U. [*senatus consultum ultimum*] . . . or the senate's decree that the men had acted *contra rem publi-*

---

cam (Sal. *Cat.* 50.3) was sufficient to deprive a citizen of his right under the *lex Sempronia* (*Catil.* 4.10; c.f. *Rab. Perd.* 12) to a trial before the people."[70] The *lex Sempronia de capite civis Romani* provided that a citizen be allowed the right of appeal to an assembly of fellow citizens before capital punishment. The senate expressed a *sententia*, an opinion, on which the consul acted; responsibility rested with the presiding magistrate.

Cicero would answer for this action for the rest of his career. His first opportunity came in the following year with the trial of Publius Sulla for complicity in the conspiracy. Cicero spends a fair amount of energy rebutting charges of tyranny for executing citizens without a trial. The *exordium*, brief and to the point, is followed immediately by a digression on Cicero's reasons for accepting the case. He defends himself from charges of inconsistency thus:

> Finally, that same powerful and fierce character which the time and the Republic imposed upon me, my own inclination and nature itself has now removed. For a short time the former demanded harshness, but the latter calls for mercy and mildness in all my life.[71]

Compare his remarks in the *De Officiis*, written in 44:

> And yet gentleness and clemency must be approved such that harshness is applied for the sake of the Republic, without which no city-state can be governed. Moreover, all punishment and reprimand should avoid insult, nor should utility redound to him who punishes someone or reprimands him verbally, but to the Republic.[72]

Cicero was only meeting the exigencies of the Republic, an argument absent from the speech of Sallust's Cato; in fact, the entirety of Cicero's Catilinarian orations is pointedly absent from the monograph. According to Sallust, Cicero had already seen to the widespread popularity of the first oration: "Then M. Tullius as consul, whether fearful of the man's presence or affected by anger (*ira conmotus*), delivered a sparkling speech of benefit to the commonwealth, of which he afterwards issued the written version."[73] This is the only nod to Cicero's speeches, and it is significant that Sallust posits anger as a possible motivation, for according to the *De Officiis*, anger must be held at bay when punishing: "Above all anger must be kept from punishment" (*prohibenda autem maxime est ira puniendo*, 1.89). We cannot pinpoint the degree of intercourse between the *Bellum Catilinae* and the *De Officiis*; allusions do not surface. Nor is it necessary to posit enmity, rivalry, or animosity between Sallust and Cicero; Syme is right to caution against absolutes.[74] Rather, the temporal proximity of the works suggests an ongoing dialogue over the legitimacy of deterrent punishment, a dialogue taken up by Tacitus when he responds to the philosophical works of Seneca.

In *Annales* 14.43–44, Tacitus recounts the speech of Gaius Cassius Longinus in the senatorial debate over the enforcement of the *senatus consultum Silanianum* that called for the summary execution of the *familia* of Pedanius Secundus, who was murdered by one of his slaves. As a secondary source embedded in the narrative of the *Annales*, the speech adheres to the conventions of historiography by which the historian reconstructs a speech according to principles of probability and necessity. In many ways, then, the speech of Cassius reveals as much (if not more) about Tacitus' way of thinking while composing the *Annales* under Trajan and Hadrian[75] as anything about Cassius' argument during the reign of Nero. The speech also contains undertones of slave conspiracy.

In form and content, this episode is uncommon. As Judith Ginsburg and others before have noted, it is the first extended senatorial speech in *oratio recta* in the Neronian books of the *Annales*, and it is the longest speech in Book 14.[76] No doubt the execution of the *familia* in 61 was of contemporary importance, if not for the momentous debate it sparked in the senate, at least for the civil unrest it caused in the streets. A legislative principle was at stake; to spare the *familia* on this particular occasion set a precedent for overturning other senatorial decrees in the future on other unspecified grounds. A moral principle was also at stake; to execute the *familia* risked extending the senate's usual severity (a virtue that was acceptable only to a degree) to the point of utter savagery. Summary execution would taint senators with cruelty that would diminish their public esteem (and consequently put them on par with the *princeps*). Of little consequence beyond public opinion was regard for the welfare of the slaves; of no consequence beyond mere speculation was the reason for conspiring to assassinate Pedanius Secundus. But if we would fully comprehend the pervasiveness of conspiracy theory in the service of persuasion, we must find a way to discern the individual tiles that compose this tessellated episode.

In the first place, it is difficult if not impossible to sort out whether a historical Cassius speaks—a Cassius characterized by Tacitus, who speaks as a representative of old senatorial aristocracy—or whether Tacitus simply dons the mask of Cassius to express his own opinions.[77] Arguments for Tacitean invention compare the description of the *senatus consultum* as "according to the ancient custom" (*uetere ex more*, 14.42.2) to Cassius' pointed appeal to the better judgment of senators of old (14.43.1). The reader is left with an impression that the *senatus consultum Silanianum* is ancient, although it dates to 10 C.E., only fifty years before.[78] Furthermore, Tacitus must have had a reason for giving so much space and attention to this speech. Invoking a metahistorical line of argument, Joseph Wolf supposes that Tacitus was growing disappointed with Trajan's reign. Trajan extended the scope of the *senatus consultum Silanianum*, an already cruel law. The speech is thus Tacitus' way of commenting on his own times.[79] Tacitean *inventio* may be located along a spectrum of authorial intrusion, from none whatsoever to complete fabrication by the historian. A prudent reader would conclude that (1) Cassius no doubt gave a speech in the senate, probably recorded in the *acta senatus*, and (2) Tacitus was constrained by this historical fact to adhere to the principles of the original speech for which he may have consulted the *acta*. One need not go so far as Wolf and posit a metahistorical explanation for this uncommon episode; Tacitus' reportage attests an abiding interest in the problem of slave revolt and conspiracy, the master's omniscience and providence, and the role of punishment in mediating the two.

Rather than sort out Cassius from Tacitus, I prefer to look at the ways the speech and the narrative in which it is embedded echo each other in tone, diction, and theme. The words of Cassius are framed by the narrative of Tacitus, but as focus shifts from narrative to speech, the distinction between historian and orator blurs. Whether Tacitus is echoing or ventriloquizing Cassius, the effect is the same. This episode conveys a preoccupation with an abiding fear of violent slave resistance and the twofold purpose of deterrence: to allay that fear among the senators and to marshal it against slaves.

The preoccupation with the behavior of the mob in Paragraphs 42 and 45 envelops the speech in a ring composition. The people rise in protest ("with a throng of people . . . it reached the point of riot," *concursu plebis . . . usque ad seditionem uentum est*, 42.2), and after the senate resolves to adhere to the terms of the *senatus consultum*, a throng blocks the streets ("a throng amassed threatening with rocks and firebrands," *conglobata multitudine et saxa ac faces minanter*, 45.1). This theme of justifiable public protest penetrates the inner logic of the speech with a dangerous insinuation. The mob that opposes the execution is analogous to the band of slaves; as the mob assaulted the *mos maiorum*, so slaves laid hands on Pedanius Secundus. If the violence of the mob is justified, then by analogy the violence of the slaves may also be justified.

Furthermore, both historian and orator attempt to explain why the slaves murdered their master. Tacitus gives alternative explanations:

Pedanius Secundus, the urban prefect, was killed by his very own slave, either because the freedom he had paid for was denied, or because he was inflamed with affection for a male prostitute and would not tolerate his master as a rival.[80]

Tacitus fulfills the duty of refining historian in that typically Tacitean way. When two alternative explanations compete for priority, he states, then suspends, discrepancy. As orator, Cassius is held to a higher standard of explanation. He elaborates only the first of these reasons:

> Or was the murderer avenging his own wrongs, because he had made a contract concerning his family finances or was robbed of a family slave?[81]

Thus, Cassius tries to explain the motives of the slaves in terms that approximate Tacitus' explanation but are somewhat more defined.[82] This brings us to Cassius' speech itself.

Wolf has analyzed the speech into its rhetorical components. The *exordium*, intended to establish the speaker's *auctoritas*, is "elaborate in design, mundane in content."[83] The *narratio* is noticeably short. The *argumentatio* has three rhetorical questions, followed by the *refutatio*, the usual place for rhetorical irony, which some say Cassius exaggerates to a fault.[84] The final and strongest arguments are marshaled before the epilogue in which Cassius incites hatred of slaves to soothe the conscience of the senators.[85] Rather than examine the individual parts of the speech, Dieter Nörr investigates the way the speech adheres to and departs from the Aristotelian categories of oratory. Judicial speeches distinguish the just from the unjust; deliberative speeches argue for utility to the public good; demonstrative speeches praise honesty and censure corruption. Elements of all three are evident in Cassius' speech.[86] Wolf and Nörr are in search of Tacitean *inventio*. Yet, whether the attitudes are Neronian or Hadrianic, the speech advocates for deterrent punishment (Neronian or Hadrianic) by recourse to conspiracy theory.

Since the speaker openly acknowledges the possibility of injustice ("But some innocent men will perish," *at quidam insontes peribunt*, 14.44.4), the punishment is admittedly not retributive. Neither does the speaker seek reform, for slaves by definition cannot be reformed. Instead, the speaker orients his audience forward, to the dreadful possibilities that lie in the future ("Go ahead, cast your vote for impunity, but whom can his rank defend, when it did not defend the urban prefect?" 14.43.3). This is a brilliant twist of the agency imperative. A conspiracy theorist demands action, but Cassius grants agency to his audience only to castigate them for missing the mark. Misguided agency is as dangerous as the threat of conspiracy itself. All depends on persuasion.

The effectiveness of deterrence depends on the publicity of the punishment, and Tacitus makes it clear that this case had an extremely high public profile. Furthermore, the uniform application of the punishment is stressed in the *exordium*, when the speaker goes to great lengths to establish the authority of the *senatus consultum Silanianum* and its inveterate stability.

If the effectiveness of deterrence also depends on the punishment of "all and only" those who have committed the crime, then on this point Cassius admits his weakness: *at quidam insontes peribunt*; some will object that innocent men will die too. In the matter of slaves, however, this injustice is of limited importance. The speaker is not as worried about the justice of the punishment as he is concerned with the senatorial self-fashioning. To convince the audience that "all and only" those who have done wrong will be executed, the speaker constructs an elaborate, fictive, counter-*narratio* within his argument to flesh out the otherwise weak *narratio* at the outset of the speech. The fact of the case is simply stated in an ablative absolute that emphasizes its syntactic distinctiveness in the sentence as well as its structural distinctiveness in the overall speech, ". . . when a man of consular rank was murdered in his own home by a slave plot" (*consulari uiro domi suae interfecto per insidias seruiles*, 14.43.2). Compare the much more detailed fiction the audience is asked to imagine, introduced by a finite, indicative verb: "Do you believe that a slave conceived the intention to kill his master?" (*creditisne seruum interficiendi domini animum sumpsisse*, 14.44.1). The contrafactual supposition is expressed not in the subjunctive mood but with an indicative question introduced by *num*, a particle that expresses the speaker's anxiety and expects of the audience a negative answer:

> Would he have been able to get past the watchmen, to unlock the bedroom doors, to bring in a lamp, and to perpetrate the murder, with everyone oblivious?[87]

In this elaborate fiction, ignorance is relegated to an ablative absolute (*omnibus nesciis*), but this ignorance is itself construed as evidence of the conspiracy. As Keeley puts it, "Conspiracy theories are the only theories for which evidence *against* them is actually construed as evidence *in favor* of them."[88] That is to say, the unsubstantiated details (hoodwinked watchmen, unlocked doors, lamp) are proof of the final deed (*caedem perpetrare*, "to perpetrate the murder"), even though everyone was oblivious.

This elaborate counter-*narratio* is an excellent example of the rhetoric of conspiracy. In the absence of testimony or evidence, the speaker constructs a plausible scenario, based on belief (*creditis*), in which even if a single slave conceives of a plot to kill his master, he still is not able to carry it out without accomplices. His success depends upon the silence of others who know of his plan. Cassius constructs a step-by-step theory that explains how Pedanius Secundus was murdered; it is a conspiracy theory that lays blame on the entire *familia* acting in secret, and it is meant to persuade his audience.

To strengthen his argument, presumably Cassius would suggest limitations to the principle of strong deterrence inherent in the *senatus consultum Silanianum*. Although not stated with the force of Pliny, for example, vigilance is suggested by the conditional clause "you will not keep them in check but by fear" (*non nisi metu coercueris*, 14.44.3). Other *familiae*, presumably, are watching and will learn from this example (another example of the consequentialist *topos*). Rather, Cassius argues most strongly and explicitly for consistency of punishment that denies discretion in individual cases. Cassius rejects outright the possibility that this case had extenuating circumstances: "Or, as some are not embarrassed to imagine, was the murderer avenging his own wrongs?" (*an, ut quidam fingere non erubescunt, iniurias suas ultus est interfector*, 14.43.4).[89] If consistency in the face of individual circumstances is Cassius' only overt attempt at limiting the severity of deterrence, then acknowledgement of the social and economic causes of the crime is not only unspoken but unthinkable.

The arguments of Cassius incorporate fear mongering and religious belief, two of the components of a conspiracy mentality. Twice fear is invoked, the first time in a simple question: "Whose *familia* will bring aid that takes notice of our dangers not even in fear?" (*in metu*, 14.43.3). When fear is adduced a second time, however, it is part of a xenophobic complex: "Now that we have foreigners among our *familiae* whose religious rights are different, or foreign, or nonexistent, you will not keep that rabble in check but by fear" (*postquam uero nationes in familiis habemus, quibus diuersi ritus, externa sacra aut nulla sunt, colluuiem istam non nisi metu coercueris*, 14.44.3). The deliberative agents of punishment hold different beliefs from the silent, powerless objects of punishment. Yet if slaves constitute a separate, unquestioned, and unquestionable subjectivity, why does Cassius need to introduce xenophobia as an argument for harsh punishment? In a conservative appeal to the good old days, when slaves were born on the estate "and immediately conceived an affection for their masters" (*cum . . . caritatemque dominorum statim acciperent*, 14.44.3), Cassius distinguishes contemporary foreign-born slaves according to their different (or nonexistent) religious practices. The weakness of the "then-versus-now" argument is (poorly) disguised by the appeal to perennial xenophobia and religious prejudice. As the slaves' religious practice degenerates—from different, to foreign, to nonexistent—so the senators' agency gains momentum, from a nondefensible appeal to the good old days, to blame of uncontrollable foreign influence, to the sovereignty of fear.

Finally, because Cassius' speech opens with a verbatim repetition from the speech of Cato in Sallust's *Bellum Catilinae*, the arguments for punishment are immediately embedded in a context of conspiracy. Both Cato and Cassius begin, "My fellow senators, I have often . . ." (*saepe numero, patres conscripti, Cat.* 52.3; *Ann.* 14.43.1). Of course, the formula was probably common and reminded the audience of the longstanding experience, the equivalent status, and the mutual respect of the speaker and audience.[90] The content of the speeches, however, suggests that the repetition is more potent. In the face of his weak-minded fellow senators, Cato throws his hands up in a desperate concession: "I propose that you take pity on them" (*misereamini censeo, Cat.* 52.26). Notice the affinity with the absolutism of Cassius' surrender: "We might as well declare that the master was murdered justly" (*pronuntiemus ultro dominum iure caesum uideri,* 14.43.4). These guys are playing for keeps in a rhetoric that paints everything black and white: either withstand or capitulate, conquer or be conquered, live or die. Yet morality resides squarely in the interstices.

Cato advocates the punishment of citizen conspirators who have been betrayed; Cassius advocates the punishment of slave conspirators who have succeeded in murdering their master. Furthermore, as Ginsburg has shown, the invocation of Cato in the words *saepe numero, patres conscripti* raises the expectation of an old-fashioned senatorial deliberation, complete with opposing speech. If so, then Tacitus has bypassed the opposing speaker's motion against capital punishment; *saepe numero* is thus an admission of omission at the outset, whereby the opposing argument is conspicuous in its absence.[91] Yet this was no longer the consulship of Cicero; this was the reign of Nero. In contrast to Cassius' artfully constructed oration, opposition could be expressed only by discordant—and unsuccessful—voices:

> As no one individual dared oppose the opinion of Cassius, so discordant voices kept on objecting to the number, or the age, or the sex and the undoubted innocence of several of the condemned. Still, the side that decreed capital punishment prevailed.[92]

Rather than speak against the senator, Nero instead issued an edict to the general populace, and though he mitigated the sentence, he did not reverse it: "Nero prohibited this, so that the ancient custom that pity (*misericordia*) had not lessened might not be strained by savagery (*per saeuitiam*)" (14.45.2). His only concern was for the appearance of *misericordia* over *saeuitia*.

Tacitus' choice to close the episode with these two catchwords strikes me as an implicit indictment of a philosophy of punishment that could not hold up under the pressure of Neronian Rome.[93] With these words the glacial narrative of Book 14 drifts toward the death of Burrus (perhaps by poison, *Ann.* 14.51.1) and the eventual retirement of Seneca (14.53–57), the philosopher so careful to distinguish *misericordia* from *clementia, saeuitia* from *seueritas*.[94] In 62, Seneca attempted to convince Nero to let him go: "Your great-great-grandfather Augustus permitted a Mytilenean retirement to Marcus Agrippa and (so to speak) a foreign furlough within the city itself to Gaius Maecenas."[95] With the *exemplum* of Augustus, Tacitus closes the circle,[96] for in the inaugural *De Clementia*, Seneca's best example is Augustus, whose treatment of a conspirator runs counter to every expectation of the age in a deliberation that runs counter to the speeches of Cato and Cassius in every respect.

When Augustus was in his forties and staying in Gaul, he was given information that Cornelius Cinna Magnus, grandson of Pompey, was plotting against him.[97] One of the conspirators (*unus ex consciis, Clem.* 1.9.2) betrayed the place, time, and manner of attack. Augustus was as angry with himself for his vulnerability as he was with Cinna for plotting against him. Livia offered advice. He had already punished a litany of conspirators to no avail. "Now, find out how clemency can turn out for you: pardon Lucius Cinna" (*nunc tempta quomodo tibi cedat clementia; ignosce L. Cinnae, Clem.* 1.9.6).[98] Delighted (*gauisus*, 1.9.7), Augustus summoned Cinna for an interview that lasted more than two hours, during which Augustus apparently did most if not all the talking (*Clem.* 1.9.11). After the pardon Cinna was most devoted and most loyal (*amicissimum fidelissimumque*, 1.9.12), and Augustus was never the target of a conspiracy again.

The anecdote is quite unlike the situations in Sallust and Tacitus.[99] First, the conspiracy of Cinna rests on the firm evidence handed over by a traitor; there is no need for a rhetoric of conspiracy that alleges a plot based on false logic and nonexistent evidence. Cinna is not dubiously accused; he is definitively betrayed. Second, he is not punished but pardoned; there is no defense of deterrence such as Cato and Cassius mount. If anything, the anecdote is a stinging indictment, for Livia rattles off an impressive catalogue of the many times punishment failed to deter conspirators.[100] Third, Seneca and Dio record the conspiracy of Cinna to showcase Augustus' capacity for forgiveness and *clementia*. Yet the amnesty granted to Cinna obfuscates the memory of the other conspirators, all of whom were executed. By pardoning the last conspirator, Augustus rehabilitates his reputation. Cato and Cassius, on the other hand, are remembered for their *seueritas*.

The speeches of Cato and Cassius are instances of deterrence in action; the *De Officiis*, the *De Ira*, and the *De Clementia* ponder punishment in theory. The concurrence of the *De Officiis* and the *Bellum Catilinae* does not necessarily put them in direct conflict but in dialogue of word and deed, as both Cicero and Sallust confront the morality of deterrence. The texts are especially congenial since both are born in the wake of the assassination of Caesar, when the morality of conspiracy was brought to the fore once again: Were Brutus and Cassius assassins or liberators? The verdict was still out. Tacitus, of course, writes long after the murder of Pedanius Secundus and the execution of his four hundred slaves. In recording the speech of Cassius, Tacitus evokes Sallust's Cato and the paradoxes of punishment, and as Sallust engaged in dialogue with Cicero, so Tacitus turns to Seneca, whether in sympathy or criticism we cannot discern. It is time, however, to reevaluate Miriam Griffin's overarching conclusion, that "Tacitus has no interest" in the philosopher Seneca.[101]

My point in this chapter is simple: The problem of punishing conspirators in ancient Rome does not go away; it is resolved neither in theory nor in practice. In every incarnation, whether senators are agents or victims, the problem of punishment poses the same dilemma, and sometimes the only way Roman senators could elucidate their intuitions about morality was to argue against their noble ideals and their hideous outcomes.

As both agents and victims, senators reflect the dual capacity of conspiracy theory to be a constructive and destructive force. How much of this goes out the window when it comes to emperors? When social status is inflated beyond measure, what is left of conspiracy theory? Does it wither into mere speculation or does it mushroom into boundless paranoia?

CHAPTER 4

SUETONIUS *and* SUSPICION

Suspicion is a recurring theme in Suetonius' *De Vita Caesarum*. From Julius Caesar to Domitian, it is inextricably woven into the fabric of the biographies, individually and as a whole. Emperors are objects of suspicion by virtue of their autocracy; however, numerous examples will attest the need to exercise suspicion. Some may have good reason for distrust, but others take it too far. Thus, a spectrum emerges, from judicious mistrust, to dysfunctional suspicion, to unbridled and deadly paranoia. This spectrum is visible only when the twelve biographies are considered as a complete unit, hence my contention that suspicion is a unifying narrative framework for Suetonius' entire enterprise. My conclusions bear upon our understanding of the Hadrianic context of production.

Such conclusions depend in part on chronology. The dates of Suetonius' birth and death are uncertain and can only be guessed, although some evidence obtains from his works, a letter of Pliny, an inscription, and a notice in the *Historia Augusta*. Suetonius describes himself as an *adulescens* when rumors of a false Nero in Parthia reached Rome in 88 C.E. (*Nero* 57.2). If an *adulescens* is between eleven and nineteen years old, Suetonius was probably born sometime in the decade between 69 and 79. From his cognomen "Tranquillus," Syme infers the year 70 and the tranquility after civil war; however, Andrew Wallace-Hadrill notes that "Tranquillus" need not refer specifically to the peace bestowed by the accession of Vespasian but may only be a pun on the father's name, Suetonius Laetus "The Happy," who was tribune of the thirteenth legion in 69 (*Otho* 10).[1]

Pliny's *Epistula* 3.8, written to Suetonius, dates to 101–103.[2] Suetonius declined the post of military tribune in Britain, asking Pliny to recommend another in his stead. If Suetonius was then about thirty years old, he would have been born between 71 and 73. An inscription from the ancient town of Hippo Regius establishes his birthplace and preserves some public distinctions and career highlights.[3] Suetonius served under Trajan as minister of libraries (*a bibliothecis*) and the related post of minister of documents (*a studiis*) and under Hadrian as minister of correspondence (*ab epistulis*).[4] Finally, according to the biography of Hadrian in the late antique collection of biographies known as the *Historia Augusta*, Suetonius was removed from his position as *ab epistulis* because his (and others') behavior toward Hadrian's wife Sabina was more informal than court etiquette tolerated. The incident is generally dated to 122, although some historians have proposed 128.[5] Therefore, on the outside estimation, Suetonius was born in 70 and is not attested after 128.

The date of composition and publication of the *De Vita Caesarum* is similarly vexing. According to the late antique Byzantine scholar Johannes Laurentius Lydus, Suetonius dedicated the biographies to Septicius Clarus, praetorian prefect; this would have been between 119 and 122.[6] Publication probably overlapped with the *Annales* of Tacitus, begun under Trajan and continued under Hadrian.[7] Yet it is not possible to gauge how many (if any) of the biographies were already written when Hadrian became emperor in 117. Did his accession inspire the *De Vita Caesarum* or did the events of 117 merely intrude upon work already underway? Surely the accession of Hadrian must have influenced the work in some perceptible way. Based on remarks about things in which Hadrian was known to have taken an interest (e.g., hunting, travel, Greek culture, advancement of provincial interests), T. F. Carney identifies a "deeply felt antipathy to all that Hadrian stood for." Eugen Cizek maintains that Suetonius slipped in some warnings, examples, and advice for Hadrian, a premise rejected by Wallace-Hadrill: "Hadrian could well have read the *Caesars* out of interest, but not to be taught lessons." Ulrich Lambrecht insists that the first two lives reflect Suetonius' own life experience under Trajan and Hadrian, while Jacques Gascou compares the ideal *princeps* according to Suetonius with the images of Hadrian available in Dio and the *Historia Augusta* to conclude that Suetonius neither criticizes nor counsels Hadrian; rather, he supports his public image.[8] I argue that Suetonius develops a composite picture of the causes and effects of suspicion that would not have been ignored by the *princeps* of the day.

In addition to chronology, the unity of the twelve lives has been a matter of debate. The first two biographies are copious, the middle four mediocre, the last six cursory.[9] Reasons for the degeneration are proposed: The first two biographies reflect Suetonius' area of particular expertise in the age of Cicero and Augustus;[10] his interest and enthusiasm waned in the course of writing;[11] he was denied access to archives after the political blunder in 122.[12] It has even been proposed (and abandoned) that the biographies are uneven because Suetonius composed the last six first, and then with increasing skill and enthusiasm lavished more attention, space, and care on the earlier lives.[13]

Controversy fades somewhat if the *De Vita Caesarum* is understood as a complete work in twelve parts; we might compare the unity of a twelve-book epic.[14] Rather than a collection of individual biographies, the *De Vita Caesarum* documents the life of a principate from its inception under Julius Caesar (dictator but never *princeps*) to its demise under Domitian, the last of the Flavians. The *De Vita Caesarum* partakes of the traditions of exemplarity[15] that characterize so much of Roman history and biography; Suetonius presents much to emulate, much to avoid. Through individual *principes*, he arrives at a composite Caesar seen in a variety of situations across time.[16] Thus, the biographies are not so much divided by deterioration in quality as they are united by skillfully articulated repetitions and allusions. Verbatim expressions and hauntingly familiar anecdotes of suspicion unite the work in tone and purpose. Suspicion creeps into each life, as each Caesar must confront it in himself or in others. Some handle it more effectively than others; however, all of them are subject to its principles.

TRUST AND SUSPICION

Suspicion and its opposite, trust, bring us to the heart of conspiracy theory, for these twin acts of mind are social and epistemic at their core. Both are human responses to a "perennial epistemological gap."[17] When faced with uncertain or unknowable outcomes, one attempts to map the available clues so as to minimize the risk of a wrong decision. For instance, an emperor conducts an unusually large number of treason trials one year; as a result, a certain senator is unsure whether he will be prosecuted. In the face of uncertainty, he can extend to the emperor either trust or suspicion so as to secure for himself a purchase on the future. Should he trust the emperor and plan on seeing his children grow up, or should he go ahead and deposit his will with the Vestal Virgins? In deciding, the senator risks his reputation, his relationship with the emperor, and even his life. Such a decision must be made carefully and prudently.

In the face of an epistemological gap, the potential truster must depend on the testimony of others. Michael Baurmann identifies three crucial factors that come into play. First, the truster must assess the competence of his informant. Has the informant proven reliable and useful in the past? Second, is the informant influenced by extrinsic incentives such as benefits, rewards, sanctions, or other forms of recognition that can influence the reliability of the testimony? Do these external factors tempt the informant to offer wrong, misleading, or useless information in his own self-interest? Finally, to what degree is the informant motivated by intrinsic incentives, bonds of solidarity, common social values and norms, and moral virtues or vices? A sympathetic informant can transmit reliable information; a hostile informant, false and deceptive testimony.[18]

Trust is more readily extended to informants who resemble the truster. Xenophobia fosters suspicion,[19] as the *Satires* of Juvenal so clearly demonstrate; however, the more inclusive the trust network, the more efficient it is. So a trust network that transgresses boundaries of status, gender, race, class, or ethnicity can offer information from a broader spectrum of sources.[20] In the *Hecyra*, Laches would have fared much better if he had not impugned the testimony of women so readily; indeed, Pamphilus is so successful precisely because his trust network extends to the courtesan Bacchis. In the case of our fictional senator, he can make a better, more informed response to the emperor's loaded docket of treason trials if he can canvass not just his fellow senators but freedmen, slaves, or any who might offer information. Of course, as his trust network widens, he must assess the attendant extrinsic and intrinsic incentives of each informant.

If trust is deeply embedded in social networks, then suspicion is the result of social isolation and what Baurmann calls "epistemic seclusion."[21] Narrow social circles limit one's accessibility to knowledge. Individuals who are systematically restricted in their options for acquiring knowledge are at the mercy of limited information that supports only a selected point of view. Potential informants may be pressured into silence; for example, fellow senators may refuse to speak to our fictional senator for fear that they too will fall victim to a *delator*.[22] Epistemic seclusion can also be the result of the truster's self-imposed social isolation. By virtue of his extraordinary and exclusive social status—there is only ever one *princeps*—an emperor is in a perpetual state of social isolation. No one resembles him; all are unlike him. His trust network is inherently compromised by the essential social difference between him and any potential informants. Such extreme asymmetry in status leads to dysfunctional distrust.

Yet the phrase "dysfunctional distrust" presupposes a positive function of distrust and indeed even suspicion. For example, in some middle-class American neighborhoods, signs can be seen such as those produced by the National Sheriff's Association: "NEIGHBORHOOD WATCH—our neighbors are watching to report suspicious activity to our law enforcement agency." Under the guidance of the authorities, neighbors can take their safety into their own hands. Suspicion is thus a form of self-policing and self-protection. It deters wrongdoers and lets potential wrongdoers know that they are being watched. Such a judicious use of suspicion can help avoid the sticky problem of punishing conspirators, since suspicion can ward off crimes and conspiracies. Suspicion is preventative and keeps society from having to deal with the paradox of punishment. Some social roles demand suspicion; border guards, airport security, and customs officials are expected to be suspicious.[23] In antiquity, the *delator* is expected to be suspicious.[24] Other roles assume suspicion; nobody expects a spy to be truthful or, in antiquity, a slave or a woman. Because certain people will be assumed to behave a certain way, necessary precautions can be taken. Therefore, suspicion lends a degree of predictability and enhances security; it is the assertion of a modicum of human control over the unknown.

Yet suspicion can also backfire for reasons epistemic and social. It can be dangerous because it posits, without proof, the existence of something evil. It is the apprehension of guilt or fault on slight grounds, without clear evidence. As conspiracy theories are phenomena for which, paradoxically, a lack of evidence may constitute evidence, so suspicions are also based on a lack of evidence. Too much surveillance can have a "boomerang effect."[25] Rather than ward off crime, posted signs can invite potential criminals to challenge proclaimed authority. The outward manifestation of suspicion not only undermines trust but generates resentment and antagonism. Instead of discouraging crime, suspicion can actually cultivate it.

Dysfunctional suspicion is generated by a distrust of the trustworthy, a misunderstanding of available information, a disregard of available information, or a disbelief in the truth. Any one of these four factors can set a vicious loop into perpetual motion, creating a culture of suspicion. When a person distrusts his faithful friends, disregards their information, or simply disbelieves them, the friends are likely to respond in kind. Reactions to unwarranted suspicion include resentment, frustration, and feelings of helplessness that lead to violence.[26]

Suspicion and conspiracy theory rely on dispositional and circumstantial explanations as their proof; in this sense, both generate stereotypes. Both destabilize authority by casting doubt on intentions and motives that cannot be proven. Yet the differences are as important as the similarities. While conspiracy theory seeks scapegoats, suspicion is deployed in the interest of security, whether personal or communal. Conspiracy theory attempts to explain past events, while suspicion attempts to prevent future events. A moral dividing line emerges as well. As the neighborhood crime watch sign suggests, "bad" citizens conspire to commit crimes, but "good" citizens are suspicious. Emperors are citizens extraordinaire,[27] and so their suspicions carry greater weight. Indeed, suspicion is a fact of life for the Roman emperors. Their lives are preserved by the suspicions they hold and can eventually be destroyed by the suspicions they generate.

CONDITIONS OF RULE

Suspicio and its cognates are the principle indicators, together with the adjective *diffidens* ("distrustful") and the verbs *credere* ("to believe"), *opinari* ("to hold as an opinion, to suppose") and *existimare* ("to think or suppose"), usually in the passive voice. Anecdotes allow for distortion, contradiction, simplification, and confusion; however, these interpretive disadvantages are counterbalanced by the way they allow Suetonius to broaden "le champ de l'histoire."[28] Anecdotes—especially of suspicion—document areas to which Roman historians and writers in general paid little attention.[29] I resist the urge to correct and criticize Suetonius' errors as much as possible to discern not only his unique conception of suspicion but also its unifying force.

Suspicion surfaces in the *De Vita Caesarum* in three ways and almost exclusively from the point of view of the emperor. First, emperors are objects of suspicion; their actions, words, and behavior arouse suspicion in others. Second, they attempt to avoid suspicion. Third, they regard others with suspicion that can be judiciously exercised to save their own lives. When taken to extremes, however, suspicion devolves into paranoia. These three aspects thus work in concert to achieve a balanced representation.[30] Just as an emperor arouses suspicion, so he seeks to avoid it. To the extent that an emperor is suspicious, he is justified by virtue of the number of plots detected against him. The three categories are not consistently evident in each individual life; rather, they appear across the twelve lives, thereby creating a composite picture of suspicion as a condition of rule.[31]

EMPERORS AS OBJECTS OF SUSPICION

Julius Caesar (hereafter referred to simply as Caesar) is suspected of complicity in a conspiracy:

> He fell under suspicion (*uenit in suspicionem*) of having conspired with the ex-consul Marcus Crassus, as well as Publius Sulla and Lucius Autronius (who had been convicted of bribery after winning the consular elections), their plan being to attack the senate on New Year's Day and, after the slaughter of their chosen victims, for Crassus to usurp the dictatorship,

while Caesar would be made his Master of Horse; then, when they had organized the state according to their wishes, the consulship would be restored to Sulla and Autronius.[32]

Suetonius is describing the so-called first Catilinarian conspiracy, a shadowy event that resists our full comprehension.[33] According to Sallust, Sulla and Autronius were charged with electoral bribery and disqualified from office (*Cat.* 18.2). A second election was held for which Catiline offered himself as candidate. His application was rejected on the grounds that he had not yet been tried for extortion committed during his governorship of Africa the year before (*Cat.* 18.3); Cotta and Torquatus were elected instead. In retaliation, a plot was formed to assassinate them on the first of January 65 B.C.E. According to Suetonius, Crassus as dictator and Caesar as *magister equitum* would then have restored the consulship to Sulla and Autronius.[34] The coup d'état was aborted, however, because Catiline, in his impatience, signaled the conspirators prematurely.

Once Cicero apprehended the Catilinarian conspirators after the ambush at the Mulvian Bridge on December 2, 63, Caesar was named among the associates of Catiline

both by the informer Lucius Vettius, at a hearing conducted by the quaestor Novius Nigrus, and in the senate house by Quintus Curius, to whom a sum of money had been publicly voted, since he was the first to unveil the plans of the conspirators.[35]

We have seen that Cato tried to implicate Caesar with innuendo: "I wonder what's going on, if in the enormous fear of all men, he alone is not afraid" (*Cat.* 52.16); here, Suetonius offers proof of complicity.

Finally, at the end of his life, Caesar is suspected of having hastened his own death:

Caesar left some of those close to him with the suspicion (*suspicionem Caesar quibusdam suorum reliquit*) that he had no wish to live much longer and had taken no precautions, since his health was deteriorating, and that it was for this reason that he took little notice either of portents or of the advice of his friends.[36]

This last suspicion is not of a political sort per se; there is no conspiracy against the *res publica* or complicity with others to usurp power. Instead, Suetonius uses the term *suspicio* in a more neutral sense to denote the general ideas that were held at the time about Caesar's death. Yet Suetonius will also invoke suspicion to implicate the emperor in another's death, as we shall see (*Aug.* 11; *Vit.* 14.5).

Each time Suetonius records Caesar under suspicion, he is careful to provide documentation for the allegation. For the first Catilinarian conspiracy, Suetonius presents four types of evidence (history, oratory, documentary edicts, and a letter), and he names four individuals who attest that Caesar came under suspicion:

> Tanusius Geminus mentions the plot in his history, as does Marcus Bibulus in his edicts and Gaius Curio the elder in his speeches. Cicero, too, seems to be referring to this in a letter to Axius.[37]

Suetonius brings to bear a variety of testimony, although the letter of Cicero is qualified by the verb *videtur*. Even for Suetonius, who is conscientious in his level of detail, this list of four seems overly fussy.

In the paragraph describing Caesar's complicity with Catiline, again Suetonius attempts to warrant the suspicion:

> Curius maintained he had his information from Catiline, while Vettius even promised a document in Caesar's handwriting that had been given to Catiline.[38]

Indicting Caesar of conspiracy is a serious matter that demands concrete evidence. In the case of the murky first Catilinarian conspiracy, Suetonius marshals four sources that he consulted, as a historian would. In the case of the second Catilinarian conspiracy, however, Suetonius reports how the accusers validated their accusation. Curius had a direct link to Catiline, and Vettius had a document in Caesar's own hand, although Vettius is not the most trustworthy of informants. The document was probably forged.[39]

In recording the suspicions that surrounded Caesar's attitude toward his own death, Suetonius brings forward unnamed sources:

> There are those who think that he had such faith in the most recent decree of the senate and their oath that he dismissed the armed guard of Spanish troops who had previously attended him. Others take a different view, holding that he preferred to fall victim just once to the plots that threatened him from all sides, rather than be perpetually on guard against them. Some say that he was even in the habit of remarking that his safety was more a matter of concern for the republic than it was for him.[40]

Three opinions are repeated. *Sunt qui putent . . . alii e diuerso opinantur . . . quidam . . . ferunt*; such is the language of historiographical research.[41] With relative clauses of characteristic, indefinite pronouns, and the ubiquitous verb *ferunt*, historians record differing opinions on a matter.[42] It seems that even the casual suspicion of Caesar demands investigation.

Twice Augustus comes under suspicion, both times in deeply political and controversial contexts. Upon becoming Caesar's heir in March 44 B.C.E., Octavian competed with Antony for a share of the dictator's estate, and whatever alliance they struck was tenuous at best.[43] Alleging that there was a conspiracy against him, Antony broke with Octavian in October.[44] Octavian levied troops (a legally questionable move).[45] In November, Antony ordered Decimus Brutus to quit his command of Cisalpine Gaul,[46] but in December Cicero proposed legislation that authorized Brutus to remain in his province until further notice.[47] In January 43, Antony besieged Brutus at Mutina; repeated efforts at arbitration were fruitless. The senate declared a state of emergency and resolved to send the consuls Hirtius and Pansa against Antony.[48] Brutus was able to hold out in Mutina until April, when at last Antony retreated. Hirtius was killed in the second battle against Antony; Pansa received two serious wounds in the first. The eventual deaths of both consuls aroused suspicion:

Since, in the course of this war, Hirtius died in the line of battle and Pansa not long afterwards from a wound, a rumour developed that both had been killed through his agency so that, with Antony routed and the state bereft of both consuls, he [Augustus] would be left with sole command over the victorious forces. Indeed, the death of Pansa aroused such suspicion (*adeo suspecta mors fuit*) that the doctor Glyco was imprisoned on the grounds that he had applied poison to the wound.[49]

The rumor was certainly persistent; in his balanced obituary of Augustus in the opening tableau of the *Annales*, Tacitus records the hesitations of some concerning the deaths of Hirtius and Pansa and the possibility of poison, or at least foul play (*Ann.* 1.10.2). Given the recurrence of the story (surely more than anecdotal), Suetonius could hardly omit the suspicions that surrounded Augustus upon the deaths of the consuls.[50]

The second time Augustus arouses suspicion is during his revision of the senate membership. In 29 B.C.E., he exercised the duties of the censor with Agrippa:

It was on this occasion that he is believed (*existimatur*) to have presided protected by a cuirass under his tunic and wearing a sword at his side, with ten strong men, friends from the senatorial order, standing around his seat.[51]

The precautions attest an uncertain political atmosphere; there was no way of knowing how his policies would be received. The bodyguard of ten men would have been visible to all, but the breastplate underneath his toga is presented as a supposition, difficult to substantiate. Yet for Suetonius, suspicion demands substantiation. Therefore, in his report of the rumors attending the suspicious deaths of Hirtius and Pansa, the biographer calls upon the otherwise unknown Aquilius Niger:

> Aquilius Niger adds to this that Octavian himself actually killed one of the consuls, Hirtius, in the heat of battle.[52]

To the claims that Augustus was unreasonably cautious during the revision of the senate roster, Suetonius adds those of the historian Cremutius Cordus:

> Cremutius Cordus writes that no member of the senate was allowed to approach him unless on his own and once his toga had been searched.[53]

The hunch that Augustus wore a breastplate under his tunic is given credence, since Cremutius records that the emperor checked the senators for weapons.

Suetonius continues the pattern of evidence in the biography of Tiberius, who arouses quite a bit of suspicion, not least because of the continual machinations of his mother Livia. He attempted to quit public life by retiring to Rhodes, but there too he was beset by scrutiny because of his position as Augustus' stepson:

> Tiberius had also fallen under suspicion (*uenit etiam in suspicionem*) of having some centurions to whom he was patron, when they returned to their camp from leave, send ambiguous messages to a number of men which seemed to suggest he was testing whether these individuals might be persuaded to join a rebellion.[54]

As evidence that Tiberius was suspected of plotting against Augustus, Suetonius records that Augustus himself knew of these suspicions:

> When he [Tiberius] was informed of this (*suspicione*) by Augustus, he insistently demanded that someone, of no matter what rank, be appointed to act as scrutineer of his actions and words.[55]

Obviously Tiberius was eager to clear his name; however, we also get the impression that Augustus is omniscient, for he is aware of rumors that appear to have escaped Tiberius' notice.

When Augustus finally died, suspicion again hounded Tiberius. Although he expressed such deep grief before the senate that he was unable to compose himself, his emotional display failed to convince. As soon as Augustus' will was read, Tiberius came under scrutiny:

> The will began as follows: "Since harsh fortune has robbed me of my sons Gaius and Lucius, Tiberius Caesar shall be heir to two-thirds of my estate." This too increased the suspicions (*quo et ipso aucta suspicio est*) of those debating the matter that he had chosen Tiberius as successor through necessity rather than preference, since he had not refrained from prefacing his will in this way.[56]

The document itself is quoted *ipsa verba*. The first two allegations, that Tiberius was plotting revolution against Augustus and that he had unduly influenced Augustus' will, seem reasonable given the conditions of rule: Augustus as sole ruler and as first *princeps* invited challenges to his power, and it is only reasonable to conjecture that his successor would have tested his authority. In a way these suspicions need only be grounded in common sense; any successor to Augustus would have been vulnerable to such accusations.

The death of Germanicus was one of the great outrages of the early empire. Tacitus records that contemporary public outcry was overwhelming, and his story resonated across the imagination for generations.[57] Germanicus was Tiberius' nephew; he married Agrippina the Elder and was the father of Caligula. In 14–15 C.E., he campaigned in Germany and recovered the standards of Varus' three legions massacred six years before, but he was recalled by Tiberius and redeployed to the East, where he campaigned successfully. He returned to the province of Syria, where Tiberius had appointed Gnaeus Calpurnius Piso to be governor. Piso was a man who made no pretense of his enmity toward Germanicus. When Germanicus fell mysteriously ill, Piso was thought to have poisoned him, acting on Tiberius' wishes:

> It is even believed (*creditur*) that he [Tiberius] was the cause of his death through the agency of Gnaeus Piso, the legate of Syria.[58]

Tiberius' part in the mysterious death of Germanicus is illuminated in two ways:

Because of this, the words "Give us back Germanicus!" were written up in many places and at night frequently called out. He himself [Tiberius] confirmed suspicions (*quam suspicionem confirmauit*) when, afterwards, he inflicted cruel treatment on Germanicus' wife and children, too.[59]

This is the closest we come to evidence that nonelites subscribed to a conspiracy theory. In search of why bad things happen to good people, that is, why the prince Germanicus died so young and so lamentably, the public answer is not Stoic resolve. There is no mention that his death can somehow make the Republic stronger or provide opportunity to prove its virtue. Instead, some invisible hand is behind the tragedy. Subliterary evidence (graffiti) is brought to bear, together with Tiberius' own actions.

Characteristic features of suspicion in the *De Vita Caesarum* begin to take shape. Evidence for suspicion is drawn from a range of literary sources, from the histories of Tanusius Geminus, Aquilius Niger, and Cremutius Cordus and the letters of Cicero; to documentary evidence such as the edicts of Marcus Bibulus and the will of Augustus; to subliterary graffiti; and finally to the actions of the *princeps* himself. The decline in the quality of evidence to corroborate statements of suspicion is perfectly in keeping with Suetonius' general pattern in the *Caesars*: later lives, less detail. If we resist being diverted by questions of occupation (bureaucrat vs. scholar) or career (pre- or post-dismissal in 122), the trend reveals an elaborate artifice that unites the biographies. Suetonius traverses the spectrum from positive to dysfunctional suspicion, from defensible to irrational behavior that can be explained only by character. The recurrence of suspicion in individual *principes*, each time with slight mutation, recapitulates the evolution of the principate itself as an institution built on suspicion.

The biography of Caligula begins with the suspicions surrounding the death of his father, in a sort of prefatory microbiography:

After he [Germanicus] had defeated the King of Armenia and made Cappadocia a province, he died at Antioch, in his thirty-fourth year, of a long-drawn-out illness—indeed there was some suspicion of poison.[60]

The legend of Germanicus spans the biographies, casting Tiberius and Caligula as perpetrator and victim in one continuous narrative.

In 39, Caligula ventured on an expedition to Germany, where it occurred to him to decimate the legions that had revolted when Tiberius came to power in 14 C.E. These legions had abused his father Germanicus, who was sent to quell the revolt, and although Caligula was an infant at the time, he harbored resentment. (This in itself contributed to the portrait of Caligula as mentally unstable.) Caligula summoned the legions without their weapons; they assembled defenseless, only to be surrounded by armed cavalry. Yet these soldiers were not stupid; they were former mutineers, after all:

> However, when he saw that quite a few of the legionaries, suspecting that something was going on (*suspecta re*), were slipping away to arm themselves in case violence broke out, he fled from the assembly.[61]

Caligula is thus suspected by the very soldiers who had beleaguered Germanicus.

Like Tiberius, Caligula too is suspected of ending his predecessor's life. Suetonius' narrative of the death of Tiberius casts agent and victim as incurring suspicion:

> He [Caligula] administered poison to Tiberius, as some believe (*opinantur*), and, while he still breathed, ordered first that his ring be pulled off, then, since Tiberius seemed to be resisting (*quoniam suspicionem retinentis dabat*, "since he was offering suspicion of resisting"), that a pillow be put over his mouth, and he himself with his own hands strangled him.[62]

The two appear to deserve each other when in this final struggle Caligula is suspected of poisoning Tiberius, while Tiberius is suspected of wanting to keep his ring, the symbol of his power.

Caligula's biography is framed by suspicion; as it began, so it ends. Report of his assassination was credited to rumor, and people suspected that he faked his own death in a last hurrah of megalomania:

> For when news broke of his assassination no one would believe it (*creditum est*) at first, and people suspected (*fuitque suspicio*) that the story had been devised and spread by Caligula himself in order to discover by this means how people felt about him.[63]

Like father like son? According to Tacitus, Germanicus was supposed to have gone to some effort to find out what his troops thought of him. In a common cloak, he descended to the tents in the camp to hear the soldiers praise his excellence, good looks, patience, affability, and temperament (*Ann.* 2.13).

No doubt Caligula is an object of suspicion, yet even in this biography, Suetonius attempts to provide grounds. For the murder of Germanicus by poison, forensic evidence obtains:

For dark patches appeared all over his body and he foamed at the mouth, and besides this, when he was cremated, his heart was found intact amongst his bones; it is thought that the heart, when infected with poison, cannot be destroyed by fire.[64]

For Caligula's implication in the death of Tiberius, unnamed sources are at hand: "For some authors report that he himself confessed, if not to the deed itself of parricide, then certainly to planning it."[65] Curiously, he admits to aborted attempts that even Tiberius was aware of—but did not act upon. But for the suspicions of the mutinous legions and the populace incredulous about his death, Caligula is on his own. His life answers for the suspicion it arouses, as doubt is transformed into fact.

The *Divus Claudius* is distinctive in form and content; like the man himself, it is somewhat off-kilter. With it commences the perceptible decline in quality in the *De Vita Caesarum*, from the well-documented lives of Julius and Augustus to the briefly executed biographies of the Flavians.[66] Yet as Cizek has demonstrated, it is the most morally neutral; Suetonius' judgments are balanced.[67] Attention to suspicion in the *Divus Claudius* enriches our understanding of the phenomenon and its importance to the composition of the individual lives, the overall structure of the *De Vita Caesarum*, and the conception of the principate as a whole.

Mistrust is cast upon Claudius only once in the *vita* and only indirectly, at the very beginning, where his father's paternity is called into question. The life opens with the requisite genealogy, a device that ought to legitimate the subject; however, doubt is immediate:

> The father of Claudius Caesar was Drusus, who first had the forename of Decimus, then later that of Nero. Livia, having married Augustus when she was pregnant, gave birth to Drusus less than three months later and it was suspected (*fuitque suspicio*) that he was the child of his stepfather, conceived in adultery.[68]

The suspicion is not imputed to Claudius himself, nor even to his father, but to his grandmother Livia: she is suspected of adultery. Thus, while Caligula's life is framed by suspicion, Claudius' life is begotten of it. As for evidence of the suspicion, Suetonius proffers the popularity of a quip from Attic comedy: "Certainly the following line was soon circulating: 'The lucky ones have children in just three months.'"[69] In the *Apocolocyntosis*, Seneca records a line of Euripides' *Cresphontes* as Claudius "gurgles his life out." In fact, "he breathed his last while listening to some comic actors."[70] From the opening of the *vita* with a line of Attic comedy to the end of his life, Claudius was an object of ridicule.

Repetition of content and diction closely bind Suetonius' biographies of Caligula and Claudius. The biography of Caligula opens with the dubious circumstances of his father's death, for which Tiberius was the object of much suspicion. The biography of Claudius begins with his father's doubtful paternity. Furthermore, a phrase from the end of the one is put squarely at the beginning of the other: *fuitque suspicio* (*Cal.* 60; *Cl.* 1.1).

Nero garners suspicion when, on the anniversary of his mother's murder, he receives news of Gallic uprisings with such indifference that "he gave the impression (*suspicionem praeberet*) of being pleased on the grounds that he would have an opportunity, in accordance with the laws of war, to despoil the most wealthy provinces."[71] At the beginning of Galba's revolt, it was believed (*creditur*, 43.1) that Nero was planning many monstrous deeds, but before enumerating them, Suetonius qualifies them as "nothing inconsistent with his own nature" (*uerum non abhorrentia a natura sua*, 43.1). The list is long and detailed: he intended to send agents to depose and assassinate the commanders of the armies on the grounds that they were united in a conspiracy against him; to massacre all exiles everywhere and all Gauls in the city; to poison the entire senate at banquets; and to set fire to the entire city, first letting wild beasts loose against the citizens. He was deterred from doing any of these things "not so much by regret as by despair of ever finishing the job" (*sed absterritus non tam paenitentia quam perficiendi desperatione*, 43.2). As a result, the suspicions do not amount to anything—except for an opportunity for conjecture about Nero's atrocities, limited by yet another character flaw: a sort of inertia caused by hopelessness at his inability to finish what he starts.

The only other mention of Nero as an object of suspicion in the biography is intricately embedded:

> He forced his adviser Seneca to kill himself, even though, when Seneca requested that he be allowed to retire and give up his properties, he had sworn that Seneca's suspicions were unfounded and that he would sooner die than harm him.[72]

Semantically, Nero is the object of Seneca's suspicions, but the statement is indirect (dependent on *iurasset*) and embedded in a concessive clause introduced by *quamuis*. So *although* Nero swore *that* Seneca's suspicions were unfounded, still he drove his adviser to suicide. Although nowhere stated explicitly, the sentence can only imply that Seneca suspected that Nero wanted him to commit suicide. Furthermore, this suspicion is stated with litotes; *frustra* ("in vain"), negates the act of suspicion: Seneca was wrong to suspect. One could consult Tacitus for the full version: Seneca, together with Lucan, Petronius, and a host of others, fell victim in the aftermath of the Pisonian conspiracy (itself rumored to be a counterconspiracy to legitimate Nero's reign of terror).[73] Here, though, the intimation of Seneca's suspicion reveals how suspicion is embedded, encrypted, and inscribed into a life.

Galba, Otho, Vitellius: three short reigns, three short lives, one long year. As a result, the rhetoric of suspicion will be comparatively uneven across these biographies; however, each of these emperors of the Long Year contributes in various ways to the project of suspicion.

Only Vitellius, perhaps the most despicable of the three,[74] is ever an object of suspicion; he is supposed to have hastened the death of his mother Sextilia (*suspectus et in morte matris fuit*, Vit. 14.5):[75] He refused her food when she was ill (*aegrae*, 14.5), because an oracle had predicted successful rule if he should survive his parent (*parenti*, 14.5). To this, Suetonius appends an alternative that is oddly familiar:

> Others record that it was she, weary of present evils and fearful of those to come (*imminentium*), who demanded poison from her son—which he willingly gave her.[76]

In the face of an unpredictable future, Sextilia exerts a degree of control over her own circumstances. Recall that Caesar aroused a similar suspicion, that he wished to die, either because of his failing health (*ualitudine minus prospera, Jul.* 86.1) or because of constant worry (*insidias undique imminentis, Jul.* 86.2). Worn out with worry over constant threats, Caesar and Sextilia are thought to have wished life away. Caesar succumbed to the hands of a band of conspirators, Sextilia to the hand of her own son. An inscription was dedicated to Julius Caesar, *parenti patria*, "To the Father of the Fatherland" (*Jul.* 85). So when Sextilia is referred to as *parenti* (*Vit.* 14.5), the repetition of *parens* in the same case transfers the suspicion from the public to the private sphere, making it all the more pervasive.

The last emperor in the *De Vita Caesarum* to incur suspicion is Titus; indeed, he is a sort of Janus-like figure when it comes to suspicion, for he is wrongfully suspected of trying to usurp power from his father, while at the same time he is rightfully suspicious of his brother Domitian. Titus captured Jerusalem and was acclaimed by his troops as *imperator*. When he tried to leave the province, the soldiers would not let him go. With entreaties and threats they urged him to stay or take them all with him:

It was this which provoked the suspicion (*suspicio*) that he had tried to rebel against his father and secure for himself rule over the East, a suspicion (*suspicionem*) which he fuelled by wearing a diadem.⁷⁷

In response to these suspicions, Titus does something radically different from any other emperor who has come under suspicion before him: he willfully proves the suspicions false by his actions alone. He hurries home to Italy, from Regium to Puteoli to Rome, then, "so as to show that the rumours were false and unfounded, he announced, to his father's surprise: 'I have come, father, I have come.'"⁷⁸

In describing the private life of Titus, Suetonius reports that "besides being suspected of cruelty, he was also suspected of self-indulgence" (*praeter saeuitiam suspecta in eo etiam luxuria erat*, 7.1), evidenced by his binge drinking. Titus was also lustful (witness the flock of catamites and eunuchs and his passion for Queen Berenice). In addition, he was suspected of excessive greed (*suspecta rapacitas*, 7.1) because he took bribes. Suetonius sums up popular sentiment: Titus was regarded as a second Nero.⁷⁹ Every last suspicion, however, is proven false and unfounded by the conduct of his life. In fact, such suspicion was to his advantage, since, "when he was found to have no vices but instead the greatest virtues, it was succeeded by the greatest praise" (*conuersaque est in maximas laudes neque uitio ullo reperto et contra uirtutibus summis*, 7.1). What about the drunken parties? The catamites and eunuchs? What about the queen? The bribes? The life of Titus erased all these (seemingly concrete) grounds for suspicion.

Thus, this survey of the suspicions cast against emperors in the *De Vita Caesarum* reveals first that repetitions, exact or with only slight variation, lend the work a sense of unity:

(1) *uenit in suspicionem* (*Jul.* 9.1), *uenit etiam in suspicionem* (*Tib.* 12.3)

(2) *fuitque suspicio* (*Cal.* 60, *Cl.* 1.1)

(3) *non sine ueneni suspicione* (*Cal.* 1.2); compare the litotes *suspectum se frustra* (*Nero* 35.5)

(4) *opinantur* (*Jul.* 86.2, *Cal.* 12.2), *opinantium* (*Tib.* 23), *opinabantur* (*Tit.* 7.1)

(5) *creditur* (*Tib.* 52.3, *Nero* 43.1), *creditum est* (*Cal.* 60)

(6) *aucta suspicio* (*Tib.* 23), *suspicionem auxit* (*Tit.* 5.3)

The diction of *suspectus et in morte matris fuit* (*Vit.* 14.5) echoes *suspecta mors fuit* (*Aug.* 11), while the content is reminiscent of *Jul.* 86.1.

Second, Suetonius initially substantiates suspicion with vigorous documentation; however, with each biography, the proof dwindles. Of course, this could be due in part to the general trend toward less documentation for the later lives. Nevertheless, when it comes to casting suspicions on the *princeps*, the decrease in documentation has an effect. The ability or inability to deflect suspicion ultimately rests on ethos. Caesar is not cleared of complicity in the Catilinarian conspiracy; on the contrary, he is deeply implicated. Rumors about his wish to die are likewise given substance by unnamed sources. During critical moments in his rise and consolidation of power, Augustus came under suspicion; Suetonius substantiates these allegations by mentioning historians by name. When Tiberius falls victim to suspicion, however, the documentation is less rigorous, and Suetonius adduces subliterary evidence. Suspicions surrounding the death of Germanicus span two lives; they are corroborated by rumor, graffiti, and forensic evidence. A line of Attic comedy attests suspicion of Drusus' paternity. For suspicions against Nero, no evidence surfaces, except his own character; he appears to deserve every aspersion cast upon him. Rumor that Vitellius poisoned his mother, given credence by unnamed sources (*alii tradunt, Vit.* 14.5), echoes the diction of Caesar's will to die. Finally, Titus can turn suspicion into praise. For those who would see in the *De Vita Caesarum* a blueprint for a successful *princeps*, lessons on suspicion make useful advice.

AVOIDING SUSPICION

Surely the more astute among the twelve knew that they were objects of suspicion, and indeed Caesar, Tiberius, Nero, Vespasian, and Domitian all attempt to avoid suspicion. Within these strategies of avoidance are echoes of diction and content that again unify the *De Vita Caesarum*. Certain passages are quickly set aside. As Suetonius progresses through the rubrics of biography, he reports of Augustus that in some aspects of his life, he was without suspicion of any vice (*sine suspicione ullius uitii, Aug.* 72.1). At games given for his grandsons, though the people were worried that the seats would collapse, Augustus sat in the "most suspicious" part of the theater, to relieve their fears (*quae suspecta maxime erat, Aug.* 43.5). While on his deathbed, Tiberius tries to avoid suspicion of ill health (*suspicionem infirmitatis, Tib.* 72.2). Although negligible, these examples of avoidance keep the theme before the reader. Suspicion is woven across the biographies, even into lesser matters, with the effect that it seems all the more pervasive.

Twice Caesar seeks to avoid suspicion: once in military maneuvers, once in domestic affairs. In 49, when diplomacy with the senate failed and Caesar and Pompey were on the brink of civil war, Caesar sent a few cohorts ahead in secrecy, and then, "so that suspicion would not be aroused, . . . he concealed his intentions"[80] with various diversions (he attended public games, inspected plans for a gladiatorial school, and entertained numerous guests) before catching up with the cohorts at the Rubicon. In 62, he married Pompeia but divorced her for her alleged complicity in the Bona Dea scandal with Publius Clodius:

> He denied that he knew anything of the matter, though his mother Aurelia and his sister Julia had faithfully told the whole story before the same judges. And when he was asked why, if he knew nothing, he had nevertheless divorced his wife, he replied, "In my view, my family needs to be as much free of suspicion as free of crime."[81]

Caesar recognizes the damaging effects of suspicion and takes steps to avoid it even in his private life.

While on Rhodes in 2 B.C.E., Tiberius learned that he had been divorced from his wife. With his tribunician power at an end, he sought to return to Rome, explaining that

> what he had hoped to avoid through his withdrawal was nothing other than the suspicion that he was a rival to Gaius and Lucius.[82]

His voluntary retirement became all but exile; when he was finally allowed to return to Rome, according to Barbara Levick, "Augustus made it clear that it was expressly by permission of Gaius."[83] Within two years, the boys were dead.

Notice of Nero's sole attempt to avoid suspicion is recorded in the *Otho*, who was privy to all of Nero's schemes and secrets. When Nero planned to murder his mother, it was Otho who made all the arrangements for the lavish and refined dinner party that was thrown "to allay suspicion" (*ad auertendas suspiciones*, 3.1).

Vespasian was more inclined to trust than to suspect:

> He was so disinclined to bring about anyone's downfall through some fear or suspicion, that when friends warned him to beware of Mettius Pompusianus, because it was commonly believed that he had an imperial horoscope, he actually made him consul, promising that he would someday be mindful of the favour.[84]

Vespasian was not superstitious; rather, he was so virtuous as to trust a potential enemy, so magnanimous as to allow Pompusianus whatever comfort about the unknown the horoscope might give, and so confident as to dismiss his own need to control the unknown and to abstain from the burdens of suspicion. Yet as Brian Jones points out, "Suetonius has conveniently not cited the execution of Julius Sabinus and his family."[85] According to Dio (66.16.1), Vespasian executed Julius Sabinus because he had taken up arms against the emperor; no mercy was shown to his wife and children.

Only later do we learn that Mettius Pompusianus was a victim of Domitian

> because it was commonly reported that his birth-signs predicted empire and because he carried around a map of the world on parchment and copies of the speeches made by kings and generals in Livy, as well as giving two of his slaves the names Mago and Hannibal.[86]

Vespasian is willing to overlook the horoscope as meaningless and therefore trust Pompusianus, whereas Domitian is overly eager to distrust the same man based on an inventory of increasingly unreliable indicators. Furthermore, Vespasian is seen to have a broad trust network of friends warning him (*monentibus amicis*, *Ves.* 14), while Domitian is isolated so that no one is able to offer stronger allegations of treason. In his isolation, Domitian is forced to overinterpret the signs and imagine Pompusianus sizing up his conquest, memorizing imperial orations for delivery, and giving his slaves Punic names.[87]

Domitian is careful to avoid suspicion: "He gave scarcely any grounds for being suspected of greed or avarice either before he became emperor or for sometime during his reign" (*cupiditatis quoque auaritiae uix suspicionem ullam . . . dedit*, 9.1). Only after he became emperor, "and, even then, not at once,"[88] as Jones remarks, does Domitian reveal his character.

The only other mention of the deliberate avoidance of suspicion in the *De Vita Caesarum* occurs in the narrative of the assassination of Domitian. Stephanus, freedman of Domitilla (Vespasian's granddaughter), suggested the plan of action. To allay suspicion (*ad aduertendam suspicionem*, 17.1), he wrapped his arm in bandages, feigning an injury so that he could conceal a dagger unnoticed. The ruse worked, and Domitian was caught unawares. Clearly the avoidance of suspicion can be a matter of life and death for the emperors.

FROM SUSPICION TO PARANOIA

Of the twelve emperors, Otho, Vitellius, and Vespasian are not credited with being suspicious. Suspicion is a defense mechanism for the absolute ruler; by keeping his guard up and his wits about him, the *princeps* can perceive plots before they come to fruition. He can preempt attempts on his authority or his life and thereby preserve civil order. Taken to an extreme, however, suspicion devolves into paranoia. From the *De Vita Caesarum* it would seem that so long as a good emperor's life is spared, suspicion is salutary, but once suspicion causes bloodshed, it is no longer a safe practice. Likewise, as long as a bad emperor's life is terminated, suspicion is good, but when suspicion prolongs the life of a bad emperor, it is undesirable. As suspicion develops from Caesar to Domitian, it extends across a continuum of morality and value judgments about what constitutes not only a good *princeps* but a good principate.

Caesar could in no way be accused of paranoia, although Suetonius describes a consulship freighted with machination, politicking, and double-dealing. Caesar confronted every obstacle to his agenda. When Marcus Cato tried to use his veto, Caesar had him dragged from the senate house to prison. When Lucius Lucullus stood up too openly to him, Caesar threatened him until he capitulated. When Cicero lamented the current state of affairs, Caesar arranged to have his archenemy Publius Clodius transferred from patrician to plebeian status (*Jul.* 20.4). Rather than deal with his opponents individually, Caesar concocted a plan to counter them all at once:

> He bribed (*inductum praemiis*) an informer to confess (according to an agreed plan) that he had been incited to murder Pompey by certain individuals and, when brought before the rostra, to name the culprits. However, after the informer named one or two to no effect and had aroused suspicions that he was a fraud, Caesar abandoned hope (*desperans*) that this hastily arranged plan would come off, and is thought (*creditur*) to have had the informer poisoned.[89]

Because the informant is not held by any bond of solidarity with Caesar but by extrinsic incentives (*praemiis*), he does not seem credible, with the result that Caesar aborts his plot. This counterconspiracy, designed to relieve Caesar of suspicion once and for all, backfires, and Caesar himself becomes an object of suspicion (*creditur*). Finally, note the shift in point of view achieved so adroitly by the participle *desperans*.[90] The nominative singular participle shifts the authorial standpoint from Suetonius to Caesar, from the external voice of the narrator to the inner thoughts of the character. The shift to internal focalization allows Suetonius to posit psychological inferences; thus, the participle is a particularly effective way to describe suspicion.[91]

It would be difficult to put a positive spin on Augustus' part in the triumvirate and the proscriptions, and Suetonius necessarily draws on hostile sources. Violence and suspicion feed each other in a vicious cycle:

When he was addressing the soldiers and a crowd of civilians had been allowed to listen, he noticed that Pinarius, a Roman knight, was writing something down and, thinking (*ratus*) that he was an informer and a spy, gave orders that he be run through on the spot.[92]

Notice how economically the participle *ratus* gives a glimpse of Augustus' inner thoughts. He reckoned he had enough information to take action, but we will never know if Pinarius intended any harm. Suspicion was reasonable, given the times. Under the triumvirate nothing was permanently settled; rather, it was a period of constant negotiation. However, Suetonius records another example that clearly exceeds the limit:

When the praetor Quintus Gallius came to pay his respects with some folded tablets covered by his cloak, Octavian, suspecting him of concealing a sword, did not dare to have him searched at once, in case it should turn out to be something else, but soon afterwards had him seized from the tribunal by centurions and their men and subjected to torture as if he were a slave. And, when he admitted nothing, he gave orders that he should be killed, first gouging out the man's eyes with his own hand.[93]

At first it seems that Octavian learned, after his hasty execution of Pinarius, to act more cautiously on his suspicions; however, the torture, mutilation, and execution of Gallius are impossible to justify. Indeed, John Carter finds it improbable that Octavian would have risked his image by committing such an atrocity.[94] So Suetonius closes this grim paragraph with a rebuttal of the hostile sources, from the emperor himself:[95]

He wrote, however, that the man had asked for an audience then treacherously attacked him and that, after he had been thrown into custody and then sent into exile, he had met his end in a shipwreck or an attack by thieves.[96]

In self-defense, prison and exile would be reasonable, even merciful responses. The hazards of the sea conveniently dispose of any evidence of mutilation.

The triumvirate was the exception. As *princeps*, Augustus was clement and rational. Suetonius documents his kindness to friends, and only when friendship was overtly betrayed did he respond in kind. So Salvidienus Rufus was punished because he plotted revolution (*res novas*, 66.2), and Cornelius Gallus was "banned from his home and from his provinces because of his ungrateful and malicious temper" (66.2). Augustus was sorely distressed at Gallus' suicide and lamented that "he alone had not the power to decide how far he wished to take his anger toward his friends."[97] The *princeps* cannot decide limits for his actions, but rather, such limits are imposed by his subjects.[98] While Augustus may be constrained by his exceptional status, Agrippa can respond to suspicion appropriately. "When he suspected Augustus' feelings had cooled" (*cum ille ex leui <f>rigoris suspicione*, 66.3), he simply took himself to Mytilene.

Tiberius exhibits the range from temperate to dysfunctional suspicion. At first he is justified and judicious. Upon completing his campaign in Germany, "he came very close to being assassinated by one of the Bructeri who had infiltrated his attendants but betrayed himself through his nervousness. A confession of his planned crime was extracted from him through torture."[99] As *imperator*, Tiberius was vulnerable to plots by the enemy. The assassin was visibly nervous enough (*trepidatione detecto*) to alert Tiberius to an impending danger. He thus had grounds to take the next step, torture, and indeed the plot was revealed. Foreign kings suspected of hostility (*reges infestos suspectosque*, 37.4) were also controlled through threat rather than force; Tiberius simply lured them to Rome and detained them. He is capable of exercising suspicion appropriately.

Yet as Tiberius' degenerate character slowly reveals itself during his life and principate, his healthy suspicion becomes increasingly dysfunctional. He could be forgiven for his first bout of paranoia because he was wracked with grief over the death of his son Drusus. Tiberius thought Drusus died as a result of disease and self-indulgence, but when he learned that his son was poisoned, tricked by his wife Livilla and Sejanus, he went on a rampage of torture and execution in retaliation for his son's murder. He was so consumed with revenge that

> when the arrival was announced of a guest from Rhodes, whom he had summoned to Rome by a friendly letter, he had the man subjected to torture without delay, supposing someone had arrived who was an important witness for the case.[100]

The knee-jerk reaction to this guest from Rhodes reminds us of Augustus' swift response to Pinarius, whom he ordered killed on the spot. Without thinking, Augustus and Tiberius assume the worst and take extraordinary measures. Tiberius immediately regrets his rashness:

> Then, when his mistake came to light, [he had the man] put to death, so that he would not publicize his mistreatment.[101]

Of course, the execution of the guest canceled any possibility for cover-up, and Tiberius' attempt at camouflage renders his paranoia more obvious. Likewise, after the fall of Sejanus, one would expect Tiberius to rest easy; on the contrary, "even when Sejanus' conspiracy was suppressed, he felt no more secure or at ease."[102] He was still distrustful and fearful (*sic quoque diffidens . . . metuens*, 65.2). Again, nominative singular participles succinctly allow for a radical shift in point of view, so that the inner thoughts of the *princeps* are made manifest.

Caligula's suspicions are altogether unfounded and his behavior, inexcusable. He had his adopted brother Tiberius Gemellus murdered suddenly and without warning, claiming that "he smelt of an antidote of the kind people take when they are afraid of poison" (23.3). Caligula even mocked his brother's feeble attempt at protecting himself:

> When he was about to kill his brother, whom he suspected of taking remedies through fear of being poisoned, he said: "Do you think you can take a remedy against Caesar?"[103]

Caligula mistakenly assumed that Gemellus was trying to assert some control over his future by inoculating himself; however, Gemellus was not drinking an antidote at all but rather medicine for a persistent and increasingly severe cough (23.3).[104]

One more anecdote illustrates Caligula's inability to judge appearances properly. When he asked a man who had been recalled from an exceptionally long exile how he spent his time, the man attempted to flatter: "I kept praying to the gods that Tiberius would die, as indeed happened, and that you would come to power" (28). The flattery backfired, however, and Caligula inferred (*opinans*) that those now in exile were hoping for his death. As a result, he had them all killed. Thus, we see in Caligula a tendency to jump to conclusions and misread cues. The smell of cough syrup becomes grounds for suspicion. An attempt at flattery testifies to imminent revolution. Caligula is unable to process information rationally.

Three full paragraphs are devoted to Claudius' fearfulness, making timidity one of his most salient characteristics: "But above all he was cowardly and suspicious."[105] He would not attend a dinner party unless guards were posted in place of slaves. He would not visit a sick friend until the room was searched and pillows and sheets were shaken. All callers were patted down, though later in his reign he spared women and children the humiliation of a body search (35.1). In fact, he was so afraid of conspiracies that he attempted to abdicate (36.1). He mistook a man about to make a sacrifice for an assassin; however, unlike Augustus, Tiberius, or Caligula, he merely complained of his precarious situation. He gave up on his marriage to Messalina not because of the humiliation she inflicted but because he feared her ability to achieve a coup d'etat (36). "Even the most insignificant suspicion or the most untrustworthy informant would provoke some minor anxiety."[106] Suetonius then records two executions prompted merely by dreams—even less compelling evidence than the smell of cough syrup.

Surprisingly, the *Nero* does not record similar suspicions or parallel anecdotes of paranoia. In passing (and in indirect discourse) we learn that he did not trust the judges at his singing competitions (*suspectosque sibi dicens*, 23.3).[107] When it came to politics, Nero never waited for even a hint before he put to death whomever he wanted (37.1). We are left with the impression that Nero had no time for suspicion.

Galba exercised a judicious amount of suspicion when dealing with the praetorians, whom he suspected of alliance with Nymphidius Sabinus;[108] however, he also "condemned without a hearing, on the slightest suspicion, certain distinguished men of the senatorial and equestrian orders."[109]

Vespasian was not paranoid, and he doubted a man only once. He suspected (*suspicatus*, 23.2) that his muleteer had stopped the carriage unnecessarily, on the pretense that he needed to shoe the mules, when he really meant to delay Vespasian's arrival in court. Rather than punish the driver, Vespasian merely insisted on a cut of the plaintiff's bribe. The anecdote is another example of the kind of ideology and humor that Trevor Luke has identified in the *Divus Vespasianus*.[110] It showcases Vespasian's good nature and distances him from the tyrant who responds to baseless suspicion.

We have already seen how Titus occupies a pivotal position between the genial Vespasian and the criminal Domitian. Titus is reported to have handled the praetorian guard in a rather uncivilized and violent fashion (*inciuilius et uiolentius*):

Whenever he had suspicions of someone (*siquidem suspectissimum*) he would send secret emissaries to the theatres and army camps to demand their punishment, as if by common consent, and then he would dispose of the suspect without delay.[111]

For example, Aulus Caecina was invited to dinner, and Titus gave the order for his immediate death since a speech had been found in Caecina's handwriting that was to be delivered to a gathering of soldiers. After all, Caecina had been a lead player in the revolution of 69. Between Caecina's expertise and his rhetoric, Titus had warrant. Then—for the first time in the *De Vita Caesarum*—Suetonius puts forward a succinct explanation of the causes and effects of suspicion:

While such measures were intended to ensure future security, they provoked a great deal of unpopularity at the time, and as a result scarcely anyone ever acceded to the principate with so bad a reputation and with everyone so against him.[112]

Whether or not Suetonius intended the *De Vita Caesarum* to instruct potential rulers, this statement describes very clearly the "boomerang effect" that a ruler can expect if he observes or oversteps the proper limits of suspicion.

Domitian seems to emerge as the pinnacle of paranoia, a portrait consistent with the caricature in Juvenal's *Satires* (especially 4). This impression of paranoia is achieved by the juxtaposition of rational with irrational behavior. The incongruity defies reason, leaving the reader to supply an explanation — or with no explanation at all — for the senselessness:[113]

> He put to death many senators, including a number of consular rank, among them Civica Cerealis, who was at that very time proconsul of Asia, also Salvidienus Orfitus and Acilius Glabrio, then in exile, on the grounds that they were planning a rebellion, while for others the reason in each case was a trifling one.[114]

The three named victims did not have clean records; suspicion was warranted. Jones suggests that Cerealis may have been connected with the appearance of the false Nero in 88; Orfitus was an aristocrat "connected with the 'opposition' and reputed to be *capax imperii*."[115] Glabrio was charged with atheism; as a member of a minority sect, he would have aroused suspicion. He also had deadly good aim.[116] Suetonius assumes knowledge of these grounds and therefore omits them; firing off three famous names in a row, without detail, enhances the impression of Domitian's cruelty.

The list of those put to death for trifling causes (*leuissima quemque de causa*, 10.2) is longer and more detailed. First in the list is Aelius Lamia because of his "suspicious jokes" (*ob suspiciosos . . . iocos*, 10.2), even though they were old and harmless.[117] Second, Salvius Cocceianus, because of his mutual birthday with Otho; Mettius Pompusianus, because of his horoscope, map, speeches, and fondness for Punic names; Sallustius Lucullus, because he named a new weapon after himself; and Junius Rusticus, because he published eulogies for the senators Thrasea Paetus and Helvidius Priscus, staunch opponents of the Neronian regime.[118] By omitting details for the warranted suspects and providing details for the unwarranted, Suetonius gives the impression that Domitian's decisions are not sound.

Then, Domitian's fear — and his ability to instill it — increases: "He was always fearful and anxious and the slightest grounds for suspicion disturbed him to an abnormal degree."[119] Domitian's natural tendency becomes manifest and continues to increase as the day of his assassination draws near:

> As the time when the danger was expected came closer, he became daily more anxious and had fitted with phengite stone the walls of the porticoes where he used to walk, so that he would be able to see in the images reflected by the gleaming surface whatever was happening behind him.[120]

The *domus Flavia* was an extraordinary complex of official palace, private residence, and hippodrome, designed for grandeur but also for security.[121] Yet how much protection would the reflective stone really offer the *princeps*? How much could he see and how clearly? Were his reflexes quick enough to counter whatever attack he might perceive? The precautionary reflective stones merely emphasize Domitian's feebleness. Physical considerations aside, the temporal ablative absolute (*tempore . . . appropinquante*) foregrounds the essential difficulty of predicting the future, a difficulty that trust and suspicion, in their competing and complementary functions, attempt to allay. By paying attention to what is behind him (*a tergo*), Domitian attempts to "see forward" (*prouideret*), which seems to make sense. When asked why bad things happen to good people, Seneca proposes not *suspicio* but *prouidentia*: a prescient force. In the face of a perennial epistemological gap, one must look forward (*pro-uidere*), not under (*sub-spicere*). In his attempt to harness *prouidentia*, however, the suspicious Domitian makes a mockery of the Stoic *sapiens*.

In the *De Vita Caesarum* suspicion runs its course from robust salvation to vapid weakness. Finally, it is the cause of death:

> [Domitian] put Clemens to death all of a sudden, on the slightest grounds (*ex tenuissima suspicione*) and when he had barely come to the end of his consulship. It was this deed in particular which precipitated (*maturauit*) his assassination.[122]

The prepositional phrase does not fully convey Clemens' potential threat; Dio records a more substantial charge of atheism.[123] Oversimplifications of this sort do little to enhance Suetonius' reputation as a credible source or to foster serious rehabilitation of his status for the study of ancient history. Instead, *ex tenuissima suspicione* contributes to the unifying theme of suspicion. Suetonius effectively draws the *De Vita Caesarum* to a close in this echo from the *Divus Julius*: "It was for this reason that the conspirators decided to speed up (*maturandi*) their planned action."[124] Caesar hastened conspiracy because of rumors of kingship; Domitian hastened it because of baseless suspicion.

Suetonius thus demonstrates the full spectrum of suspicion, including justifications, when possible.[125]

In eight of the twelve lives, Suetonius catalogues plots and conspiracies that lend credence to an emperor's suspicion. Caesar exercised *clementia* although he was aware of conspiracies, nightly meetings, and scurrilous pamphlets (*Jul.* 75.5). Augustus was able to suppress a number of conspirators: the young Lepidus, Varro Murena and Fannius Caepio, Marcus Egnatius, Plautius Rufus, Lucius Paulus, Lucius Audasius, Asinius Epicadus, and finally Telephus (*Aug.* 19). Tiberius too was the object of plots by Clemens and Libo, in addition to the mutinous armies in Pannonia and Germany (*Tib.* 25). Caligula's sisters were privy to plots against him (*Cal.* 24.3). Nero's safety was threatened by the conspiracy of Piso at Rome and of Vinicius at Beneventum (*Nero* 36). Titus was always the target of Domitian's machinations (*Tit.* 9.3).

Domitian pronounces the last word on suspicion in the *De Vita Caesarum*, in a quotation that recapitulates and summarizes the notion of suspicion that has been developed across the twelve biographies:

> He used to say that the situation of emperors was a most wretched one, for everyone thought that their suspicions of conspiracy were groundless until they were killed.[126]

The iterative sense of *aiebat* ("used to say") generalizes the sentiment across time and circumstances so that repetition universalizes the proverb. The same quotation survives in the late antique biography of Avidius Cassius, where it is attributed instead to Hadrian:

> Hadrian said, "Unhappy is the lot of emperors, who are never believed when they accuse anyone of pretending to the throne, until after they are slain." I have preferred, moreover, to quote this as his, rather than as Domitian's, who is reported to have said it first, for good sayings when uttered by tyrants have not as much weight as they deserve.[127]

Jones also notes that a similar idea is attributed to Augustus in Dio:

> Whatever measures a ruler takes, either personally or through the senate, for the punishment of men for alleged plots against himself, are generally looked upon with suspicion as having been done out of spite, no matter how just such measures may be.[128]

All three passages attest an abiding concern about the general conditions of rule. Of course we have no way of knowing whether Hadrian latched on to the proverb after reading Suetonius' *Domitianus* or whether Hadrian's pithy saying found a comfortable home in the earlier biography. I would like to think that with the repetition, Hadrian would have seen in the *De Vita Caesarum* a reflection of himself, his conditions of rule, and strategies for survival. Bradley describes the impact of contemporary politics on Suetonius:

> The years of Trajan's reign, with their promise that autocracy would not again degenerate into despotism, were a formative period in the biographer's life, encouraging reflection on the performance of earlier rulers that perhaps became more urgent under the climate of unease under which the reign of Hadrian began.[129]

To this climate of unease we turn at last.

The GOLDEN AGE *of* CONSPIRACY THEORY

On August 9, 117 C.E., Hadrian in Syria received a letter stating that Trajan had adopted him. On August 11, Trajan died at Selinus, a city on the coast of Cilicia. The description of his symptoms (peripheral edema, hemostasis, and stroke) suggests cardiovascular disease that would explain his rapid deterioration and death.[1] Yet around these seemingly straightforward facts, rumors accumulate, starting with poison: "Trajan himself suspected that he had fallen ill because of poison" (Dio 68.33.2). According to the *Historia Augusta*, Trajan was supposed to have favored Neratius Priscus as his successor (SHA *Hadr.* 4.8) and said to have wanted to die, like Alexander the Great, without naming one (SHA *Hadr.* 4.9). Dio records that Hadrian owed the adoption to the schemes of Attianus, Trajan's praetorian prefect, and Plotina, Trajan's wife:

> [Hadrian] became Caesar and emperor owing to the fact that when Trajan died childless, Attianus, a compatriot and former guardian of his, together with Plotina, who was in love with him [Hadrian], secured him the appointment, their efforts being facilitated by his proximity and by his possession of a large military force.[2]

The adoption was abrupt (received just two days before Trajan's death) and the signatures uncustomary:

> . . . The death of Trajan was concealed for several days in order that Hadrian's adoption might be announced first. This was shown also by Trajan's letters to the senate, for they were signed, not by him, but by Plotina, although she had not done this in any previous instance.[3]

In the *Historia Augusta*, too, Plotina is implicated in a scheme. After Trajan died, she smuggled an impostor onto the deathbed to whisper the adoption in a muffled voice (SHA *Hadr.* 4.10). Then there is the matter of Trajan's personal attendant, a healthy twenty-eight-year-old man, who died on August 12; did he know something?[4]

The beginning of Hadrian's reign was further marred by political difficulty. He did not reach Rome until July 118, and in the intervening months the senate executed four former consuls on the charge of conspiracy. Palma and Celsus supposedly plotted to kill Hadrian while hunting (Dio 69.2.5), Nigrinus and Lusius while sacrificing (likely before the hunt, SHA *Hadr.* 7.1). Coincidentally all four had served under Trajan.[5] Yet Hadrian denounced the senate's rash verdict, "as he himself says in his autobiography" (*ut ipse in vita sua dicit,* SHA *Hadr.* 7.2). It appears that his first priorities as *princeps* were to clear himself of blame and to establish his credibility as a just ruler (SHA *Hadr.* 7).

At work in Dio and the *Historia Augusta* is the usual bias in imperial historiography that transmits a negative portrait deriving from irretrievable, and consistently hostile, senatorial sources disappointed in Hadrian's abandonment of Trajan's conquests.[6] When the facts are examined, the execution of four potential usurpers becomes a prudent safeguard against opposition and an important step toward securing political stability: Hadrian had rivals and there was widespread opposition to his policy of retreat.[7] As for the implication of Plotina, a woman's part in a conspiracy is a predictable feature of Roman historiography.[8]

This political conspiracy theory is part of the cultural landscape that Juvenal, Tacitus, and Suetonius inhabited. According to Syme, it suffuses Tacitus' *Annales*:

> The early chapters of Book I depict political behaviour, pitilessly—the fraudulent protestations of loyal subjects, discreetly modulated between mourning and rejoicing, and the eager rush to voluntary enslavement. State ceremonial, public professions, and secret conflicts—the whole thing may seem to hint and foreshadow the accession of Hadrian.[9]

Such a metahistorical move allows Syme to press Tacitus into service as a more credible source for the accession of Hadrian than the mangled epitome of Dio or the spurious tales spun by a late antique biographer who styles himself, *inter alia,* "Aelius Spartianus."[10] Syme makes Tacitus' *Annales* into a legible commentary on the reign of Hadrian, in which "allusion to Hadrian is also covert, but not perhaps always discreet."[11] More discreet is Suetonius, whose *De Vita Caesarum,* if it offers any advice to Hadrian, does so without ever even mentioning Trajan's name. When Juvenal finally gets around to Hadrian in *Satire* 7, he trades in overt anger for subtle irony.[12]

The Pisonian conspiracy left visible scars on Neronian literature: Seneca, Lucan, and Petronius were forced to commit suicide.[13] Relatively bloodless by comparison, the conspiracy theory surrounding the accession of Hadrian gives rise to conspiracy and suspicion as major themes in the literary imaginations of Juvenal, Tacitus, and Suetonius, who do not articulate presumptions of fear so much as they reassert the vitality of their familiar and comforting models of the self. Unlike the postwar American culture of conspiracy that is symptomatic of political disaffection and deteriorated autonomy, the intimations of conspiracy in the Roman literature under consideration here champion the Roman value system. While modern conspiracy theory is a marginalized discourse deriving from the fringe, conspiracy theory in Rome is, like nearly all that remains of Roman discourse, the prerogative of the elite. What this tells us is slightly less than we might have liked about conspiracy theory per se and slightly more than we might have expected about the informal mechanisms by which the Romans safeguarded their subjectivity.

The rhetoric of conspiracy theory is evident in ancient Rome in a wide variety of historical and literary contexts. In the courtroom, Cicero's fifth Verrine oration is a tour de force; he constructs a complex explanation for Verres' outlandish behavior and bases the jury's sense of duty and obligation on an oxymoron: *suspicio certa*, "a sure doubt" (*Ver.* 2.5.65). On the comic stage, conspiracy theory entertains. It also embodies the deep-seated moral dilemmas caused by ignorance and the manipulation of knowledge. In Terence's *Hecyra*, Pamphilus explains away the mystery of his wife's disappearance with the stereotype of the wicked mother-in-law. Ripped from context, allusions to conspiracy give the impression that it is omnipresent, atemporal, and therefore relevant in every situation. Such impressions are given substance by reports of conspiracies, whether averted or crushed. At the core of these representations is a conspiracy mentality that articulates a response to permanent conditions, reasserts a capacity for social control, and operates through a kind of story telling that makes claims to truth and credibility—claims made all the more convincing by noticeable inoculations of indisputable common sense. Thus, another difference between modern and ancient conspiracy theory emerges: For modern Americans, to explain something based on unsubstantiated conjecture risks credibility; for ancient Romans, *not* to explain something risks exposing the inherent weaknesses in the essential tenets of a society predicated on inequality. Conspiracy theory was one more way to negotiate the social hierarchies that defined the Roman world.

As Fenster has shown, modern American conspiracy theory assumes the domination of a relatively secret elite "power bloc" over "the people." The tradition of consensus posits a dominant society as "normal" so that those outside—on the fringe—are by definition abnormal to the point of pathological.[14] Therefore, conspiracy theory of the so-called paranoid style is a discourse that emanates from the socially, politically, and culturally antagonized. Against this viewpoint, proponents of conspiracy theory argue that if you cannot enumerate universal criteria sufficient to warrant belief in conspiracy theory, then you cannot dismiss it either: if you cannot dictate the warranted, then you cannot dictate the unwarranted. So in a liberal, democratic society that values transparency and freedom of expression, conspiracy theory should not be silenced. To allow conspiracy theory to exist is less harmful than to impose a restriction that would erode a fundamental right to freedom of expression. Furthermore, even when the conspiracy theorist is wrong, he does less harm in speaking than if he is right and silenced.

If these defenses of conspiracy theory seem less than airtight, it is because they are conditional and comparative, forms of syntax that operate by approximations that conceal their imprecision so ideology can rush into the breach. For example, the "birther" movement in American politics posits that President Barack Obama was not born in the United States and is thus ineligible to be president.[15] This radically misinformed conspiracy theory is "easily marginalized as irrational,"[16] and because the White House produced the long form of his birth certificate, the matter is proven completely baseless.[17] Yet conspiracy theory is nothing if not tenacious; there are those who say that the long form is a forgery, evidence of an even larger network of conspirators.[18] With their persistent conspiracism couched in patriotism, birthers are able to cling to a dispositional explanation instead of a situational explanation and vent abject racism. Thus, as David Owen puts it, "we are not entering a post-racial era, but an era in which racial oppression functions in ever more subtle and invidious ways."[19] All the while, awareness is deflected from the collapsed economy that will ensure an American political culture well stocked with conspiracy theories for decades to come.[20] We can easily reject doubts of President Obama's citizenship. We cannot so easily reject the residue of such doubt.

Although the literature of Juvenal, Tacitus, and Suetonius offers examples nowhere near as stark, the conspiracy theory evident in their works adumbrates an underlying ideology about the legitimacy of Hadrian's adoption, as well as the existence of a readership disposed to take pleasure in such designs. Much can happen in the ungovernable zone between evidence and conjecture, where aspects of ideology not articulated in the manifest discourse can operate all the more artfully.

Juvenal is for many reasons an ideal centerpiece for the study of conspiracy theory in Latin literature. He represents the culmination of the tradition of Roman verse satire, which I take to be a literary expression unique to Rome.

In his poems he sometimes refers to the ancient past; at the same time, he offers some of the most vivid commentary on contemporary society. Juvenal is the photojournalist of Hadrianic Rome, and his vignettes convey a sense of the here and now, the day and age in which he lived and wrote. In his xenophobic diatribes and numerous allusions to historical conspiracies, Juvenal uses synecdoche to assimilate foreigner and conspirator so that one stroke can level two adversaries. Yet it is possible that such strident blame can backfire; angry tirades may in fact belie weakness and inability to control the enemy. It is difficult to explain authoritatively why bad things happen to good people and doubly so for the satirist, whose mask is in constant danger of slipping. Thus, to maintain his persona, the speaker of *Satire* 10 throws in a hedge clause that neatly absolves him of accountability: "After all, what is rational about our fears and desires?" (10.4–5). Such crafted insecurity gives the speaker the purchase necessary to stake his claim in the social order.

Roman politics routinely involved conspiracy, and protection was complicated because sufficient proof to convict and punish conspirators was never forthcoming. The legitimacy and efficacy of arguments for deterrence depend on persuasion. In the speeches of Cato on the execution of the Catilinarian conspirators and Cassius on the summary execution of a *familia* of four hundred slaves, Sallust and Tacitus are able to probe the principles of punishment set forth by Cicero and Seneca. As for the lavish attention that Tacitus devotes to the murder of Pedanius Secundus and the speech of Cassius, one further explanation obtains: Wolf detects in Tacitus a mounting dissatisfaction with the reign of Trajan, who extended the scope of the *senatus consultum Silanianum*—an already cruel law—to unprecedented levels, including the torture of citizens.[21] If sometimes it seems difficult for Tacitus to write the history of the Julio-Claudian dynasty because of sources or bias or relatives who might complain, we should remember that it was probably even more difficult to write about Trajan.[22] Twice Tacitus promised but never delivered.[23] In "that rare time when you can think what you want and say what you think," indirect methods prevail.[24]

Suetonius shows how conspiracy and suspicion permeate the principate and how the emperors use suspicion to their advantage when possible. The verbal and thematic repetitions of suspicion unite the twelve biographies as the story of the life of the principate. Such a reading exonerates Suetonius from charges of uneven or faulty composition. Yet by making it an underlying organizational principle for the twelve lives, Suetonius also harnesses the power of conspiracy theory to his own advantage; namely, it allows him to enter an uncharted region where, in the absence of certainties, he can explore the larger implications of suspicion surrounding the accession of Hadrian.

Conspiracy theory allows us to assess critical disjunctions and glean as much as possible from Roman literature, not only to learn more about the Romans but to confront with less reluctance the epistemic dissatisfaction that circumscribes the human condition. For although we would very much like to think that knowledge is power, the persistence of conspiracy theory with its intractable and resolute unsolvability demonstrates that compromised knowledge too has a measurable valence.

ABBREVIATIONS

In the text, names of authors, works, or words in square brackets [ ] indicate spurious or questionable attributions or interpolations.

ad, ad loc.	*ad locum*, at the line being discussed in the commentary
App. *BC*	Appian *Bella Civilia*
c.	*circa*, about or approximately
CAF	T. Kock, *Comicorum Atticorum Fragmenta*, 3 vols. (1880–1888)
cf.	compare
Cic.	Cicero
ad Brut.	*Epistulae ad Brutum*
Att.	*Epistulae ad Atticum*
Cael.	*Pro Caelio*
Catil.	*In Catilinam*
Clu.	*Pro Cluentio*
Off.	*De Officiis*
Phil.	*Philippicae*
Rab. Perd.	*Pro Rabirio Perduellionis Reo*
Sest.	*Pro Sestio*
Sul.	*Pro Sulla*
Vat.	*In Vatinium*
Ver. 1.x	*In Verrem (actio prima)*
Ver. 2.x.x	*In Verrem (actio secunda)*
Dio	Dio Cassius
Flor.	Lucius Annaeus Florus (or Julius Florus)
ILS	H. Dessau, *Inscriptiones Latinae Selectae* (1892–1916)
Jos. *AJ*	Josephus *Antiquitates Judaicae*
Juv.	Juvenal
Sat.	*Saturae*

Liv.	Livy
Luc.	Lucan
Lys.	Lysias
n.	note
p.	page
Paus.	Pausanias
Plato *Rep.*	Plato *Respublica*
Pliny *Nat.*	Pliny the Elder *Naturalis Historia*
Plin.	Pliny the Younger
Ep.	*Epistulae*
Pan.	*Panegyricus*
Plu.	Plutarch
Cic.	*Cicero*
Luc.	*Lucullus*
Num.	*Numa*
Quint. *Inst.*	Quintilian *Institutio Oratoria*
Sal.	Sallust
Cat.	*Bellum Catilinae*
Hist. fr.	*Historiae*; B. Maurenbrecher, ed., *C. Sallusti Crispi Historiarum reliquiae* (1893)
Sen. *Suas.*	Seneca the Elder *Suasoriae*
Sen.	Seneca the Younger
Ap.	*Apocolocyntosis*
Ben.	*De Beneficiis*
Clem.	*De Clementia*
Dial.	*Dialogi*
Ep.	*Epistulae Morales*
Ira	*De Ira*
Marc.	*Consolatio ad Marciam*
Thy.	*Thyestes*
SHA	Scriptores Historiae Augustae
Hadr.	*Hadrian*
Statius *Theb.*	Statius *Thebaid*
Suet.	Suetonius
Aug.	*Divus Augustus*
Cal.	*Gaius Caligula*
Cl.	*Divus Claudius*
Dom.	*Domitianus*
Jul.	*Divus Julius*
Tib.	*Tiberius*
Tit.	*Divus Titus*

Ves.	*Divus Vespasianus*
Vit.	*Vitellius*
Tac.	Tacitus
Ag.	*Agricola*
Ann.	*Annales*
Hist.	*Historiae*
Ter. *Hec.*	Terence *Hecyra*
trans.	translated by
V. Max.	Valerius Maximus
Varro *Rust.*	Varro *De Re Rustica*
Vell.	Velleius Paterculus

Unattributed translations are my own.

NOTES

INTRODUCTION

1. Sen. *Dial.* 1.2.1: *quare multa bonis viris adversa eveniunt?*

2. Sen. *Dial.* 1.4.6: *calamitas virtutis occasio est.*

3. Groh 1987.

4. Pigden 1995, 5. See also Coady 2006a, 1, who nuances the definition but keeps the two essentials, secrecy and plurality.

5. Coady 2006a, 1; cf. Keeley 1999, 116: "A conspiracy of one is no conspiracy at all." This is in sharp contrast to Roisman's "notion of a single conspirator, a semantic oxymoron, [who] posed no difficulties for the Athenians" (2006, 158). A semantic oxymoron may in fact be the misapplication of the term, for just as the repetition of the prefix in the word *co-conspirator* is a tautology, so a single conspirator runs counter to the very etymology of the word in Greek, Latin, and English, with its recurrent prefix *syn* and *con* denoting togetherness that assumes more than one agent. However, if we accept Roisman's "notion of a single conspirator," then he has identified an abiding difference between Athenian and Roman conspiracy. For Keeley 2007, 140, the regular definition of a conspiracy as composed of a "group of agents" is restrictive and relativized to "non-omnipotent" agents—that is, humans; an omnipotent agent (such as God) has no need to conspire with others to bring about his plans.

6. On the strategies of containment and deterrence, see Pagán 2004, 6, 16, 22–23, 40, 56, 61, 88, 90, 98–99, 124, 129. Phillips 2006, 293, objects that the strategy of containment is not sufficiently proved in the Roman historians' accounts of conspiracies; however, Roisman 2006, 7, 158–159, discerns similar attempts at containment and deterrence at work in the corpus of Attic orators.

7. Pagán 2004, 6.

8. Keeley 1999, 116. Mandik 2007, 206, synthesizes Keeley 1999 (accepted by Clarke 2002) and the revisions of Coady 2006b, 116–117.

9. Pigden 1995, 20.

10. Moscovici 1987, 154.

11. Moscovici 1987, 162.

12. Tac. *Ann.* 15.38.1: *sequitur clades, forte an dolo principis incertum (nam utrumque auctores prodidere)* . . .

13. Tac. *Ann.* 15.44.2: *quin iussum incendium crederetur,* ". . . but that it was believed that the arson had been ordered."

14. Tac. *Ann.* 15.44.4: *deinde indicio eorum multitudo ingens haud proinde in crimine incendii quam odio humani generis*, "then, on their information, a great host was convicted not so much on the charge of arson as for hatred of the human race." See also Moscovici 1987, 157–158. Tacitus' text presents significant interpretive obstacles. Does he describe Roman attitudes toward Christians under Nero, or does he import the attitudes of his own time into his account of the fire? What exactly were the Christians charged with? See Bodinger 2002, who asserts that there was no persecution of the Christians under Nero; the persecutions did not take place until the '70s of the second century C.E. As usual, we must be content to learn more about the historian than the history he records.

15. Louis Blanc, *The History of Ten Years, 1830–1840, Vol. II*, trans. W. K. Kelley (Philadelphia, Lea & Blanchard, 1848), p. 416. Cf. Popper 1966, 95: "Conspirators rarely consumate their conspiracy," and Pipes 1997, 39: "Familiarity with the past shows that most conspiracies fail."

16. For the term "refining historians," see Pigden 1995, 11, citing Lord John Hervey, *Lord Hervey's Memoirs*, edited by Romney Sedgwick (London, William Kimber, 1952). At the brink of epistemological uncertainty, historians make plausible connections. "Refining historians" attribute causality in the face of what may simply be accident. Such refining historians are in a sense guardians of history; by asserting causality at critical moments of epistemological uncertainty, they ensure logical explanations impervious to (other) conspiracy theories. To question and probe the refining historians' assertions of causality are to exhibit a degree of distrust in the sources, their credibility, integrity, and sincerity, and any warrant for such distrust must be justified.

17. This is not to be confused with the cock-up theory, Pigden 1995, 7: "A cock-up is a situation in which an event X is explained by a plan (or perhaps a conspiracy) to bring about Y that somehow goes astray."

18. Graumann 1987, 247; Groh 1987, 7; Kruglanski 1987; Moscovici 1987, 152–153; Roisman 2006, 157.

19. Girardet 1986, 61.

20. Lincoln 1989, 23–26.

21. E.g., Tiffen 2005: "Felt's . . . public identification . . . confirmed that 'Deep Throat' existed as they had said, and was not, as some had speculated, a composite of several sources or even an intention."

22. Lincoln 1989, 24 (emphasis original), 25.

23. Keeley 1999, 117–118, identifies the role of "errant data" in the conspiracy theorist's agenda; data can be unaccounted for or contradictory. "Conspiracy theories are the only theories for which evidence *against* them is actually construed as evidence *in favor* of them" (p. 120, emphasis original).

24. Groh 1987, 5: "'When bad things happen to good people' then something is wrong in the world, and this inconsistency must be able to be explained!" See also Girardet 1986, 13, on political myth as an appeal to action.

25. Lincoln 1989, 25.

26. Graumann 1987, 251; cf. Pigden 1995, 5, on the presumption that conspiracies are morally suspect, and 2007, 219; Husting and Orr 2007, 127, on the power of the label to "turn the tables."

27. See Pagán 2004, 10–14; Nousek 2010, 158–159. Spencer 2001, 78–133, examines the use of *coniuratio, coniurare,* and *coniurati* in Cicero, Livy, Tacitus, Caesar, Sallust, and Suetonius; the consistency in diction points to a larger narrative framework.

---

28. *Coniuratio* experiences a semantic shift from neutral to negative. "Conspiracy," on the other hand, currently appears to be experiencing a semantic shift in the opposite direction, from negative to neutral. To judge from the illustrative quotations cited in the *Oxford English Dictionary*, "conspiracy" has had a consistently negative semantic history. Its use in a good or neutral sense, as listed under Definition 3, "Union or combination (of persons or things) for one end or purpose; harmonious action or effect," is labeled obsolete or archaic, with examples of the word in its strictly etymological sense ("the act of breathing together"). Given the rising interest in conspiracy as a subject of study, the word does not necessarily raise negative expectations. The scholar's attempt at detachment would seem to neutralize the force of the word, lending it credence as a valid critical perspective.

29. Moscovici 1987, 156.

30. According to Comaroff and Comaroff 2003, 288, "If conspiracy is the autonomous explanatory trope of our age, its conceptual grounding lies in its obverse, in transparency." The contributions in West and Sanders 2003 explore the opposition between transparency and conspiracy, the seen and visible, and the unseen and invisible.

31. Hofstadter 2008, 29–40.

32. On Left and Right politics of conspiracy theory, see Pipes 1997, 154–170; Coady 2006a, 3–4. Knight 2000, 37–43, discusses "fusion paranoia," in which the political language of the dissenting fringe is folded into mainstream expressions of conspiratorial uneasiness. Conspiracy theory is no different from other contested value terms (see Goodnight and Poulakos 1981 on the contest over the political language of conspiracy). See Coady 2007b, 202, on how we should talk about conspiracy theory.

33. See Goshorn 2000 on anticonspiracy discourse as a strategy of deterrence from dissent; Pigden 2007, 219, on the dismissal of critical allegations; Husting and Orr 2007 on the "transpersonal strategy of exclusion;" Bratich 2008, 11, on conspiracy theory "as an intolerable line and an antagonism."

34. Groh 1987, 2: "We as historians would be taking our task too lightly if we characterized theories of conspiracy as simply irrational or pathological."

35. Basham 2001, 276.

36. According to the psychological study by Abalakina-Paap et al. 1999, beliefs in conspiracies are related to feelings of alienation, powerlessness, hostility, and disadvantage; however, the need to seek explanations for complex events was not supported by their study (p. 644). While the need for explanation may not be a cause of conspiracism, simplified explanations are certainly the result of belief in conspiracy. Theorists work out their feelings of alienation, powerlessness, hostility, and disadvantage by streamlined explanations embedded in narratives.

37. Fenster 1999, 225–226.

38. Knight 2000, 13.

39. Melley 2000, 44.

40. See also Zukier 1987, 90–91.

41. See also Clarke 2002, 148.

42. Pigden 1995, 25; cf. 2006, 165: "The idea that conspiracy theories *as such* are somehow intellectually suspect is a superstitious or irrational belief, since there is no reason whatsoever to think it true" (emphasis original).

43. Coady 2007a, 133.

44. Coady 2007b, 196.

45. Coady 2007b, 202.

46. Roisman 2006, 160.

47. Coady 2006a, 10: "The legitimacy of conspiracy theorizing depends, not only on the content of the conspiracy theory in question and the content of its official rival, but also on the social and political context in which it takes place."

48. Levy 2007, 182 (emphasis original).

49. Levy 2007, 188. Levy's description of radically social knowledge reads much like a defense of Wikipedia; experts on individual topics band together to create a knowledge base that is greater than the sum of its parts. For a study of the epistemology of Wikipedia, see *Episteme: A Journal of Social Epistemology* 2009 (Volume 6.1), "The Epistemology of Mass Collaboration."

50. Levy 2007, 190, 191.

51. Coady 2007b, 199.

52. Clarke 2002, 133.

53. Clarke 2002, 136.

54. Clarke 2002, 146.

55. Clarke 2002, 144.

56. Pigden 2006, 162.

57. Coady 2006b, 124–125.

58. Clarke 2006, 130, 131.

59. Coady 2006c, 170.

60. Fenster 1999, xv (emphasis original).

61. Melley 2000, 14; see also 135 for a disavowal of theories about the assassination of John F. Kennedy. Cf. Keeley 1999, 111.

62. Roisman 2006, 9.

63. Coady 2007b, 202–203.

64. Horn and Rabinbach 2008, 7.

65. Spencer 2001, 5.

66. Roisman 2006, 35.

67. Roisman 2006, 64.

68. Roisman 2006, 141.

69. Roisman 2006, 158. Difficulties with this conclusion have been registered above, n. 5.

70. Hinds 2007, 218–219.

71. Sukic 2006, 221.

72. Lowrie 2008, 12.

73. Lowrie 2008, 25.

74. The closest we have to an ancient treatise on conspiracy is the tenth-century collection *Excerpta Historica iussu Imp. Constantini Porphyrogeniti*, Vol. III: *Excerpta de Insidiis* (de Boor 1905), which catalogues numerous examples of men and women who conceived and executed treacherous plots: e.g., Clytemnestra, Cambyses, Romulus, Tarquinius Priscus and Tarquinius Superbus, Darius, Jugurtha, Mithridates, Brutus, and Cassius. The epitome spans Greek and Roman, mythological and historical, and military and political events and lists plots from the Trojan War to the time of John of Antioch (early seventh century).

75. Pagán 2008, 30–32.

76. Edwards 1993, 11.

77. Basham 2006, 134, takes an extreme position on the ubiquity of conspiracy

theory: "Far from a nefarious fringe activity, conspiracy and its theory are common place within the most profound personal experiences and commitments of billions of human beings. Far from a rarity, both conspiracy and its theory are fundamental modes of human cognition and have been for millennia." See also Basham 2003.

78. Tac. *Hist.* 1.1.4: *rara temporum felicitate, ubi sentire quae velis et quae sentias dicere licet.*

79. Ahl 1984, 207. On the value of Tacitus, Suetonius, and Juvenal as sources for the Flavian era, see Wilson 2003.

80. Syme 1958, 500.

81. Keane 2012, 403.

82. Sen. *Thy.* 487: *serum est cavendi tempus in mediis malis.*

83. Sal. *Cat.* 52.4: *nam cetera maleficia tum persequare ubi facta sunt; hoc nisi provideris ne adcidat, ubi evenit, frustra iudicia inplores.*

84. Lintott 1999, 90: "[The *senatus consultum*] is an example of an institution created by *mos* over a period . . . that not only owed nothing to *lex* (statute) but had the precise object of rendering temporarily void certain *leges*. Secondly, it raises the perennial question, how far can one save law and order by using illegal violence, how far can *ius* be based on *vis* without ceasing to be *ius*."

85. Melley 2000, 16, 17.

86. Melley 2000, 30.

87. Coady 2006a, 10.

88. Suet. *Dom.* 21.1: *condicionem principum miserrimam aiebat, quibus de coniuratione comperta non crederetur nisi occisis.*

CHAPTER 1

1. Groh 1987, 11–13, on the "boom" and "slump" periods in the history of conspiracy theory.

2. Cowles 1917 is an indispensable historical study.

3. Cowles 1929; Stockton 1971, 41–48; Habicht 1990, 25.

4. *Ver.* 2.1.20. Pseudo-Asconius 126.14–15 (Stangl), following Cicero's hint at *Ver.* 2.3.205. Alexander 1976 and Venturini 1980 argue that Hortensius did in fact give a speech in defense of Verres.

5. Frazel 2004 carefully demonstrates how the second act resembles other delivered speeches in form and technique.

6. Greenwood 1978, xix, asserts that the *actio secunda* could not have been merely a rhetorical exercise and that Cicero must have composed it in advance for delivery in court. To Stockton (1971, 43), Cicero published the *Verrines* to enhance his reputation and as "a detailed and overwhelming justification for the cause of moderate administration and constitutional reform." Crawford 1984, 7: "In all probability, a combination of didacticism and political considerations was responsible for Cicero's publication of his speeches." Nisbet 1992 adds literary purposes to the political aims of publication. Butler 2002, 71–84, also argues for a combination of motives and adds Cicero's ever-nagging anxiety about his status to the list. Frazel 2004, 140, is unconvinced that status anxiety had anything to do with it; publication bolstered Cicero's self-promotion. On the general question of published versus delivered speeches, see Riggsby 1999, 178–184.

7. Plin. *Ep.* 1.20.10: "We find in many of the best orations . . . even where we are sure they were only published, as for instance in this passage from the *Against Verres.*" Pliny goes on to quote *Ver.* 2.4.5. Quint. *Inst.* 6.1.3, 9.2.22, 11.1.40; Levens 1980, n. 18.

8. Parts (also called chapters or books) of the *actio secunda* are named for the aspect of Verres' maladministration under examination by Cicero: *De Juris Dictione* (*Ver.* 2.2), *De Frumento* (*Ver.* 2.3), *De Signis* (*Ver.* 2.4), and *De Suppliciis* (*Ver.* 2.5). Levens 1980, xxxix n. 13, objects to the "misleading" title *De Suppliciis* ("On Punishment"), bestowed by grammarians because the last section of the speech, on Verres' punishments of Roman citizens, was held up as a model of rhetoric in antiquity.

9. *Ver.* 2.5.5: *num tibi illius victoriae gloriam cum M. Crasso aut Cn. Pompeio communicatam putas?* Attempts to cross to Sicily: Flor. 2.8.13; Verres fortifies the island: Sal. *Hist.* fr. IV.32 (Maurenbrecher). Cowles 1917, 137, reminds us that Verres must have been somewhat helpful; see also Maróti 1961, esp. 45–46.

10. *Ver.* 2.5.7: *contagio autem ista servilis belli cur abs te potius quam ab iis omnibus qui ceteras provincias obtinuerunt praedicatur?* The Latin text is by Greenwood (1978), whose translations of the Verrine orations I adapt.

11. *Ver.* 2.5.9: *tamen coeptum esse in Sicilia moveri aliquot locis servitium suspicor. id adeo non tam ex re quam ex istius factis decretisque cognosco.*

12. *Ver.* 2.5.11: *vincam tamen exspectationem omnium. homines sceleris coniurationisque damnati, ad supplicium traditi, ad palum alligati, repente multis milibus hominum inspectantibus soluti sunt et Triocalino illi domino redditi.*

13. *Ver.* 2.5.14: *quis dubitet quin servorum animos summa formidine oppresserit, cum viderent ea facilitate praetorem ut ab eo servorum sceleris coniurationisque damnatorum vita vel ipso carnifice internuntio redimeretur?*

14. *Ver.* 2.5.15: *iste motus servitiorum bellique subita suspicio utrum tibi tandem diligentiam custodiendae provinciae an novam rationem improbissimi quaestus attulit?*

15. *Ver.* 2.5.15: *quod nuper ipse iuratus docuit quem ad modum gestum esset,* "which he himself in sworn evidence showed"; *dixit ipse Matrinius,* "Matrinius himself has stated."

16. *Ver.* 2.5.16: *homines statim loqui: "mirabar quod Apollonius, homo pecuniosus, tam diu ab isto maneret integer; excogitavit nescio quid, attulit; profecto homo dives repente a Verre non sine causa citatur."*

17. *Ver.* 2.5.18: *cum servorum bellum metueretur, quo supplicio dominos indemnatos afficiebat, hoc servos damnatos liberabat.*

18. *Ver.* 2.5.22: *tantumque in hoc crimine suspicionis esse affirmabo ut iam ipsis iudicibus sine mea argumentatione coniecturam facere permittam.*

19. Roisman 2006, 5.

20. On cases involving violence and the laws *de vi*, see Riggsby 1999, 79–119.

21. *Sul.* 21: *an tum in tanto imperio, tanta potestate non dicis me fuisse regem, nunc privatum regnare dicis?* One could of course argue that all references to the conspiracy are defensive.

22. *Cael.* 70: *quaeque lex sedata illa flamma consulatus mei fumantis reliquias coniurationis exstinxit.* On this unspecified law, see Austin 1960, 42–43.

23. *Sest.* 9: *qua de causa et tum conventus ille Capuae, qui propter salutem illius urbis consulatu conservatam meo me unum patronum adoptavit, huic apud me P. Sestio maximas gratias egit.*

24. Liv. 34.2.3–4: *equidem fabulam et fictam rem ducebam esse, virorum omne genus in aliqua insula coniuratione muliebri ab stirpe sublatum esse; ab nullo genere non summum periculum est, si coetus et concilia et secretas consultationes esse sinas.*

---

25. The Flavian poet Statius describes in vivid detail the conspiratorial oath, *Theb.* 5.159–163: *natum Charopeia coniunx / obtulit. accingunt sese et mirantia ferro / pectora congestis avidae simul undique dextris / perfringunt, ac dulce nefas in sanguine vivo / coniurant,* "The wife of Charops offered her son. They gird themselves and greedily slice through the perplexed breast with steel, hands stretching from every side at once. They seal the conspiracy, a sweet crime, in living blood." For the ancient sources for this myth, see Burkert 1970, 6 n. 5.

26. Milnor 2005, 168–169, notes that much of Cato's vocabulary, including the word "conspiracy" (*coniuratio*), is drawn from Roman public life, the very sphere from which Cato sought to exclude women.

27. Groh 1987, 13.

28. Juv. 6.655–661: *occurrent multae tibi Belides atque Eriphylae / mane, Clytaemestram nullus non vicus habebit. / hoc tantum refert, quod Tyndaris illa bipennem / insulsam et fatuam dextra laevaque tenebat; / at nunc res agitur tenui pulmone rubetae, / sed tamen et ferro, si praegustarit Atrides / Pontica ter victi cautus medicamina regis.* Trans. Braund 2004. On poison and the reference to Mithridates, see below, Chapter 2 n. 55.

29. Richlin 1992.

30. Plato, *Rep.* 606c: "Does not the same argument hold about ridicule? You greatly enjoy on the comic stage, or even in private conversation, things at which you would be ashamed to provoke laughter yourself, and there you do not hate them as wicked. Indeed you do the same as in the case of the pitiful, for that part of you which wants to provoke laughter was held back by your reason, for fear of being thought a buffoon, but you let it loose in the theatre, not realizing that, by making that part strong there, you will be led to being a comedian in your own life." Trans. Grube 1974.

31. On the meaning of "Philumena" and the passivity that it suggests, see Penwill 2004, 140, 148 n. 54.

32. On these protatic characters, see Duckworth 1952, 108; R. Hunter 1985, 34.

33. "The mother-in-law joke is part of the human condition," remarks Ferguson 1979, 195, of Juv. 6.231–241, a passage that shares many features with the *Hecyra*: disruption of domestic harmony, pretense of sickness, opportunity for adultery; however, Juvenal's *socrus* is malignant, whereas Terence's Sostrata is innocent. See Braund 1992, 76–77, for the *topos.*

34. Of this speech in particular, R. Hunter 1985, 85, warns that the context of speeches by male characters is important. This attack on women is not indicative of a general misogynist tone of comedy. Boyle 2004, 6, notes that the "prejudicial 'truisms'" of this speech are undercut by their context.

35. Ter. *Hec.* 198–204: *pro deum atque hominum fidem, quod hoc genus est, quae haec est coniuratio! / utin omnes mulieres eadem aeque studeant nolintque omnia / neque declinatam quicquam ab aliarum ingenio ullam reperias! / itaque adeo uno animo omnes socrus oderunt nurus. / viris esse advorsas aeque studiumst, simili' pertinaciast, / in eodemque omnes mihi videntur ludo doctae ad malitiam; et / ei ludo, si ullus est, magistram hanc esse sati' certo scio.* The Latin text is Kauer and Lindsay 1990.

36. Anderson 2000, 316, 317.

37. Ter. *Hec.* 865–868: PAM. *dic mi, harunc rerum numquid dixti iam patri?* BA. *nil.* PAM. *neque opus est / adeo muttito. placet non fieri hoc itidem ut in comoediis / omnia omnes ubi resciscunt. hic quos par fuerat resciscere / sciunt; quos non autem aequomst scire neque resciscent neque scient.*

38. See Pierce 1997, 163, on patterns in the portrayal of rape in New Comedy.

39. The play inverts the customary order of events; in New Comedy, a play ends with a marriage; Norwood 1923, 93; Konstan 1983, 133; Slater 1988, 251; Braund 2005 shows that Plautus anticipated the innovation in the *Amphitryo* and *Menaechmi*. For Sharrock 2009, 236, with the marriage already in place, the plot is driven by "compulsive repetition." On Terence's adaptation of the Greek original by Apollodorus, see Lefèvre 1999.

40. Slater 1988, 251.

41. James 1998.

42. Konstan 1974, 33; Goldberg 1986, 168 ("not a play easy for a Roman audience to love"); James 1998, 46; notably, Anderson 2000, 2002; most recently, Penwill 2004, 137.

43. Konstan 1983, 140.

44. On the theme of *morbus* vs. *odium*, see Gilula 1979/1980; Ireland 1990, 158–162.

45. On the many ways that the *Hecyra* subverts the familiar generic expectations of New Comedy, see Duckworth 1952, 148, 259, 270. It is the only play of Terence that does not have two simultaneous love stories; Beare 1951, 95; Forehand 1985, 95; Ireland 1990, 8.

46. Ter. *Hec.* 179–181: *odisse coepit Sostratam: / neque lites ullae inter eas, postulatio / numquam.*

47. Ter. *Hec.* 187–188: *postquam accersunt saepius, / aegram esse simulant mulierem*, "after they summoned her quite often, they pretended the woman was ill."

48. Ter. *Hec.* 466–467: LA. *heri Philumenam ad se accersi hic iussit. dic iussisse te. / PH. noli fodere. iussi.* LA. *sed eam iam remittet.* PH. *scilicet.*

49. Ter. *Hec.* 654: *redduc uxorem ac noli advorsari mihi.*

50. Ter. *Hec.* 299: *tum matrem ex ea re me aut uxorem in culpa inventurum arbitror.*

51. Ter. *Hec.* 323: *quid morbi est? . . . quid? nemon medicum adduxit?*

52. Ter. *Hec.* 477–481: PAM. *sed quando sese esse indignam deputat matri meae / quae concedat cui(u)sque mores toleret sua modestia, / neque alio pacto componi potest inter eas gratia, / segreganda aut mater a me est, Phidippe, aut Philumena. / nunc me pietas matri' potiu' commodum suadet sequi.*

53. Goldberg 1986, 161.

54. Forehand 1985, 97, 102–103, acknowledges the importance of stereotyping and its effects in this play, but he does not show how the characters are made to reinforce stereotypes. See R. Hunter 1985, 85, for the ability of contradicted stereotype to generate humor, Boyle 2004, 6, for contradicted stereotypes as a compelling force in the works of Terence.

55. Ter. *Hec.* 600: *sine me obsecro hoc effugere volgu' quod male audit mulierum.*

56. As Slater 1988, 259, has noted.

57. Penwill 2004 indicts him categorically—and convincingly.

58. My interpretation of Bacchis contradicts Norwood 1923, 99, for whom she is Terence's "noblest achievement"; "her sunny kindliness pervades the close," of the play, which Norwood calls Terence's "most charming feat of artistry" (pp. 97, 105). See also Duckworth (1952, 259), for whom Bacchis is almost a paragon of "virtue and generosity," in the way she brings about the reconciliation; however, he does entertain the possibility that "she is too noble to be true to life," p. 260. For Rosivach 1998, 136, Bacchis is a "good" *meretrix* who knows her place in polite society. Gilula 1980 argues convincingly that Bacchis is a *mala meretrix* and that, in fact, there is no such thing as a *bona meretrix* in Terence.

59. Anderson 2002, 4.

60. Anderson 2000, 313.

61. On the slave conspiracies of 198, 196, and 185 B.C.E., see Jähne 1986, 66–67; Bradley 1989, 41–44; Briscoe 1973, 216–219, 317–318; Toynbee 1965, II, 318–321.

62. On the Bacchanalian conspiracy, see Pagán 2004, 50–67.

63. Jähne 1986, 67–77; Bradley 1989, 46–65; Toynbee 1965, II, 327–331. On difficulties with the chronology of the beginning of the revolt, see Green 1961; Forrest, Stinton, and Green 1962, 90.

64. Athenaeus 6.104: σύγγραμμα δὲ ἐκδέδωκε περὶ τῶν δουλικῶν πολέμων Καικίλιος ὁ ῥήτωρ ὁ ἀπὸ Καλῆς ἀκτῆς, "A History of the Slave Wars was written by Caecilius, the rhetor from Kale Acte."

65. Diodorus Siculus 34/35.2.1–24 = Photius 384–386B. The principal source was probably Posidonius. On the weaknesses of Diodorus as a source for this period, see Verbrugghe 1972. Other minor sources for the revolt are collected in Shaw 2001, 79–106. For a general discussion with an appendix on chronology, see Green (1961), who shows that the First Sicilian Slave War was not a socialist economic revolt or ideologically emancipatory; rather, it was generated and sustained by models of Hellenistic kingship and syncretic mystery cults, neither of which aim at emancipation. Forrest, Stinton, and Green (1962) register objections to Green's source criticism, chronology, and textual criticism.

66. This leads Westerman 1945 to hypothesize that the revolt was the result of a breakdown of a slave code, an extralegal or partly legalized adjustment between slave labor and ownership that guaranteed slaves customary food, clothing, shelter, and protection from unreasonable punishment. Bradley 1989, 50–54 (and especially n. 8), puts Westerman's reading of the causes of the slave revolt into the broader (less idealized and more realistic) context of slave existence. See also Bradley 1987, 113–137. For a critique of Bradley's "empassioned" approach, see McKeown 2007a, 77–96.

67. The parallel passage is worded similarly: ὅτι συνετίθεντο πρὸς ἀλλήλους οἱ δοῦλοι περὶ ἀποστάσεως καὶ φόνου τῶν κυρίων (34/35.2.24b; cf. Excerpta de Insidiis 23 de Boor). The description of the conspiracy is more vivid: συνθέμενοι δὲ πρὸς ἀλλήλους καὶ πίστεις ἐπὶ σφαγίων ἐνόρκους νυκτὸς ποιησάμενοι καθωπλίσθησαν, "Having formed an agreement among themselves and having pledged oaths over sacrificial victims at night they armed themselves" (34/35.2.24b). John of Antioch also mentions the nocturnal oaths: σύνθεμα νυκτερινὸν ἐπαγγείλαντες παντὶ τῷ δουλικῷ πλήθει (Excerpta de Insidiis 23 de Boor = Roberto fr. 138; according to Roberto 2005, XLI–XLII, the contents of the fragment belong to the slave revolt of 134–132; see also Müller fr. 61).

68. On the second slave war (104–101 B.C.E.), see Toynbee 1965, II, 227–231; Jähne 1986, 77–90; Bradley 1989, 66–82; sources, Shaw 2001, 107–129.

69. The parallel source is identical: τριάκοντα οἰκετῶν συνωμοσίαν ποιησαμένων, 36.2a.

70. The parallel source is a bit more descriptive: τοῖς μὲν ἀπαιτοῦσι τὴν τιμὴν ἀνέλπιστον ἐπιβουλὴν συνεστήσατο (36.2a).

71. See Keaveney 1992, 3–5, on the political career of Lucius Licinius Lucullus.

72. Jähne 1986, 91–171; Bradley 1989, 83–101; sources, Shaw 2001, 130–165; Nachleben, Griffith 1981; Stanev 1981; Jähne 1986, 171–179; Wyke 1997, 34–72; Futrell 2001; Hardwick 2003, 37–43; Urbanczyk 2004, 92–130; Balina 2007, 325–326, 348–352. For a dramatic and factual account of the Spartacus war, see Strauss 2009.

73. It is interesting to note that, once again, a member of the Licinian family is sent to mop up slave rebellion. According to Keaveney 1992, 1, the revival of the gens was due to the Crassi and Luculli.

74. E.g., Dyson 1992, 38.

75. Toynbee 1965, II, 317, 318. Brunt 1971 attributes the rise in the number of slaves to peasant displacement, the growth of latifundia ("estates") and the constant drain on fami-

lies whose adult males were continuously taken off to war. After assessing Toynbee 1965 and Brunt 1971, Cornell 1996, 113, concludes that peasant displacement and depopulation were most pronounced in the areas that had suffered most from the Hannibalic war.

76. Hopkins 1978, 120.

77. Alföldy 1985, 70. Bradley 1989, 132, speaks of "an improved stability in the master-slave relationship of the Imperial age [that] implies that established society came eventually to perceive the need for making social adjustments that would go some way toward accommodating the interests of certain elements within the overall slave population." On the other hand, Tatum 1991, 257, suggests that this adjustment could just as easily have been an increase in cruelty, violence, and oppression.

78. Patterson 1982.

79. Bradley 1994, 131.

80. Bradley 1987, 136; cf. Callahan and Horsley 1998, 148, on the American South.

81. On the difficulties of calculating the slave population in ancient Rome, see Brunt 1971, 121–130 (on 225 B.C.E.–14 C.E.); Hopkins 1978, 99–101.

82. Plin. *Ep.* 3.14.5: *vides, quot periculis, quot contumeliis, quot ludibriis simus obnoxii; nec est, quod quisquam possit esse securus, quia sit remissus et mitis; non enim iudicio domini, sed scelere perimuntur.*

83. Williams 2006, 414–415. McKeown 2007b is less convinced of Pliny's transparency; *Ep.* 3.14 does not express paranoia, a destructive contradiction within Roman society, or a repression of unwelcome truth. Rather, either Pliny conveys a real fear or he is being ironic and the fear should not be taken seriously.

84. Varro *Rust.* 1.17.5: *neque eiusdem nationis plures parandos esse; ex eo enim potissimum solere offensiones domesticas fieri. praefectos alacriores faciendum praemiis dandaque opera ut habeant peculium et coniunctas conservas, e quibus habeant filios. eo enim fiunt firmiores ac coniunctiores fundo.* Trans. Hooper 1993, adapted.

85. Tac. *Ann.* 14.44.3: *suspecta maioribus nostris fuerunt ingenia seruorum, etiam cum in agris aut domibus eisdem nascerentur caritatemque dominorum statim acciperent. postquam uero nationes in familiis habemus, quibus diuersi ritus, externa sacra aut nulla sunt, colluuiem istam non nisi metu coerceris.* On the murder of Pedanius Secundus, see Chapter 3.

86. Cic. *Clu.* 16.47; on the trope of the loyal slave, see Parker 1998.

87. I follow Oakley 1998, 600–601, who moves the phrase *in conspectu omnium*, "in the sight of all," from its illogical position in the manuscript, after *submoto populo*, "at a distance from people," to the preferable placement within the ablative absolute, *epoto <in conspectu omnium> medicamento*, "with the drug swallowed in the sight of all."

88. The manuscript transmits *Quinctilius*; however, I follow Oakley 1998, 601–602, who prefers *Quinct[il]ius* on the basis of the *Fasti Capitolini*, which preserves *Cn. Q[u]inctius T. f. T. n. Capitolinus dict(ator) claui figendi c[aussa]*. On the dictatorship *claui figendi causa*, see Oakley 1998, 73–76 with full bibliography. According to Kaplan 1973, 172–173, in 435 a plague was mitigated when a dictator drove a nail into a wall of the inner chamber of the temple of Minerva on the Capitoline; thereafter, the chief magistrate was supposed to repeat the act annually. However, the custom lapsed and was reinstated only in times of extreme trouble. Livy's statement that a nail was driven during a plebian secession is not attested anywhere else.

89. Liv. 8.18.2–3: *ceterum in eo parvi refert quid veri sit. illud pervelim, nec omnes auctores sunt, proditum falso esse venenis absumptos quorum mors infamem annum pestilentia fecerit; sicut proditur tamen res, ne cui auctorum fidem abrogaverim, exponenda est.* From

this Fantham 1991, 282, concludes that "the story is apocryphal, probably garbled beyond retrieval."

90. Luce 1965, 213 n. 10: "The remark at 8.18.2 is typical."

91. The essence of Liv. 8.18 is distilled in Juv. 6.634–640: *fingimus haec altum satura sumente coturnum / scilicet, et finem egressi legemque priorum / grande Sophocleo carmen bacchamur hiatu, / montibus ignotum Rutulis caeloque Latino? / nos utinam vani! sed clamat Pontia "feci, / confiteor, puerisque meis aconita paravi, / quae deprensa patent; facinus tamen ipsa peregi,"* "I'm making all this up, am I, letting satire put on tragic high heels? I've exceeded the legal limits of my predecessors and I'm ranting with rotundity worthy of Sophocles a grand song that's new to the Rutulian hills and the Latin sky? If only this were really nonsense! But Pontia declares: 'Guilty! I admit it! I gave aconite to my own boys. The murder was discovered and made public. Yet it was I who performed the crime myself." Trans. Braund 2004. For Fantham 1991, 283, "the main import of the story [Livy 8.18] is to reflect the suspect, alien nature of women"; the same is true of Juvenal. Martial mentions a poisoner called Pontia (4.43, 6.75), and so Juvenal, like Cato, expresses anxiety over the evaporating boundary between myth and real life; see above, n. 24. Interested in Juvenal's manipulation of generic expectations, Morford 1972 and Keane 2003, 265–266, remark that Juv. 6.634–638, conflates tragedy and satire. The similarities in content to Liv. 8.18 have gone unnoticed.

92. Oakley 1998, 594–595, suggests that Fabius Pictor may have told the story.

93. Livy records three times when a dictator *claui figendi causa* was elected (7.3, 8.18, 9.28); each time, the ritual is apotropaic. According to Oakley 1998, 73–74, at 8.18.12, Livy's statement that there had been a dictatorship *in secessionibus quondam plebis,* "during a secession of the plebs," is unsupported by external evidence and cannot be identified with a particular event. Poma 1978, 43–45, suggests that Livy confused different traditions about the dictatorship. For our purposes it matters only that Livy gives an impression that the office had a precedent and that the unusual circumstances demanded a ritual intended to heal extreme civil disturbance.

94. Liv. 4.45.1–2: *annus <fuit>, felicitate populi Romani, periculo potius ingenti quam clade insignis. servitia urbem ut incenderent distantibus locis coniurarunt, populoque ad opem passim ferendam tectis intento ut arcem Capitoliumque armati occuparent. avertit nefanda consilia Iuppiter, indicioque duorum comprehensi sontes poenas dederunt. indicibus dena milia gravis aeris, quae tum divitiae habebantur, ex aerario numerata et libertas praemium fuit.*

95. Levene 1993, 169–173, on the favor of the gods in Book 4; however, for Ogilvie 1965, 603, this passage is not evidence of Livy's belief in divine intervention.

96. A little too schematically, according to Ogilvie 1965, 603; the rewards would not have been paid from the public treasury at so early a date. For a similar formulation of rewards to conspirators, see Liv. 22.33.1: *et servi quinque et viginti in crucem acti, quod in campo Martio coniurassent; indici data libertas et aeris gravis viginti milia,* "and twenty-five slaves were crucified because they conspired in the Campus Martius. The informant was given his freedom and twenty thousand sesterces." Punishment and rewards are treated more fully below, Chapter 3.

97. Tac. Ann. 4.27: *eadem aestate mota per Italiam seruilis belli semina fors oppressit. auctor tumultus T. Curtisius, quondam praetoriae cohortis miles, primo coetibus clandestinis apud Brundisium et circumiecta oppida, mox positis propalam libellis ad libertatem uocabat agrestia per longinquos saltus et ferocia seruitia, cum uelut munere deum tres biremes adpulere ad usus commeantium illo mari. et erat isdem regionibus Cutius Lupus quaestor, cui prouincia uetere*

ex more calles euenerat. is disposita classiariorum copia coeptantem cum maxime coniuratio-
nem disiecit. missusque a Caesare propere Staius tribunus cum ualida manu ducem ipsum et
proximos audacia in urbem traxit, iam trepidam ob multitudinem familiarum, quae gliscebat
inmensum, minore in dies plebe ingenua. The Latin text is Borzsák 1992.

98. Thompson 1974, 305. We may compare the recent scholarly controversy over the Denmark Vesey conspiracy of 1822; the state of the evidence is such that historians can argue whether there ever was a conspiracy or whether the slaves were victims of the prejudice of the South Carolina Supreme Court. The debate is waged in Gross 2001 and 2002. Similarly, the evidence for the New York Conspiracy of 1741 tells us less about the details of the conspiracy and more about how the threat of black rebellion served to shape a nascent white political consciousness, according to Lepore 2005. On the historiography of the New York Conspiracy of 1741, see Doolen 2004, 377–379. It would seem that slave revolts and conspiracies open the door to revisionist history, a risk inherent whenever primary sources are compromised or lacking.

CHAPTER 2

1. Braund 2004, 24; see also 1988, 1992, 1996, 1997. Following Braund, I shall refer to the individual poems using the English word *Satires* and not the Latin *Saturae.*

2. 2.47: *magna inter molles concordia,* "The solidarity among effeminates is enormous." Unless otherwise indicated, the Latin text is from Braund 2004; I use or adapt her translations. My own translations of Juvenal are identified.

3. Walters 1998, 356, 357.

4. 3.222: *suspectus tamquam ipse suas incenderit aedes,* "He's suspected of having set fire to his own house." Cf. Martial 3.52.3–4.

5. 14.28–29: *conscia matri / virgo fuit,* "As a little girl she was her mother's accomplice."

6. Hooley 2007, 134–135, is sensitive to Juvenal's over-the-top mode: exaggeration becomes the subject matter of the poems. Thus, the satires showcase not only excessive xenophobia but the excess itself. Coffey 1976, 123–124, would attribute this in part to the influence of rhetorical training, especially the practice of declamation. For Gowers 1993, 188–190, excess is accompanied by deflation.

7. E.g., 4.147, 5.52–55, 13.162–165, 14.187.

8. 10.1–5: *omnibus in terris, quae sunt a Gadibus usque / Auroram et Gangen, pauci dinoscere possunt / vera bona atque illis multum diversa, remota / erroris nebula. quid enim ratione timemus / aut cupimus?*

9. Braund 1988 demonstrates that in *Satires* 7–9 (Book 3) anger is no longer the main feature of the speaker's persona, but he has moved to a new and more subtle level of criticism; irony emerges as the predominant register, in a sense more brutal than anger because it is double-edged. With irony the speaker can cut his victim two ways at the same time.

10. Braund 1996, 182, *ad* 3.49–50, with citations; Braund 1988, 164–177.

11. I follow Braund 1988, 1, and refer to the speaker of the poems so as to draw the distinction between Juvenal the poet and the voice that speaks in the *Satires.*

12. Hatred: 6.272, 451; 7.35; 9.96; 10.73; 15.37; and especially 15.71: *ergo deus, quicumque aspexit, ridet et odit,* "So any god that takes a look is filled with laughter and loathing." Throughout the poems the speaker has been, in many ways, like this god, observing human nature and reacting with laughter and loathing.

13. Highet 1954, 52, on Juvenal as the "first satirist to blend the past with the present. . . . It was this sense of history that made him, not merely the scourge of a single emperor, but the satirist of all Rome."

14. Lutz 1950, 118, calls these lines a "hedge clause," identifiable in other authors, by which Juvenal avoids matter-of-fact statements and buffers himself from criticism for departing from historical facts.

15. On Juvenal's dates, see Syme 1958, 774–778; Coffey 1976, 119–123; Braund 1996, 15–16.

16. See Morgan 2006, 261–262, on the effects of the civil wars of 69 on everyday Roman life and, in particular, a rise in criminal activity such as Juvenal describes at 3.306–308. The absence of the praetorian and urban cohorts "cannot have encouraged a sense of security in citizens at any level of society in Rome" (p. 262).

17. Chronology defies exactitude. Syme 1958, 776, declares, "There is no proof that Juvenal published anything earlier than 115, perhaps even 117." Hardie 1997–1998, 120, demonstrates that *Satire* 4 was written in a post-accession period so as "to present implicit contrasts between Domitian and the early Hadrianic era." Braund 1996, 16, suggests that some poems may have been composed under Trajan but does not mention this at 2004, 19.

18. 1.147–171 resounds with themes found in Tacitus' programmatic paragraphs at *Ann.* 4.32–33: *apologia* for subject matter, *ingenium* necessary for the task at hand, talents of earlier authors, dangers of recent history, and events within living memory. E.g., *Ann.* 4.33.4: *quod antiquis scriptoribus rarus obtrectator, neque refert cuiusquam, Punicas Romanasue acies laetius extuleris*, "But rare is the detractor of ancient historians, nor does it matter to anyone whether you praise Carthaginian or Roman battle lines more happily." Juvenal may point to Tacitus' name at 1.167, *tacita sudant praecordia culpa*, "His heartstrings sweat with silent guilt." The phrase at 1.168, *inde ira et lacrimae*, "whence anger and tears," suggests (and is metrically equivalent to) Tac. *Ann.* 1.1.3: *sine ira et studio*, "without anger or eagerness." See Bartsch 1994, 98–147, for a comparison of the *Dialogus* and Juvenal's seventh satire. I disagree with Townend 1972, 383, who questions the degree to which the *Annales* can be detected in Juvenal: "Nothing in the first nine satires displays any acquaintance with the Tacitean version [of Barea's prosecution and death]." On the correspondences between Juvenal and Tacitus, see Keane 2012.

19. Shumate 2006, 22, 27.

20. Shumate 2006, 38.

21. On the literary allusions in Juvenal, see Townend (1973, esp. 160), who advocates a fine-tuned sensitivity to possible allusions, although it is impossible to tell whether contemporary readers would have sensed them. On historical allusions in *Satire* 5, see Morford 1977, 235.

22. Claudius: 5.146–148, 6.114–135, 6.620–626, 10.329–345, 14.330. Nero: general conspiracies at 1.155, 3.116–118, 5.36–37, 8.40, 12.129; Pisonian conspiracy at 6.615–617, 6.638, 7.79, 7.91, 8.212, 10.15–16; 69 C.E. at 6.[559], 10.20–21, 13.17. Domitian: 1.26–27, 4.153–154, 6.385.

23. For two possible indirect allusions, see 9.145–146: *sit mihi praeterea curvus caelator, et alter / qui multas facies pingit cito*, "In addition, I'd like an engraver, stooped by his work, and an artist who can do multiple portraits in moments." Verres kept such artists on his payroll (Cic. *Ver.* 2.4.54). 16.29–30: *"da testem" iudex cum dixerit, audeat ille / nescio quis, pugnos qui vidit, dicere "vidi,"* "When the judge says, 'Call your witness,' suppose the person who saw the attack has the nerve to say 'I saw it.'" Cf. Cic. *Ver.* 2.5.165: *adhuc enim*

testes ex eo genere a me sunt dati, non qui novisse Gavium, sed se vidisse dicerent, "For so far I have called witnesses not from among those who were to state that they knew Gavius, but who were to state that they saw him."

24. Spencer 2001, 134–135, although see Classen 1980 on Cicero's exaggeration of Verres' gang.

25. 2.24–28: *quis tulerit Gracchos de seditione querentes? / quis caelum terris non misceat et mare caelo / si fur displiceat Verri, homicida Miloni, / Clodius accuset moechos, Catilina Cethegum, / in tabulam Sullae si dicant discipuli tres?*

26. 3.49–54: *quis nunc diligitur nisi conscius et cui fervens / aestuat occultis animus semperque tacendis? / nil tibi se debere putat, nil conferet umquam, / participem qui te secreti fecit honesti. / carus erit Verri qui Verrem tempore quo vult / accusare potest.*

27. Braund 1996, 183, 184.

28. 8.105–107: *inde Dolabella †atque hinc† Antonius, inde / sacrilegus Verres referebant navibus altis / occulta spolia et plures de pace triumphos.* The text is corrupt, hence Braund's asterisks. For *sacrilegus,* cf. Cic. *Ver.* 2.1.9, 47; 2.5.4, 188.

29. According to Livy, Romulus was the first to obtain *spolia opima,* and he dedicated them at the Temple of Jupiter Feretrius in a public ceremony (Liv. 1.10.7). On the development of the tradition, see Flower 2000. Twice more in the early Republic, generals won *spolia opima,* but in 27 B.C.E. Octavian denied Marcus Licinius Crassus the honor of dedicating spoils the latter won in his conquest of the Bastarnae; Flower 2000, 49–53.

30. 6.105, 112.

31. Muse 2007, 591, 593.

32. 10.123–125: *Antoni gladios potuit contemnere si sic / omnia dixisset. ridenda poemata malo / quam te, conspicuae divina Philippica famae,* "He could have laughed at Antony's swords if everything he said had been like this. I rank his ridiculous verses above you, immortal *Philippic.*" At *Satire* 7.199, Cicero is adduced as an example of one whose fortunes rose and fell. Cicero and Verres were both victims of Antony's proscription.

33. See Pagán 2004, 8–9.

34. 8.231–239: *quid, Catilina, tuis natalibus atque Cethegi / inveniet quisquam sublimius? arma tamen vos / nocturna et flammas domibus templisque parastis, / ut bracatorum pueri Senonumque minores, / ausi quod liceat tunica punire molesta. / sed vigilat consul vexillaque vestra coercet. / hic novus Arpinas, ignobilis et modo Romae / municipalis eques, galeatum ponit ubique / praesidium attonitis et in omni monte laborat.* Trans. Braund 2004, adapted.

35. Sal. *Cat.* 45.1.

36. On the development of fire imagery in the first satire, see Bertman 1968.

37. Tac. *Ann.* 15.44.4: *et pereuntibus addita ludibria, ut ferarum tergis contecti laniatu canum interirent, aut crucibus adfixi, ut flammandi, ubi defecisset dies, in usum nocturni luminis urerentur.* Trans. Woodman 2004.

38. Cic. *Catil.* 1.8: *iam intelleges multo me vigilare acrius ad salutem quam te ad perniciem rei publicae,* "Now you will understand that I have been much more keenly vigilant for the safety of the republic than you have been for its destruction." 2.19: *primum omnium me ipsum vigilare,* "First of all that I myself have been vigilant." 3.3: *semper vigilavi et providi,* "I was always vigilant and on the lookout."

39. 8.39–40: *his ego quem monui? tecum mihi sermo, Rubelli / Blande* (my translation).

40. Duff 1970, 293.

41. He was consul in the year 18; marriage: Tac. *Ann.* 6.27.1. Syme 1982, 72.

42. Tac. *Ann.* 3.23 (the trial of Lepida occurs in the aftermath of the trial of Piso for the murder of Germanicus), 3.51.1.

43. Tac. *Ann.* 13.19.3: *per maternam originem pari ac Nero gradu a diuo Augusto.* Trans. Woodman 2004.

44. Syme 1982, 79.

45. Tac. *Ann.* 13.19.3: *ad res nouas extollere coniugioque eius et imperio rem publicam rursus inuadere,* "to exalt him for revolution and by his marriage and subsequent command to assail the state once more."

46. Courtney 1980, 391, with stemma.

47. Syme 1982, 81.

48. Praetorian cohort: Tac. *Ann.* 4.1; Capri: Tac. *Ann.* 4.57 (Tacitus is dubious); consulship: Suet. *Tib.* 65, Dio 58.4.4.

49. Jos. *AJ* 18.181.

50. Dio 58.9–11; Cic. *Catil.* 3.21, cf. 4.14. Levick 1976, 178: "Now it [the temple] was witness to the condemnation of a latter day Catiline." On Cicero's "metaphysical topography" in the Catilinarian orations, see Vasaly 1993, 40–87. For a further point of comparison between Catiline and Sejanus, cf. Tacitus' character sketch of Sejanus at *Ann.* 4.1 with Sal. *Cat.* 5, the portrait of Catiline.

51. 10.65–67: *pone domi laurus, duc in Capitolia magnum / cretatumque bovem: Seianus ducitur unco / spectandus, gaudent omnes* (my translation).

52. 10.69–72: *"sed quo cecidit sub crimine? quisnam / delator quibus indicibus, quo teste probavit?" / "nil horum; verbosa et grandis epistula venit / a Capreis." "bene habet, nil plus interrogo"* (my translation).

53. Syme 1958, 777; Townend 1972, 383–384 and 1973, 159; Keane 2012.

54. On *Ann.* 11.26–38, Colin 1956; Pagán 2006, 66–85; von Stackelberg 2009.

55. 5.146–148, 6.620–623. Poison is a recurrent subject in the poems; cf. 1.69–72 for Locusta the notorious poisoner from Gaul, who is supposed to have supplied Agrippina and Nero with the drugs to kill Claudius and Britannicus; 6.133–134 for poisons served to stepsons; 6.630 for advice not to trust one's food; 14.252–253, 6.660–661 for Mithridates' development of antidotes to poison. See Cilliers and Retief 2000 for a brief overview of poisons, antidotes (especially "mithridatum"), and recorded crimes by poison; most occurred under Julio-Claudian emperors. On Mithridates, see Mayor 2010.

56. Nero mentioned by name: 4.137, 6.615, 8.72, 8[170], 8.193, 8[223], 10.308.

57. 8.211–212: *libera si dentur populo suffragia, quis tam / perditus ut dubitet Senecam praeferre Neroni.*

58. 10.15–18: *temporibus diris igitur iussuque Neronis / Longinum et magnos Senecae praedivitis hortos / claudit et egregias Lateranorum obsidet aedes / tota cohors.*

59. Longinus: Tac. *Ann.* 16.9.1; Seneca: 15.60.2–64; Lateranus: 15.60.1.

60. Juvenal mentions that Petronius' daughter Pontia was a famous pharmacologist, *Sat.* 6.638; see Bagnani 1954, 86. Pontia is also mentioned at Martial 2.34.6, 4.43.5, 6.75.

61. Barea: 7.91, 3.116–118; Thrasea: 5.36–37.

62. Plu. *Galba* 15.2; Suet. *Galba* 11; cf. Dio 63.23.

63. Tac. *Hist.* 1.7; cf. the obituary of Valens, 3.62.

64. Tac. *Hist.* 4.13.1: *Paulum Fonteius Capito falso rebellionis crimine interfecit,* "A little later Fonteius Capito was killed on the false charge of rebellion."

65. The Long Year 69 is also mentioned at 2.99–103; a transvestite holds a mirror, identified as the characteristic prop of Otho: "It's a matter that deserves its mention in recent annals and modern history that a mirror was part of the kit for civil warfare" (2.102–103). The "recent annals" may refer to Tacitus' *Historiae.* Otho may be alluded to once more in a rant against astrologers, 6[558–559]: [*cuius amicitia conducendaque tabella / mag-*

nus civis obit et formidatus Othoni], "by whose friendship and by whose venal horoscope a great citizen died, one whom Otho dreaded." However, Duff 1970, Courtney 1980, and Ferguson 1979 *ad loc.* regard the lines as an interpolation.

66. 10.19–21: *pauca licet portes argenti vascula puri / nocte iter ingressus, gladium contumque timebis / et mota ad lunam trepidabis harundinis umbra* (my translation).

67. Luc. 8.5–8: *pavet ille fragorem / motorum ventis nemorum, comitumque suorum / qui post terga redit trepidum laterique timentem / exanimat.* Cf. Stat. *Theb.* 6.157–159: *tantum caeli violentior aura / impulsaeque Noto frondes cassusque valeret / exanimare timor*, "But merely a breeze blowing strong or leaves shaken by Notus or idle terror might have been enough to cause his end."

68. Dio 63.28.2: ἔκ τε τῆς ὁδοῦ ἀπετράπη καὶ ἐς καλαμώδη τόπον τινὰ κατεκρύφθη. καὶ ἐνταῦθα μέχρι τῆς ἡμέρας ὑπέμεινεν ἐρριμμένος, ὅπως ὡς ἥκιστα διορῷτο. καὶ πάντα μὲν τὸν παριόντα ὡς καὶ ἐφ' ἑαυτὸν ἥκοντα ὑποπτεύων, πᾶσαν δὲ φωνὴν ὡς καὶ ἀναζητοῦσαν αὐτὸν ὑποτρέμων, εἴ τέ που κυνίδιον ὑλάξεν ἢ καὶ ὀρνίθιον ἐφθέγξατο ῥωπίον τε καὶ κλάδος ὑπ' αὔρας ἐσείσθη, δεινῶς ἐταράττετο. Trans. Carey 2000. Suet. *Nero* 48 also recounts the flight in great detail but does not mention fear caused by stirring reeds.

69. Baldwin 1983, 175, conjectures about Suetonius' source for his description of the *exitus Neronis* at *Nero* 47–49: "The hapless Epaphroditus may have left written and verbal memories of Nero's passing" (see also pp. 510–511).

70. Cf. the death of Vitellius as described by Tac. *Hist.* 3.84.4: Vitellius attempts to escape (*perfugeret*), flees to an abandoned place (*uastum desertumque*), is frightened by the solitude (*terret solitudo*), and hides himself until the executioners arrive (*semet occultans*).

71. 4.37–38: *cum iam semianimum laceraret Flavius orbem / ultimus et calvo serviret Roma Neroni* (my translation).

72. See Braund 1996, 244. Charles 2002 explores the ways in which portrayals of Domitian adhere to and depart from portrayals of Nero; later tradition sought to blacken Domitian's character by comparing him to the tyrant Nero. The identification of Domitian as another Nero is a later tradition with a distinct ideological purpose.

73. On Domitian's paranoia, see Dio 67.1.1; Plin. *Pan.* 48–49. On Suetonius' portrait of Domitian's paranoia, see below, Chapter 4.

74. 4.46–48: *quis enim proponere talem / aut emere auderet, cum plena et litora multo / delatore forent?*

75. Braund 1996, 258, identifies themes of terror, weakness, and corruption. Highet 1954, 169, on satire as "σπουδαιογέλοιον, 'serious joking.'"

76. 4.110: *Pompeius tenui iugulos aperire susurro.* On Pompeius as *delator*, see Rutledge 2001, 257–258.

77. Braund 1996, 258. It was an age of adultery and hypocrisy. Juvenal alludes to Domitian's incest with his niece Julia; she died after he allegedly forced her to have an abortion (*Sat.* 2.29–35).

78. Suet. *Dom.* 10.2, as noted by Braund 1996, 269. See also 6.385 for an allusion to the Aelii Lamiae. Lamia may also refer to Juvenal's contemporary, Lucius Aelius Lamia Aelianus, consul of 116 c.e. This would lend further support to Hardie's 1997–1998 metahistorical interpretation of *Satire 4*.

79. 8.259–268: *ancilla natus trabeam et diadema Quirini / et fascis meruit, regum ultimus ille bonorum. / prodita laxabant portarum claustra tyrannis / exulibus iuvenes ipsius consulis et quos / magnum aliquid dubia pro libertate deceret, / quod miraretur cum Coclite Mucius et quae / imperii finis Tiberinum virgo natavit. / occulta ad patres produxit crimina*

servus / matronis lugendus; at illos verbera iustis / adficiunt poenis et legum prima securis (my translation).

80. According to Fredericks 1971, 130–131, a parody of Livy.

81. Shumate 2006, 38.

82. 15.78–81: *ast illum in plurima sectum / frusta et particulas, ut multis mortuus unus / sufficeret, totum corrosis ossibus edit / victrix turba.* Gowers 1993, 198–200, discusses this poem and the intimations of cannibalism elsewhere in the satires (1.34–35, 8.90, 13.84).

83. Suet. *Nero* 37.2: *creditur etiam polyphago cuidam Aegypti generis crudam carnem et quidquid daretur mandere assueto, concupisse vivos homines laniandos absumendosque obicere.*

84. Littman 1976; Baldwin 1977.

85. 15.83, 87–88: *contenta cadauere crudo. / . . . sed qui mordere cadauer / sustinuit nil umquam hac carne libentius edit.*

86. Baldwin 1977, 407.

87. Gaius Fannius and Titinius Capito wrote works in commemoration of the "deaths of famous men" (*exitus illustrum virorum*) that were hostile to Nero: Plin. *Ep.* 5.5, 5.8, 8.12. Theirs was a contemporary fashion that Suetonius participated in; see Baldwin 1983, 76–79, esp. 508; see also Syme 1958, 91–93, who minimizes the contribution of Capito ("Titinius is a document of social mimicry," p. 92). Wallace-Hadrill 1983, 58, denies the importance of Fannius and Capito to Suetonius. Of historians who are possible, Fabius Rusticus was hostile to Nero, although his use by Tacitus suggests a degree of seriousness that would preclude sensationalism. Cluvius Rufus is also a possibility, though Wardle 1992 is hesitant. Given his wide-ranging interests and his comprehensive approach to information, the polymath Pliny the Elder is a ready candidate.

88. Shumate 2006, 147, identifies the "fear of indifferentiation" that the incident in Egypt inspires in the speaker, which "culminates in wanton disregard for the bodily integrity of individuals and in the physical fusion of self and other, inside and outside, that is represented in the taboo act of cannibalism."

89. 15.142–143, 146–149: *separat hoc nos / a grege mutorum . . . / sensum a caelesti demissum traximus arce, / cuius egent prona et terram spectantia. mundi / principio indulsit communis conditor illis / tantum animas, nobis animum quoque.*

90. Sal. *Cat.* 1.1: *omnis homines qui sese student praestare ceteris animalibus summa ope niti decet ne uitam silentio transeant, ueluti pecora quae natura prona atque uentri oboedientia finxit. Sed nostra omnis uis in animo et corpore sita est.*

91. Cf. 2.25: *quis caelum terris non misceat et mare caelo,* "Who would not confuse sky and land, sea and sky."

92. 15.171–174: *quid diceret ergo / vel quo non fugeret, si nunc haec monstra videret / Pythagoras, cunctis animalibus abstinuit qui / tamquam homine et ventri indulsit non omne legumen?*

93. With this closing, Juvenal uses cannibalism to reinforce the central topic of satire: "man's behavior toward his fellows." The act becomes "a vehicle for the fundamental themes of *humanitas* and civilization," Braund 1986, 17. On *humanitas* as a near-synonym for *Romanitas*, see Braund 1997, also Shumate 2006, 140. The speechlessness of Pythagoras suggests to me a sort of poetic cannibalism, whereby the poem consumes words themselves, producing desperate silence.

94. Harrill 2008, 136.

95. Braund 1986, 17.

96. 15.27: *consule Iunco,* Courtney 1980 *ad loc.*

97. Shumate 2006, 144–146, on the hostile tradition.

98. I refer to the story of Antinous, Hadrian's young male lover who drowned in the Nile; Hadrian founded Antinoopolis in his honor. Paus. 8.9.7; Dio 69.11.2–4; SHA *Hadr.* 14.5–7. For an assessment of the literary and iconographic evidence of Antinous, see Vout 2007, 52–135.

99. At 4.1–33, Crispinus is again targeted.

100. 1.102–105: *"prior" inquit "ego adsum. / cur timeam dubitemve locum defendere, quamvis / natus ad Euphraten, molles quod in aure fenestrae / arguerint, licet ipse negem?"* Apparently the foreigner has pierced ears (my translation).

101. The translation is Braund 1996, *ad loc.* Juvenal alludes to Tiberius Julius Alexander, who was a Jew. Here, he is scorned for his connection to Egypt. Thus, in one stroke the speaker tars twice.

102. See Keane 2003, 260–263, for a discussion of the ways Juvenal exploits the negative perception of actors.

103. Walters 1998.

104. Edwards 1997.

105. Though tempting in its implications of conspiracism, the next line (3.113) is best regarded as an interpolation: [*scire volunt secreta domus atque inde timeri*], "They wish to know household secrets and as a result to be feared"; see Braund 1996, *ad loc.*

106. Braund 1996, 183.

107. Cf. 14.96–106 for a more sustained attack on Jewish customs of keeping kosher, circumcision, the Ten Commandments, and observance of the Sabbath. See Hardie 1998 for a discussion of the inspirational topography of the grove of Egeria; the dramatic setting raises issues of credibility and skepticism. Numa's secret, erotic meetings with the nymph were a cause of speculation; Plu. *Num.* 4.1–2: ὅθεν οὐχ ἥκιστα τὴν ἀρχὴν ὁ περὶ τῆς θεᾶς ἔλαβε λόγος, ὡς ἄρα Νομᾶς ἐκεῖνος οὐκ ἀδημονίᾳ τινὶ ψυχῆς καὶ πλάνῃ τὸν μετὰ ἀνθρώπων ἀπολέλοιπε βίον, ἀλλὰ σεμνοτέρας γεγευμένος ὁμιλίας καὶ γάμων θείων ἠξιωμένος, Ἠγερίᾳ δαίμονι συνὼν ἐρώσῃ καὶ συνδιαιτώμενος, εὐδαίμων ἀνὴρ καὶ τὰ θεῖα πεπνυμένος γέγονεν, "Not least from this did the story about the goddess arise, that Numa hadn't left behind life among men because of any distress or aberration of the spirit, but because he had had a taste for more august company and had been thought worthy of divine marriage; that Egeria fell in love with him and by being with him and living with her, he had become a blessed man and one wise in divine matters."

108. 11.117–118: *illa domi natas nostraque ex arbore mensas / tempora viderunt.*

109. 25.40.2: *ceterum inde primum initium mirandi Graecarum artium opera licentiaeque hinc sacra profanaque omnia uolgo spoliandi factum est,* "But then came the beginning of our admiration for works of Greek art and hence of license and spoliation of every kind of treasure, both sacred and profane alike." Cf. Polybius 9.10.

110. 39.6.7: *luxuriae enim peregrinae origo ab exercitu Asiatico invecta in urbem est. ii primum lectos aeratos, vestem stragulam pretiosam, plagulas et alia textilia, et quae tum magnificae supellectilis habebantur, monopodia et abacos Romam advexerunt,* "For the beginnings of foreign luxury were introduced into the city by the army from Asia. These soldiers were the first to bring to Rome bronze couches, costly coverlets, counterpanes and other woven cloths, as well as what was regarded at the time as sumptuous furniture—tables supported on a single pedestal, and sideboards." Trans. Walsh 1994. Sal. *Cat.* 11.6 dates the importation of foreign luxuries to the conquests of Sulla (87–83 B.C.E.).

111. At work in such indeterminancy is what Barthes 1972, 153, calls "Ninisme"

("Neither-Norism"), a rhetorical form that generates conservative myth, whereby historical contingency is naturalized (p. 129).

112. Cf. Shumate 2006, 155, on Juvenal's "failure in the end to come down on the side of either progress or decline. . . . Juvenal's speaker, like later colonialists, wants to have it both ways."

113. Cf. 15.110–112; Shumate 2006, 137–138.

114. Richlin 1984, 67.

115. Girardet 1986, 61: the accusations of power mongering hurled against conspirators are a reflection of the accuser's own desire for power.

CHAPTER 3

1. Treggiari 1985, 258, would have us question the veracity of such an extraordinary number. Ginsburg 1993, 96, takes Tacitus at his word.

2. On Sallustian allusions in Cassius' speech, see Syme 1958, 355; Koestermann 1968, 107; Nörr 1983, 204–205; Wolf 1988, 25 n. 76; Martin 1990, 1558–1569; Ginsburg 1993, 97–98. D'Ippolito 1969, 56–58, is skeptical of overtly Sallustian language, on the grounds that Tacitus may simply be reproducing the speech of Cassius, who affected archaic, technical language.

3. The trial was held between May and October 62; Berry 1996, 14. On Cicero's reasons for accepting the case, see Berry 1996, 26–33. The arguments of the prosecution have been teased out by Alexander 2002, 189–205.

4. On the date and circumstances of production, see Dyck 1996, 8–10.

5. Braund 2009, 70–73, on the affinities between the *De Ira* and the *De Clementia*.

6. Griffin 1976, 407–411.

7. On the development of Plato's radical theory of punishment, as evidenced in the *Gorgias, Protagoras, Republic*, and *Laws*, see Mackenzie 1981, 133–239; D. Allen 2000, 245–281; Cohen 2005, 171–178, 186–190. For a summary of the Roman adaptations of the tripartite theory, see Robinson 2007, 180–187.

8. Sen. *Ira* 1.6.2–3: *nec ulla dura videtur curatio, cuius salutaris effectus est. Ita legum praesidem civitatisque rectorem decet, quam diu potest, verbis et his mollioribus ingenia curare, ut facienda suadeat . . . transeat deinde ad tristiorem orationem . . . novissime ad poenas et has adhuc leves, revocabiles decurrat; ultima supplicia sceleribus ultimis ponat, ut nemo pereat, nisi quem perire etiam pereuntis intersit.* Text and translations of the *De Ira* are Basore 1985, adapted.

9. Sen. *Ira* 1.6.4: *sed ut documentum omnium sint, et quia vivi noluerunt prodesse, morte certe eorum res publica utatur.*

10. The Pisonian conspirators defended themselves for the attempt on Nero's life by arguing that "there was no way except by death that they could help a man disgraced by every kind of wickedness" (Suet. *Nero* 36.2: *tamquam aliter illi non possent nisi morte succurrere dedecorato flagitiis omnibus*); Tac. *Ann.* 15.68.1: *percunctanti Neroni, cur in caedem suam conspirauisset, breuiter respondens non aliter tot flagitiis eius subueniri potuisse,* "To Nero's question, why he conspired to assassinate him, he briefly replied that he could not otherwise be helped for so many crimes"; cf. Dio 62.24: "They desired at the same time to be rid of these evils and to give Nero his release from them." On the Pisonian conspiracy, see Pagán 2004, 68–90.

11. Sen. *Ira* 1.15.1: *tollantur e coetu mortalium facturi peiora quae contingunt.*

12. Mackenzie 1981, 225; however, this mixed theory is then open to criticism from both sides, demonstrating that the three types of penal theory are strongest when held alone, but alone are also vulnerable to objections (p. 63).

13. Sen. *Clem.* 1.22.1: *in quibus uindicandis haec tria lex secuta est quae princeps quoque sequi debet: aut ut eum quem punit emendet, aut ut poena eius ceteros meliores reddat, aut ut sublatis malis securiores ceteri uiuant.* The Latin text and English translations of the *De Clementia* in this chapter are from Braund 2009.

14. Mackenzie 1981, 25.

15. Cf. Sen. *Ira* 2.32.1: *inhumanum verbum est et quidem pro iusto receptum ultio, et talio non multum differt nisi ordine,* "Revenge is an inhuman word and yet one accepted as legitimate, and retaliation is not much different except in rank."

16. Fenster 1999, 42–51, and Knight 2000, 39–40, discuss McVeigh as part of a culture of conspiracy that not only produced him but attempts to explain him. The conspiracy theories of right-wing militias (controlled by shadowy racists) feed on a fear of a conspiracy of Big Government.

17. Braund 2009, 23.

18. Sen. *Clem.* 1.21.1: *Vltio duas praestare res solet: aut solacium adfert ei qui accepit iniuriam aut in reliquum securitatem.*

19. Mackenzie 1981, 33.

20. Sen. *Ira* 1.19.7: *nam, ut Plato ait, nemo prudens punit, quia peccatum est, sed ne peccetur; revocari enim praeterita non possunt, futura prohibentur, et quos volet nequitiae male cedentis exempla fieri, palam occidet, non tantum ut pereant ipsi, sed ut alios pereundo deterreant,* "For, as Plato says, no wise man punishes because a sin has been committed but that a sin not be committed; for the past cannot be recalled, but the future can be forestalled. And he will openly kill those whom he wishes to have serve as examples of the wickedness that is slow to yield, not so much that they themselves may be destroyed as that they *may deter others from destruction.*" Trans. Basore 1985, adapted (my emphasis).

21. Mackenzie 1981, 34–37.

22. Goldman 1995, 35.

23. D. Allen 2000, 99.

24. Mackenzie 1981, 43. Mackenzie's three-part study of punishment in Plato begins with a discussion of the three theories of punishment and then traces notions of punishment in literature from Homer to the tragedies before analyzing the principle texts of Plato. Her underlying assumption throughout is that punishment is unjustifiable. C. C. W. Taylor 1982, 198, objects, citing Hart's 1968 seminal essay; however, Goldman 1995 successfully (to my mind) argues that the paradox of punishment is that it is both required and unjustified. Hence, I argue that deterrence is difficult, if not impossible, to justify, and attempts to justify it must rely on rhetoric (persuasion).

25. Mackenzie 1981, 45.

26. Mackenzie 1981, 50.

27. D. Allen 2000, 197.

28. Cohen 2005, 178, in describing the Mytilenian debate in Thucydides.

29. Sal. *Cat.* 51.36: *ubi hoc exemplo per senatus decretum consul gladium eduxerit, quis illi finem statuet aut quis moderabitur?* The Latin text is Reynolds 1991; translations are my own.

30. Goldman 1995, 36–46.

31. V. Hunter 1994; Roisman 2006, 7–9.

32. *Vigiles* placed throughout the city: Cic. *Catil.* 1.1, 8; 2.26; 3.29. Cicero's personal watchfulness: 1.8: *iam intelleges multo me vigilare acrius,* "Now you will understand that I have been much more keenly vigilant"; exhortations to watchfulness: 4.4: *circumspicite omnis procellas quae impendent nisi providetis,* "Watch from every side for all the storms that threaten unless you take caution"; 4.18: *vos ne populo Romano deesse videamini providete,* "Take caution lest you seem to fail the Roman people"; 4.19: *hodierno die providendum est,* "Today caution must be taken." On Ciceronian providence, see Batstone 1994, 253–254.

33. Cic. *Catil.* 2.19: *primum omnium me ipsum vigilare, adesse, providere rei publicae.*

34. Cic. *Catil.* 2.27: *qui vero se in urbe commoverit cuius ego non modo factum sed vel inceptum ullum conatumve contra patriam deprehendero, sentiet in hac urbe esse consules vigilantis, esse egregios magistratus, esse fortem senatum, esse arma, esse carcerem.*

35. Cic. *Catil.* 3.3: *semper vigilavi et providi, Quirites, quem ad modum in tantis et tam absconditis insidiis salvi esse possemus.*

36. Upon Athens' defeat in the Peloponnesian war (404), the Spartans installed thirty oligarchs who reigned for less than a year. See the discussion of Wolpert 2002, 85–86.

37. Lys. 12.85: ἀλλὰ ἡγούμενοι πολλὴν ἄδειαν σφίσιν ἔσεσθαι τῶν <τε> πεπραγμένων καὶ τοῦ λοιποῦ ποιεῖν ὅ τι ἂν βούλωνται, εἰ τοὺς μεγίστων κακῶν αἰτίους λαβόντες ἀφήσετε. Text and translations of Lysias are Lamb 1988.

38. Lys. 12.88: καίτοι οὗτοι μὲν σωθέντες πάλιν ἂν δύναιντο τὴν πόλιν ἀπολέσαι.

39. Lys. 26.14: ὑμῖν δὲ πρὸς ἅπασαν τὴν πόλιν, ἢ σκοπεῖ νυνὶ τίνα ὑμεῖς γνώμην περὶ αὐτῆς ἕξετε.

40. Lys. 27.7: ἤκουσι δὲ πάντες οἱ τὰ τῆς πόλεως πράττοντες οὐχ ἡμῶν ἀκροασόμενοι, ἀλλ' ὑμᾶς εἰσόμενοι ἥντινα γνώμην περὶ τῶν ἀδικούντων ἕξετε. ὥστ' εἰ μὲν ἀποψηφιεῖσθε τούτων, οὐδὲν δεινὸν δόξει αὐτοῖς εἶναι ὑμᾶς ἐξαπατήσαντας ἐκ τῶν ὑμετέρων ὠφελεῖσθαι· ἐὰν δὲ καταψηφισάμενοι θανάτου τιμήσητε, τῇ αὐτῇ ψήφῳ τούς τε ἄλλους κοσμιωτέρους ποιήσετε ἢ νῦν εἰσι, καὶ παρὰ τούτων δίκην εἰληφότες ἔσεσθε.

41. On the consequentialist *topos,* see Lanni 2004, 166; on the accountability necessitated by bystanders, see Lanni 1997.

42. *Ver.* 1.46: *nunc autem homines in speculis sunt; observant quem ad modum sese unus quisque vestrum gerat in retinenda religione conservandisque legibus.* This vigilance is, in part, the result of the precarious position of the extortion court, which the jury must secure once and for all. On allusions to Attic oratory in the Verrine orations, see Tempest 2007.

43. Goldman 1995, 46 and 1982, 66.

44. Sen. *Ira:* 1.6.5: *"vir bonus," inquit, "non laedit." poena laedit; bono ergo poena non convenit, ob hoc nec ira, quia poena irae convenit. Si vir bonus poena non gaudet, non gaudebit ne eo quidem adfectu, cui poena voluptati est,* "'The good man,' he says, 'does no injury.' Punishment injures; therefore punishment is not consistent with good, nor, for the same reason, is anger, since punishment is consistent with anger. If the good man rejoices not in punishment, neither will he rejoice in that mood which takes pleasure in punishment." Trans. Basore 1985.

45. Katz 1987, 165–209, explores the ranges of possibility in determining intention, knowledge, recklessness, and negligence.

46. Kavka 1978, 292.

47. On forestalling violence, see Pagán 2010.

48. Sal. *Cat.* 55.

49. See Habicht 1990, 35–52.

50. Plu. *Cic.* 28–29.

51. For an assessment of Clodius, see Gruen 1966; on his legislation, 1974, 244–246.

52. Plu. *Cic.* 46.2–3; Stockton 1971, 331.

53. The date need not be specific. In the words of Last 1948, 361: "Any conceivable date for the publication of this monograph falls within the years during which the world was still under the shadow of the Dictator's death." See also Syme 1964, 214–239, on the historical circumstances of Sallust's literary production.

54. Last 1948. White 1973, 26–27, describes the pervasive force of metahistory: "Even the works of those historians and philosophers whose interests were manifestly nonpolitical . . . have specific ideological implications. These works . . . are at least *consonant with* one or another of the ideological positions of the times in which they were written" (original emphasis).

55. The matter is fully enough discussed by Tannenbaum 2005.

56. Sal. *Cat.* 52.4: *nam cetera maleficia tum persequare ubi facta sunt; hoc nisi prouideris ne adcidat, ubi euenit, frustra iudicia inplores.* [The Latin text is Reynolds 1991; translations are my own.]

57. 52.29: *ubi socordiae tete atque ignauiae tradideris, nequiquam deos inplores.*

58. 52.6: *libertas et anima nostra in dubio est.*

59. 52.10: *nunc uero non id agitur, bonisne an malis moribus uiuamus, neque quantum aut quam magnificum imperium populi Romani sit, sed haec, quoiuscumque modi uidentur, nostra an nobiscum una hostium futura sint.*

60. 52.12: *dum paucis sceleratis parcunt, bonos omnis perditum eant.* Cicero will later invoke the retributive calculus of five lives in payment for the lives of all the citizens, *Sul.* 33.

61. 52.16: *si in tanto omnium metu, solus non timet.*

62. 52.17: *quare quom de P. Lentulo ceterisque statuetis, pro certo habetote uos simul de exercitu Catilinae et de omnibus coniuratis decernere.*

63. 52.18: *si paululum modo uos languere uiderint, iam omnes feroces aderunt.* Cf. Sen. *Clem.* 1.22, where too much punishment can also cause people to become even more delinquent. One must strike a balance between not punishing enough and punishing too much.

64. 52.25: *uos cunctamini etiam nunc et dubitatis quid intra moenia deprensis hostibus faciatis?*

65. 52.35: *undique circumuenti sumus; Catilina cum exercitu faucibus urget; alii intra moenia atque in sinu urbis sunt hostes, neque parari neque consuli quicquam potest occulte: quo magis properandum est.*

66. 51.7: *hoc item uobis prouidendum est, patres conscripti, ne plus apud uos ualeat P. Lentuli et ceterorum scelus quam uostra dignitas, neu magis irae uostrae quam famae consulatis.*

67. 51.37: *maiores nostri, patres conscripti, neque consili neque audaciae umquam eguere; neque illis superbia obstabat quominus aliena instituta, si modo proba erant, imitarentur.*

68. 51.42: *profecto uirtus atque sapientia maior illis fuit.* On the contest with the *maiores* and its reception by Tacitus in the *Annales*, see Ginsburg 1993.

69. 51.36: *ubi hoc exemplo per senatus decretum consul gladium eduxerit, quis illi finem statuet aut quis moderabitur?*

70. Berry 1996, 178.

71. Cic. *Sul.* 8: *denique istam ipsam personam uehementem et acrem, quam mihi tum tempus et res publica imposuit, iam uoluntas et natura ipsa detraxit. illa enim ad breue tempus seueritatem postulauit, haec in omni uita misericordiam lenitatemque desiderat.*

72. Cic. *Off.* 1.88: *et tamen ita probanda est mansuetudo atque clementia, ut adhibeatur rei publicae causa seueritas, sine qua administrari ciuitas non potest. omnis autem animaduersio et castigatio contumelia uacare debet neque ad eius, qui punitur aliquem aut uerbis castigat, sed ad rei publicae utilitatem referri.*

---

73. Sal. *Cat.* 31.6: *tum M. Tullius consul, siue praesentiam eius timens siue ira conmotus, orationem habuit luculentam atque utilem rei publicae, quam postea scriptam edidit.*

74. Syme 1964, 105–111.

75. For a succinct synthesis of arguments on the date of composition of the *Annales*, see Rutledge 1998, 141–143, who follows Potter 1991 in positing that the *Annales* were begun under Trajan but not completed until after the accession of Hadrian.

76. Nörr 1983, 190–191; Wolf 1988, 47; Ginsburg 1993, 97. Ginsburg's analysis of the speech demonstrates the ongoing dialectic between past and present that pervades the *Annales*, a theme that she pursued for several articles.

77. According to Nörr 1983, 215, Tacitus reworks the speech that he probably found in the *acta senatus*. Wolf 1988, 21, 27, 32, 37–39, 44–46, traces the ways that the speech accords with Tacitus' own opinion.

78. Nörr 1983, 194; Wolf 1988, 21–22; on the date of the *senatus consultum*, see d'Ippolito 1969, 50–51 and 55, on Tacitus' exaggeration of the antiquity.

79. Wolf 1988, 48.

80. 14.42.1: *praefectum urbis Pedanium Secundum seruus ipsius interfecit, seu negata libertate, cui pretium pepigerat, siue amore exoleti infensus et dominum aemulum non tolerans.* The Latin text is Wellesley 1986; the translations are my own.

81. 14.43.4: *an . . . iniurias suas ultus est interfector, quia de paterna pecunia transegerat aut auitum mancipium detrahebatur?*

82. Woodman 2004, 295, regards the allusion to 14.42.1 as "sarcastic," since technically slaves had no legal rights and therefore could not manage family finances or own property over which to be aggrieved. "But the sarcasm makes no allowance for the reality, which was that slaves might be allowed to administer assets and that these assets might be extensive." Hence, the slaves who murdered Pedanius Secundus may have done so for a reason.

83. Wolf 1988, 24: "kunstvoll die Gestaltung, banal der Inhalt."

84. Wolf 1998, 28.

85. Wolf 1988, 34.

86. Nörr 1983, 198–201. On the deliberative elements in the *Annales*, see van den Berg 2012.

87. 14.44.1: *num excubias transire, cubiculi fores recludere, lumen inferre, caedem patrare poterat omnibus nesciis?*

88. Keeley 1999, 120, original emphasis.

89. Notice the affinity with the absolutism of Cato's concession: Sal. *Cat.* 52.26: *misereamini censeo*, "Go ahead, take pity on them."

90. For Vretska 1976, 572, the adverb is an exaggeration; it is imitated by Tacitus, *pace* d'Ippolito 1969, 56–58, who argues that *saepenumero* is archaic and technical. Tacitus' use of the term may simply reflect his adherence to his source for Cassius' speech and not any intrusions of Sallustian language or style.

91. Ginsburg 1993, 97–98.

92. Tac. *Ann.* 14.45.1: *sententiae Cassii ut nemo unus contra ire ausus est, ita dissonae uoces respondebant numerum aut aetatem aut sexum ac plurimorum indubiam innocentiam miserantium: praeualuit tamen pars, quae supplicium decernebat.*

93. In the words of Sørensen 1984, 179, Seneca's humanism "met with a decisive defeat." Sørensen (pp. 178–181) suggests that Seneca's thoughts on slavery in *Ben.* 3 and *Ep.* 47 were likely written in the wake of the murder of Pedanius Secundus; *Ep.* 47.18 (on fear and slaves) "can be read as a reply to Cassius Longinus' speech in the Senate" (p. 180).

Thus, the dialogue between Seneca and Cassius is continued by Tacitus. According to Griffin 1976, 396, 399, the *Ben.* was written between 59 and 62; the *Ep.*, after 62.

94. *misericordia: Clem.* 2.4.4–2.6.4; *seueritas*: 1.22.2, 2.4.1. According to Braund, 2009, 396, Seneca explains *clementia* by constructing a spectrum of *crudelitas— seueritas—clementia—misericordia*.

95. Tac. *Ann.* 14.53.3: *atauus tuus Augustus Marco Agrippae Mytilenense secretum, C. Maecenati Vrbe in ipsa uelut peregrinum otium permisit.*

96. On the echoes of Seneca's works in the interview with Nero, see Griffin 1976, 442; Ker 2012.

97. *Clem.* 1.9. Dio 55.14.1–22.2 treats the same incident; see Braund 2009, 259 and 424–431.

98. On Dio's portrayal of Livia in this episode, see Adler 2011.

99. Most obvious are generic differences: historiography vs. philosophy. On the narrative technique of 1.9 and the four carefully structured passages of Augustus' direct speech, see Braund 2009, 258–259.

100. *Clem.* 1.9.6: *Saluidienum Lepidus secutus est, Lepidum Murena, Murenam Caepio, Caepionem Egnatius, ut alios taceam, quos tantum ausos pudet*, "After Salvidienus there was Lepidus, after Lepidus there was Murena, after Murena there was Caepio, after Caepio there was Egnatius, not to mention the others whose great audacity is shameful." See Braund 2009, 270–272.

101. Griffin 1976, 444. Similarly, my reading calls for a reassessment of Devillers 2003, 52: "Quant au *de Clementia*, bien que Tacite l'ait sans doute connu, il a laissé peu de trace dans les *Annales*" ("As for the *De Clementia*, although Tacitus undoubtedly knew it, it has left little trace in the *Annales*"). The *De Clementia* was not a direct historical source, but I hope to have shown that its detailed discussion of mercy and punishment had a discernible effect on the way Tacitus wrote about mercy and punishment in *Annales* 14.

CHAPTER 4

1. Syme 1977, 44, proposes that "Laetus" commemorates a birth in the "happy" year of Caligula's accession, "Tranquillus" commemorates a birth in the "peaceful" year of Vespasian's accession; Wallace-Hadrill 1983, 3, is skeptical.

2. Sherwin-White 1966, 229–230. Suetonius is also the recipient of *Ep.* 1.18, 5.10, and 9.34; in *Ep.* 1.24 Pliny negotiates the purchase of a farm for Suetonius, and in 10.94 he secures for Suetonius the *ius III liberorum* (the right of privilege granted to the parent of three children).

3. The inscription was first published by Marec and Pflaum 1952. Townend 1961 settles the alternatives; for a summary, see Birley 1984, 249–251.

4. Townend 1961, 103–105; Wallace-Hadrill 1983, 5 n. 8; Birley 1984, 245; Hurley 2001, 4 n. 15. On the vague difference between *a bibliothecis* and *a studiis*, see Dack 1963.

5. SHA *Hadr.* 11.3. 122 C.E.: Townend 1959 argues that Suetonius wrote the lives of Augustus through Claudius before dismissal; 128 C.E.: Crook 1956–1957. Baldwin 1975, 69, and 1997, 256, suggests that Suetonius may still have had access to archives after 122 and that no solid line of demarcation can be drawn.

6. *De magistratibus rei publicae Romanae* 2.6.

7. For the date of the *Annales*, see Ch. 3 n. 75.

8. Carney 1968, 20; Cizek 1977, 193, 196, "Voilà pourquoi il a glissé, de manière

feutrée, dans les *Douze Césars*, certains avertissements, conseils et exemples à l'usage d'Hadrien" ("this is why he slipped, so subtly, into the *Twelve Caesars*, some warnings, advice, and examples for Hadrian's use"), rejected by Wallace-Hadrill 1983, 24; Lambrecht 1984; Gascou 1984, 758–773.

9. E.g., Hurley 2001, 8. Syme 1980a, 117–120, briefly entertains the possibility that Suetonius originally intended to write the lives of only six Caesars, but he dismisses it because of "the haste and incompetence of the author" (p. 120).

10. Wallace-Hadrill 1983, 56–57.

11. Macé 1900, 182–185, on the lack of revision in the later lives.

12. Townend 1959.

13. Bowersock 1969 proposes that Galba through Domitian were composed first, while Trajan was still emperor, but the thesis is abandoned after the works of Bradley 1973; Syme 1980a, 117.

14. According to Smith 1901, 39, and 1905, 7–8, later manuscripts present a simple subdivision into twelve books, one for each life; others number the emperors without mention of books. The division into eight books is attested by the Suda; see Ihm 1933. Macé 1900, 211–212, is certain that Suetonius intended eight books; see most recently Power 2009.

15. See Braund 2002, xi–xii, for a succinct definition: "the essentially Roman habit of mind which we can label exemplarity—the deployment of historical figures as positive and negative role models."

16. Momigliano 1971, 13, Hellenistic and Roman biographers "seem to have cared for the type rather than the individual."

17. Sztompka 1999, 19.

18. Baurmann 2007, 152.

19. Sztompka 1999, 80.

20. Baurmann 2007, 156.

21. Baurmann 2007, 161.

22. For a description of the archetypal *delator*, see Rutledge 2001, 11; *delatores* denounce or lay information, but they can also serve as prosecutors. The term is less neutral than *index*, "informant."

23. Sztompka 1999, 109.

24. On the negative connotations of the term *delator*, see Rutledge 2001, 12–14.

25. Sztompka 1999, 19, 149.

26. On the causes and effects of dysfunctional distrust, see Sztompka 1999, 109.

27. Wallace-Hadrill 1982 insists on the essential ambiguity in the civil status of the *princeps* who ceremonially distanced himself from his subjects but also ritually condescended to represent himself as a simple citizen.

28. Gascou 1984, 674, "the field of history."

29. On anecdotes as historical evidence, see Saller 1980.

30. Cizek 1977, 154, tabulates the symmetry of virtue and vice in the *De Vita Caesarum*; while his "point-scoring system" (Wallace-Hadrill 1983, 114 n. 18) may be somewhat primitive, his conclusions lead me to regard balance as a fundamental principle of Suetonius' composition.

31. Gascou 1984, 758–773; Lambrecht 1984, 156–159.

32. *Jul.* 9.1: *uenit in suspicionem conspirasse cum Marco Crasso consulari, item Publio Sulla et L. Autronio post designationem consulatus ambitus condemnatis, ut principio anni senatum adorirentur, et trucidatis quos placitum esset, dictaturam Crassus inuaderet, ipse ab eo*

magister equitum diceretur constitutaque ad arbitrium re publica Sullae et Autronio consulatus restitueretur. The Latin text is Ihm 1933. All translations of Suetonius are from Edwards 2000.

33. Beesly 1878, 25–26, denies there was a conspiracy. Hardy 1917, 160–166, argues that (1) it was covered up by the senate, (2) Caesar and Crassus were behind it, and (3) at the very least it fostered an atmosphere of suspicion and distrust. F. L. Jones 1939 finds enough references to a second attempt to suggest that there was a first. Frisch 1947 catalogues the sources and concludes that there was no conspiracy proper; cf. Brunt 1957. Henderson 1950, 13–14, debunks the myth of the first Catilinarian conspiracy; *contra* Stevens 1963, who sees in the sources a belief in the plot (that is, a conspiracy theory, instead of a conspiracy per se). Earl 1963, 127, and 1966, 309; Seager 1964; Syme 1964, 88–102; Gruen 1969; and Bringmann 1972, 102–108, find the account of Sallust (*Cat.* 18–19) fundamentally flawed. See also the review of literature in Drexler 1976, 86–106 and the remarks of Berry 1996, 150–154, 265–272.

34. Caesar as complicit in the first Catilinarian conspiracy, Salmon 1935; Gruen 1969 rejects that Crassus and Caesar originated the plan.

35. *Jul.* 17.1: *et apud Nouium Nigrum quaestorem a Lucio Vettio indice et in senatu a Quinto Curio, cui, quod primus consilia coniuratorum detexerat, constituta erant publice praemia.*

36. *Jul.* 86.1: *Suspicionem Caesar quibusdam suorum reliquit neque uoluisse se diutius uiuere neque curasse quod ualitudine minus prospera uteretur, ideoque et quae religiones monerent et quae renuntiarent amici neglexisse.*

37. *Jul.* 9.2: *meminerunt huius coniurationis Tanusius Geminus in historia, Marcus Bibulus in edictis, C. Curio pater in orationibus. de hac significare uidetur et Cicero in quadam ad Axium epistula . . .*

38. *Jul.* 17.1: *Curius e Catilina se cognouisse dicebat, Vettius etiam chirographum eius Catilinae datum pollicebatur.*

39. Butler and Carey 1982, 60.

40. *Jul.* 86.1–2: *sunt qui putent, confisum eum nouissimo illo senatus consulto ac iure iurando etiam custodias Hispanorum cum gladiis †adinspectantium se removisse. alii e diverso opinantur insidias undique imminentis subire semel quam cavere <semper sollicitum maluisse. Quidam dicere etiam> solitum ferunt: non tam sua quam rei publicae interesse, uti saluus esset.* Ihm omits the supplement of Roth's Teubner of 1858, which Edwards retains in her translation.

41. Pauw 1980, 91–93, attributes Suetonius' use of "unnamed spokespersons" to a cautious self-protection; he can record the sensational (or at least the unverifiable) without taking responsibility. To the modern ear, the phrases sound evasive; however, in ancient historiography, such phrases signal the historian's consultation of (often multiple) sources.

42. On methods of recording variant versions, see Marincola 1997, 280–282.

43. Dio 45.11–17. It is likely that Antony was irritated by Caesar's favoritism toward Octavian, and Octavian, by Antony's lukewarm reception; A. H. M. Jones 1970, 11–15.

44. *Jul.* 10.3; App. *BC* 3.39; A. H. M. Jones 1970, 16.

45. *Res Gestae* 1–2; Brunt and Moore 1967, 38–39; A. H. M. Jones 1970, 16–17.

46. App. *BC* 3.49. Brutus retained the province of Gaul in spite of Antony's legal title to the province.

47. Cic. *Phil.* 3; Syme 1939, 162–163. Brutus stocked Mutina with provisions and waited for senatorial reinforcements until January, when the newly elected consuls took office.

---

48. Cic. *Phil.* 9; Syme 1939, 170; A. H. M. Jones 1970, 19.

49. *Aug.* 11: *hoc bello cum Hirtius in acie, Pansa paulo post ex uulnere perissent, rumor increbruit ambos opera eius occisos, ut Antonio fugato, re p. consulibus orbata, solus uictores exercitus occuparet. Pansae quidem adeo suspecta mors fuit, ut Glyco medicus custoditus sit, quasi uenenum uulneri indidisset.*

50. Dio 46.39.1; App. *BC* 3.71 reports that Octavian rescued the corpse of Hirtius, giving opportunity for foul play; Vell. 2.61.4 is characteristically reticent; at Cic. *ad Brut.* 1.6.2, Brutus pleads the innocence of Glyco and asks Cicero to help release him from prison. See Scott 1933, 18.

51. *Aug.* 35.1: *quo tempore existimatur lorica sub ueste munitus ferroque cinctus praesedisse, decem ualentissimis senatorii ordinis amicis sellam suam circumstantibus.*

52. *Aug.* 11: *adicit his Aquilius Niger, alterum e consulibus Hirtium in pugnae tumultu ab ipso interemptum.*

53. *Aug.* 35.2: *Cordus Cremutius scribit ne admissum quidem tunc quemquam senatorum nisi solum et praetemptato sinu.* Cremutius Cordus, testimonia: Tac. *Ann.* 4.34; Dio 57.24; Sen. *Marc.* 1.3, 22.4, 26.1, 3, 5; Suet. *Tib.* 61, *Cal.* 16; Quint. *Inst.* 10.1.104; fragmenta: Sen. *Suas.* 6.19, 23; Tac. *Ann.* 4.34; Pliny *Nat.* 10.74, 16.108.

54. *Tib.* 12.3: *uenit etiam in suspicionem per quosdam beneficii sui centuriones a commeatu castra repetentis mandata ad complures dedisse ambigua et quae temptare singulorum animos ad nouas res uiderentur.*

55. *Tib.* 12.3: *de qua suspicione certior ab Augusto factus non cessauit efflagitare aliquem cuiuslibet ordinis custodem factis atque dictis suis.*

56. *Tib.* 23: *testamenti initium fuit: quoniam atrox fortuna Gaium et Lucium filios mihi eripuit, Tiberius Caesar mihi ex parte dimidia et sextante heres esto. quo et ipso aucta suspicio est opinantium successorem ascitum eum necessitate magis quam iudicio, quando ita praefari non abstinuerit.*

57. E.g., Soubiran 1964, 63, compares Lucan's Caesar and Tacitus' Germanicus.

58. *Tib.* 52.3: *etiam causa mortis fuisse ei per Cn. Pisonem legatum Syriae creditur.*

59. *Tib.* 52.3: *<propter> quae multifariam inscriptum et per noctes celeberrime adclamatum est: redde Germanicum! quam suspicionem confirmauit ipse postea coniuge etiam ac liberis Germanici crudelem in modum afflictis.*

60. *Cal.* 1.2: *cum Armeniae regem deuicisset, Cappadociam in prouinciae formam redegisset, annum agens aetatis quartum et tricensimum diuturno morbo Antiochiae obiit, non sine ueneni suspicione.*

61. *Cal.* 48.2: *sed cum uideret suspecta re plerosque dilabi ad resumenda si qua uis fieret arma, profugit contionem.*

62. *Cal.* 12.2: *ueneno Tiberium adgressus est, ut quidam opinantur, spirantique adhuc detrahi anulum et, quoniam suspicionem retinentis dabat, puluinum iussit inici atque etiam fauces manu sua oppressit.*

63. *Cal.* 60: *nam neque caede uulgata statim creditum est, fuitque suspicio ab ipso Gaio famam caedis simulatam et emissam, ut eo pacto hominum erga se mentes deprehenderet.*

64. *Cal.* 1.2: *nam praeter liuores, qui toto corpore erant, et spumas, quae per os fluebant, cremati quoque cor inter ossa incorruptum repertum est, cuius ea natura existimatur, ut tinctum ueneno igne confici nequeat.*

65. *Cal.* 12.3: *cum sint quidam auctores, ipsum postea etsi non de perfecto, at certe de cogitato quondam parricidio professum.*

66. Baldwin 1983, 278: "The *Divus Claudius* is one of Suetonius' poorest efforts." Cf. 282: "an inept performance."

---

67. Cizek 1977, 109–110, 154.

68. *Cl.* 1.1: *Patrem Claudi Caesaris Drusum, olim Decimum mox Neronem praenomine, Liuia, cum Augusto grauida nupsisset, intra mensem tertium peperit, fuitque suspicio ex uitrico per adulterii consuetudinem procreatum.*

69. *Cl.* 1.1: *statim certe uulgatus est uersus,* τοῖς εὐτυχοῦσι καὶ τρίμηνα παιδία (*CAF* 449, no. 213). Hurley 2001, 57, points out that the adverb *certe* is an attempt to lend at least some credibility.

70. Sen. *Ap.* 4.2: *Claudium autem iubent omnes* χαίροντας, εὐφημοῦντας ἐκπέμπειν δόμων . . . *expirauit autem dum comoedos audit.*

71. *Nero* 40.4: *ut gaudentis etiam suspicionem praeberet tamquam occasione nata spoliandarum iure belli opulentissimarum prouinciarum.*

72. *Nero* 35.5: *Senecam praeceptorem ad necem compulit, quamuis saepe commeatum petenti bonisque cedenti persancte iurasset suspectum se frustra periturumque potius quam nociturum ei.*

73. Tac. *Ann.* 15.73.1.

74. Cizek 1977, 132–133, 154.

75. Her name is attested at Suet. *Vit.* 3.1 and Tac. *Hist.* 2.64.2; cf. Tac. *Hist.* 2.89.2, 3.67.1.

76. *Vit.* 14.5: *alii tradunt ipsam taedio praesentium et imminentium metu uenenum a filio impetrasse, haud sane difficulter.*

77. *Tit.* 5.3: *unde nata suspicio est, quasi desciscere a patre Orientisque sibi regnum uindicare temptasset; quam suspicionem auxit . . . diadema gestauit.*

78. *Tit.* 5.3: *uelut arguens rumorum de se temeritatem: ueni, inquit, pater, ueni.*

79. *Tit.* 7: *denique propalam alium Neronem et opinabantur et praedicabant,* "People thought of him and even publicly spoke of him as another Nero."

80. *Jul.* 31.1: *ne qua suspicio moueretur . . . per dissimulationem interfuit.*

81. *Jul.* 74.2: *negauit se quicquam comperisse, quamuis et mater Aurelia et soror Iulia apud eosdem iudices omnia ex fide re<t>tulissent; interrogatusque, cur igitur repudiasset uxorem: quoniam, inquit, meos tam suspicione quam crimine iudico carere oportere.*

82. *Tib.* 11.5: *nihil aliud secessu deuitasse se quam aemulationis cum C. Lucioque suspicionem.*

83. Levick 1976, 46.

84. *Ves.* 14: *nam ut suspicione aliqua uel metu ad perniciem cuiusquam compelleretur tantum afuit, ut monentibus amicis cauendum esse Mettium Pompusianum, quod uolgo crederetur genesim habere imperatoriam, insuper consulem fecerit, spondens quandoque beneficii memorem futurum.*

85. B. W. Jones 2000, 87.

86. *Dom.* 10.3: *quod habere imperatoriam genesim uulgo ferebatur et quod depictum orbem terrae in membrana[s] contionesque regum ac ducum ex Tito Liuio circumferret quodque seruis nomina Magonis et Hannibalis indidisset.*

87. On Mettius Pompusianus, see B. W. Jones 1992, 186. On the political dangers of astrology, see MacMullen 1966, 128–162.

88. B. W. Jones 1996, 80.

89. *Jul.* 20.5: *<indicem . . . > inductum praemiis, ut se de inferenda Pompeio nece sollicitatum a quibusdam profiteretur productusque pro rostris auctores ex conpacto nominaret; sed uno atque altero frustra nec sine suspicione fraudis nominatis desperans tam praecipitis consilii euentum intercepisse ueneno indicem creditur.* According to Ihm 1933, Ursinus (Fulvio

Orsini, 1529–1600) was the first to propose that the *index* is Vettius (cf. *Jul.* 17.1); for the edition containing the notes of Ursinus, see Macé 1900, 25. For this incident, cf. Cic. *Att.* 2.24, *Vat.* 24, *Sest.* 132; Plu. *Luc.* 42.7; App. *BC* 2.2.12; Dio 38.9. On the date of the affair, see L. R. Taylor 1950 (*pace* Brunt 1953). On Caesar's instigation of Vettius, see McDermott 1949; Caesar used Vettius to alienate Cicero from Pompey, W. Allen 1950.

90. On the preponderance of participles in Suetonius, see Hurley 2001, 20: "The emperor is the grammatical subject of virtually every [participle]."

91. On Sallust's use of internal focalization, see Pagán 2004, 36–37.

92. *Aug.* 27.3: *nam et Pinarium equitem R., cum contionante se admissa turba paganorum apud milites subscribere quaedam animaduertisset, curiosum ac speculatorum ratus coram confodi imperauit.*

93. *Aug.* 27.4: *et Quintum Gallium praetorem, in officio salutationis tabellas duplices ueste tectas tenentem, suspicatus gladium occulere, nec quicquam statim, ne aliud inueniretur, ausus inquirere, paulo post per centuriones et milites raptum e tribunali seruilem in modum torsit ac fatentem nihil iussit occidi prius oculis eius sua manu effossis.*

94. Carter 1982, 123–124.

95. For the eyeballs, cf. Sulla in V. Max. 9.2.1.

96. *Aug.* 27.4: *quem tamen scribit conloquio petito insidiatum sibi coniectumque a se in custodiam, deinde urbe interdicta dimissum naufragio uel latronum insidiis perisse.*

97. *Aug.* 66.2: *quod sibi soli non liceret amicis, quatenus uellet, irasci.*

98. Cf. Sen. *Clem.* 1.8: sovereignty is a noble slavery; the ruler cannot escape his position.

99. *Tib.* 19: *non multum afuit quin a Bructero quodam occideretur, cui inter proximos uersanti et trepidatione detecto tormentis expressa confessio est cogitati facinoris.*

100. *Tib.* 62.1: *ut Rhodiensem hospitem, quem familiaribus litteris Romam euocarat, aduenisse sibi nuntiatum torqueri sine mora iusserit, quasi aliquis ex necessariis quaestioni adesset.*

101. *Tib.* 62.1: *deinde errore detecto et occidi, ne uulgaret iniuriam.*

102. *Tib.* 65.2: *uerum et oppressa coniuratione Seiani nihilo securior aut constantior.*

103. *Cal.* 29.1: *trucidaturus fratrem, quem metu uenenorum praemuniri medicamentis suspicabatur: antidotum, inquit, adversus Caesarem?*

104. On the murder of Gemellus, see Barrett 1989, 74–77.

105. *Cl.* 35.1: *sed nihil aeque quam timidus ac diffidens fuit.*

106. *Cl.* 37.1: *nulla adeo suspicio, nullus auctor tam leuis extitit, a quo non mediocri scrupulo iniecto . . . compelleretur.*

107. Here the participle *dicens* not only shifts point of view but lets Nero speak his suspicions for himself in the text.

108. *Galba* 16.1: *ut suspectos et Nymphidi socios*; see also Tac. *Hist.* 1.25.2.

109. *Galba* 14.3: *quosdam claros ex utroque ordine uiros suspicione minima inauditos condemnauit.*

110. Luke 2010.

111. *Tit.* 6.1: *siquidem suspectissimum quemque sibi summissis qui per theatra et castra quasi consensu ad poenam deposcerent, haud cunctanter oppressit.*

112. *Tit.* 6.2: *quibus rebus sicut in posterum securitati satis cauit, ita ad praesens plurimum contraxit inuidiae, ut non temere quis tam aduerso rumore magisque inuitis omnibus transierit ad principatum.*

113. On Suetonius' ability to manipulate his readers' perceptions, see Cizek 1977, 156; Gascou 1984, 675–706.

114. *Dom.* 10.2: *Complures senators, in iis aliquot consulares, interemit; ex quibus Ciuicam Cerealem in ipso Asiae proconsulatu, Saluidienum Orfitum, Acilium Glabrionem <in> exilio, quasi molitores rerum nouarum, ceteros leuissima quemque de causa.*

115. B. W. Jones 1996, 88.

116. Dio 67.14.3: ὅτι ὑπατεύοντα αὐτὸν ἐς τὸ Ἀλβανὸν ἐπὶ τὰ Νεανισκεύματα ὠνομασμένα καλέσας λέοντα ἀποκτεῖναι μέγαν ἠνάγκασε, καὶ ὃς οὐ μόνον οὐδὲν ἐλυμάνθη ἀλλὰ καὶ εὐστοχώτατα αὐτὸν κατειργάσατο, "[Domitian] had summoned him to his Alban estate to attend the festival called the Juvenalia and had imposed on him the task of killing a large lion; and [Glabrio] not only had escaped all injury but had killed the lion with most accurate aim." B. W. Jones 1996, 88.

117. See Chapter 2 n. 78 on the death of Lamia.

118. For a discussion of the cultural and literary significance of the Stoic martyrs Thrasea and Helvidius, and their biographers Arulenus Rusticus and Herennius Senecio, see Sailor 2008, 6–50, esp. 11–24. Suetonius mistakenly attributes both biographies to Rusticus.

119. *Dom.* 14.2: *quare pauidus semper atque anxius minimis etiam suspicionibus praeter modum commouebatur.*

120. *Dom.* 14.4: *tempore uero suspecti periculi appropinquante sollicitior in dies porticuum, in quibus spatiari consuerat, parietes phengite lapide distinxit, e cuius splendore per imagines quidquid a tergo fieret prouideret.* Cf. Plin. *Pan.* 48–49. On architecture and surveillance under Domitian, see Fredrick 2003, esp. 210–211.

121. B. W. Jones 1992, 95–96.

122. *Dom.* 15.1: *repente ex tenuissima suspicione tantum non in ipso eius consulatu interemit. quo maxime facto maturauit sibi exitium.*

123. Dio 67.14.1; B. W. Jones 1996, 121.

124. *Jul.* 80.1: *quae causa coniuratis maturandi fuit destinata negotia.*

125. The balanced treatment of suspicion is in keeping with Suetonius' objectivity and impartiality; see Ektor 1980.

126. *Dom.* 21.1: *condicionem principum miserrimam aiebat, quibus de coniuratione comperta non crederetur nisi occisis.*

127. SHA *Avidius Cassius* 2.5–6: *Hadrianus dixerit: 'misera condicio imperatorum, quibus de adfectata tyrannide nisi occisis non potest credi.' eius autem exemplum ponere malui quam Domitiani, qui hoc primus dixisse fertur. tyrannorum enim etiam bona dicta non habent tantum auctoritatis quantum debent.* A collection of cases heard by Hadrian, "Sentences of the Divine Hadrian," is preserved in the *Corpus Glossariorum Latinorum*, see Wallace-Hadrill 1983, 124.

128. Dio 54.15.2–3: πολλὰ γὰρ ὧν ἂν ὁ κρατῶν πρὸς τιμωρίαν, ὡς καὶ ἐπιβεβουλευμένος, ἤτοι δι' ἑαυτοῦ ἢ καὶ διὰ τῆς γερουσίας πράξῃ, ὑποπτεύεται κατ' ἐπήρειαν, κἂν ὅτι μάλιστα δικαιότατα συμβῇ, γεγονέναι. See B. W. Jones 1996, 146.

129. Bradley 1991, 3729.

EPILOGUE

1. Everitt 2009, 164.

2. Dio 69.1.2: ἀλλὰ καὶ Καίσαρα αὐτὸν καὶ αὐτοκράτορα τοῦ Τραϊανοῦ ἄπαιδος μεταλλάξαντος ὅ τε Ἀττιανὸς πολίτης αὐτοῦ ὢν καὶ ἐπίτροπος γεγονώς, καὶ ἡ Πλωτῖνα ἐξ ἐρωτικῆς φιλίας, πλησίον τε ὄντα καὶ δύναμιν πολλὴν ἔχοντα ἀπέδειξαν. Trans. Cary 2000. The

phrase "was in love with him" probably means only that she had an affectionate regard for Hadrian.

3. Dio 69.1.3–4: καὶ ὅτι ὁ θάνατος τοῦ Τραϊανοῦ ἡμέρας τινὰς διὰ τοῦτο συνεκρύφθη ἵν' ἡ ποίησις προεκφοιτήσοι. ἐδηλώθη δὲ τοῦτο καὶ ἐκ τῶν πρὸς τὴν βουλὴν γραμμάτων αὐτοῦ· ταῖς γὰρ ἐπιστολαῖς οὐχ αὐτὸς ἀλλ' ἡ Πλωτῖνα ὑπέγραψεν, ὅπερ ἐπ' οὐδενὸς ἄλλου ἐπεποιήκει. Trans. Cary 2000.

4. M. Ulpius Phaedimus was buried at Rome thirteen years later, *ILS* 1792; Syme 1958, 240 n. 7; Bennett 1997, 202; Everitt 2009, 166–167.

5. The evidence is so scant that the conspiracy can be doubted; Syme 1958, 244 and 1980b, 67; Birley 1997, 88.

6. Marius Maximus and another, Syme 1971, 30–53, and Benario 1980, 4. See Bennett 1997, 203–204, on Hadrian's policy.

7. Birley 1997, 75, 80.

8. Pagán 2004, 87–88.

9. Syme 1958, 481.

10. Although the manuscripts of the *Historia Augusta* transmit six biographers, the single-author hypothesis is now generally accepted; see Syme 1971, 1–16.

11. Syme 1958, 498.

12. See Braund 1988 on the transition from anger to irony. Braund 2004, 296, suggests that *Satire 7* is (momentarily) optimistic about the emperor's patronage.

13. On the Pisonian conspiracy, see Pagán 2004, 72–87.

14. Fenster 1999, 66–68.

15. McGee 2011 explores the impact of the internet on the "birther" movement.

16. Owen 2010, 118.

17. A certified copy of the long form was provided by Hawaii's health director to the White House on April 25 and released on April 27, 2011. It is available to the public at http://www.whitehouse.gov/sites/default/files/rss_viewer/birth-certificate-long-form.pdf.

18. Zernike 2011.

19. Owen 2010, 118.

20. Cf. Moscovici 1987, 162: "Whoever feels deprived of something instinctively looks for a cause of the deprivation."

21. Wolf 1988, 47–48, on the growing dissatisfaction evident in *Hist.* 1.1.4, where Tacitus refers to Divine Nerva's principate but Trajan's rule: *principatum divi Nervae et imperium Traiani.*

22. Rutledge 1998, 141: Tacitus "questions even as [he] reaffirms Trajan as *princeps.*"

23. *Ag.* 3.3: *non tamen pigebit vel incondita ac rudi voce memoriam prioris servitutis ac testimonium praesentium bonorum composuisse*, "Yet it will not be an unpleasant task to compose even in an uncouth and rough style a history of earlier servitude and a testimony to present happiness." *Hist.* 1.1.4: *quod si vita suppeditat, principatum divi Nervae et imperium Traiani, uberiorem securioremque materiam, senectuti seposui, rara temporum felicitate, ubi sentire quae velis et quae sentias dicere licet*, "But should my life be long enough, I have set aside for my old age the principate of Divine Nerva and the rule of Trajan, subjects richer and safer, in that rare happiness of the times, when you can think what you wish and say what you think."

24. Ahl 1984, 207, wisely cautions against taking Tacitus at his word: "The verdict of extant literature is very different. Latin poetry flourished under Domitian. The closest thing to epic Trajan's reign has left is his column."

BIBLIOGRAPHY

Abalakina-Paap, M., Stephan, W. G., Craig, T., and Gregory, W. L. 1999. "Beliefs in Conspiracies." *Political Psychology* 20: 637–647.

Adler, Eric. 2011. "Cassius Dio's Livia and the Conspiracy of Cinna Magnus." *Greek, Roman, and Byzantine Studies* 51: 133–154.

Ahl, Frederick. 1984. "The Art of Safe Criticism in Greece and Rome." *American Journal of Philology* 105: 174–208.

Alexander, Michael C. 1976. "Hortensius' Speech in Defense of Verres." *Phoenix* 30: 46–53.

———. 2002. *The Case for the Prosecution in the Ciceronian Era*. Ann Arbor: University of Michigan.

Alföldy, Géza. 1985. *The Social History of Rome*. Translated by D. Braund and F. Pollock. Totowa, NJ: Barnes and Noble Books.

Allen, Danielle. 2000. *The World of Prometheus: The Politics of Punishing in Democratic Athens*. Princeton: Princeton University.

Allen, Walter. 1950. "The 'Vettius Affair' Once More." *Transactions of the American Philological Association* 81: 153–163.

Anderson, William S. 2000. "The Frustration of Anagnorisis in Terence's *Hecyra*." In *Rome and Her Monuments: Essays on the City and Literature of Rome in Honor of Katherine A. Geffcken*, S. K. Dickison and J. P. Hallett, eds. Wauconda, IL: Bolchazy-Carducci: 311–323.

———. 2002. "Resistance to Recognition and 'Privileged Recognition' in Terence." *Classical Journal* 98: 1–8.

Austin, R. G., ed., 1960. *M. Tulli Ciceronis "Pro M. Caelio Oratio."* Oxford: Clarendon.

Bagnani, Gilbert. 1954. *Arbiter of Elegance: A Study of the Life and Works of C. Petronius*. Toronto: University of Toronto.

Baldwin, Barry. 1975. "Suetonius: Birth, Disgrace and Death." *Acta Classica* 18: 61–70.

———. 1977. "*Polyphagus*: Glutton or Crocodile?" *American Journal of Philology* 98: 406–409.

———. 1983. *Suetonius*. Amsterdam: Adolf M. Hakkert.

———. 1997. "Hadrian's Dismissal of Suetonius: A Reasoned Response." *Historia* 46: 254–256.

Balina, Marina. 2007. "Ancient Rome for Little Comrades: The Legacy of Classical Antiquity in Soviet Children's Literature." In *The Sites of Rome: Time, Space, Memory*, D. H. J. Larmour and D. Spencer, eds. Oxford: Oxford University: 323–352.

Barrett, Anthony A. 1989. *Caligula: The Corruption of Power*. New York: Simon and Schuster.

Barthes, Roland. 1972. *Mythologies*. Translated by A. Lavers. New York: Noonday.

Bartsch, Shadi. 1994. *Actors in the Audience: Theatricality and Doublespeak from Nero to Hadrian*. Cambridge, MA: Harvard University.

Basham, Lee. 2001. "Living with the Conspiracy." *The Philosophical Forum* 32: 265–280. = 2006. "Living with the Conspiracy." In *Conspiracy Theories: The Philosophical Debate*, D. Coady, ed. Hampshire: Ashgate: 61–75.

———. 2003. "Malevolent Global Conspiracy." *Journal of Social Philosophy* 34: 91–103. = 2006. "Malevolent Global Conspiracy." In *Conspiracy Theories: The Philosophical Debate*, D. Coady, ed. Hampshire: Ashgate: 93–105.

———. 2006. "Afterthoughts on Conspiracy Theory: Resilience and Ubiquity." In *Conspiracy Theories: The Philosophical Debate*, D. Coady, ed. Hampshire: Ashgate: 133–137.

Basore, J. W. 1985 (reprint). *Seneca: Moral Essays*. Vol. 1. Cambridge, MA: Loeb Classical Library.

Batstone, William W. 1994. "Cicero's Construction of Consular *Ethos* in the *First Catilinarian*." *Transactions of the American Philological Association* 124: 211–266.

Baurmann, Michael. 2007. "Rational Fundamentalism? An Explanatory Model of Fundamentalist Beliefs." *Episteme: A Journal of Social Epistemology* 4: 150–166.

Beare, William. 1951. *The Roman Stage: A Short History of Latin Drama in the Time of the Republic*. Cambridge, MA: Harvard University.

Beesly, Edward Spencer. 1878. *Catiline, Clodius, and Tiberius*. London: Chapman and Hall.

Benario, Herbert W. 1980. *A Commentary on the "Vita Hadriani" in the "Historia Augusta."* Chico, CA: Scholars Press.

Bennett, Julian. 1997. *Trajan Optimus Princeps: A Life and Times*. Bloomington: Indiana University.

Berry, D. H., ed. 1996. *Cicero: "Pro P. Sulla" Oratio*. Cambridge: Cambridge University.

Bertman, Stephen S. 1968. "Fire Symbolism in Juvenal's First Satire." *Classical Journal* 63: 265–266.

Birley, Anthony R. 1984. "Review of Baldwin, *Suetonius*; Wallace-Hadrill, *Suetonius: The Scholar and His Caesars*; De Coninck, *Suetonius en de Archivalia*." *Journal of Roman Studies* 74: 245–251.

———. 1997. *Hadrian: The Restless Emperor*. London: Routledge.

Bodinger, Martin. 2002. "Deux problèmes d'histoire des religions au monde antique: II. Tacite et la 'persécution néronienne'." *Archaeus: Studies in the Histories of Religions* 6: 261–281.

Boor, Carl de, ed. 1905. *Excerpta Historica iussu Imp. Constantini Porphyrogeniti, Vol. III: Excerpta de Insidiis*. Berlin: Weidmann.

Borzsák, Stephan, ed. 1992. *Cornelii Taciti "Ab Excessu Divi Augusti Libri I-VI."* Leipzig: Teubner.

Bowersock, Glen W. 1969. "Suetonius and Trajan." In *Hommages à Marcel Renard*, J. Bibauw, ed. Brussels: Latomus: 119–125.

Boyle, Anthony J. 2004. "Introduction: Terence's Mirror Stage." *Ramus* 33: 1–9.

Bradley, Keith R. 1973. "The Composition of Suetonius' *Caesares*, Again." *Journal of Indo-European Studies* 1: 257–263.

———. 1987. *Slaves and Masters in the Roman Empire: A Study in Social Control*. Oxford: Oxford University.

————. 1989. *Slavery and Rebellion in the Roman World, 140 B.C.–70 B.C.* Bloomington: Indiana University.

————. 1991. "The Imperial Ideal in Suetonius' 'Caesares'." *Aufstieg und Niedergang der römischen Welt* 2.33.5: 3701–3732.

————. 1994. *Slavery and Society at Rome.* Cambridge: Cambridge University.

Bratich, Jack Z. 2008. *Conspiracy Panics: Political Rationality and Popular Culture.* Albany: State University of New York.

Braund, Susanna. 1986. "Juvenal on How to (Tr)Eat People." *Omnibus* 11: 15–17.

————. 1988. *Beyond Anger: A Study of Juvenal's Third Book of Satires.* Cambridge: Cambridge University.

————. 1992. "Juvenal—Misogynist or Misogamist?" *Journal of Roman Studies* 82: 71–86.

————. 1996. *Juvenal Satires Book 1.* Cambridge: Cambridge University.

————. 1997. "Roman Assimilations of the Other: *Humanitas* at Rome." *Acta Classica* 40: 15–32.

————. 2002. *Latin Literature.* London: Routledge.

————. 2004. *Juvenal and Persius.* Cambridge, MA: Loeb Classical Library.

————. 2005. "Marriage, Adultery, and Divorce in Roman Comic Drama." In *Satiric Advice on Women and Marriage from Plautus to Chaucer,* W. S. Smith, ed. Ann Arbor: University of Michigan: 39–70.

————. 2009. *Seneca: "De Clementia."* Oxford: Oxford University.

Bringmann, K. 1972. "Sallusts Umgang mit der historischen Wahrheit in seiner Darstellung der Catilinarischen Verschwörung." *Philologus* 116: 98–113.

Briscoe, John. 1973. *A Commentary on Livy Books XXXI–XXXIII.* Oxford: Oxford University.

Brunt, Peter A. 1953. "Cicero: *Ad Atticum* 2.24." *Classical Quarterly* n.s. 3: 62–64.

————. 1957. "Three Passages from Asconius." *Classical Review* n.s. 7: 193–195.

————. 1971. *Italian Manpower, 225 B.C.–A.D. 14.* Oxford: Clarendon.

Brunt, Peter A., and Moore, J. M. 1967. *Res Gestae Divi Augusti: The Achievements of the Divine Augustus.* Oxford: Oxford University.

Burkert, Walter. 1970. "Jason, Hypsipyle, and New Fire at Lemnos: A Study in Myth and Ritual." *Classical Quarterly* n.s. 20: 1–16.

Butler, H. E., and Cary, M., eds. 1982 (reprint). *Suetonius "Divus Julius."* With new introduction, bibliography, and notes by G. B. Townend. Bristol: Bristol Classical.

Butler, Shane. 2002. *The Hand of Cicero.* London: Routledge.

Callahan, Allen Dwight, and Horsley, Richard A. 1998. "Slave Resistance in Classical Antiquity." *Semeia* 83/84: 133–151.

Carney, T. F. 1968. "How Suetonius' Lives Reflect on Hadrian." *Proceedings of the African Classical Associations* 11: 7–21.

Carter, John M., ed. 1982. *Suetonius: "Divus Augustus."* Bristol: Bristol Classical.

Cary, Earnest. 2000 (reprint). *Dio Cassius: Roman History Books LXI–LXX.* Cambridge, MA: Loeb Classical Library.

Charles, Michael. 2002. "*Calvus Nero*: Domitian and the Mechanics of Predecessor Denigration." *Acta Classica* 45: 19–49.

Cilliers, L., and Retief, F. P. 2000. "Poisons, Poisoning and the Drug Trade in Ancient Rome." *Akroterion* 45: 88–100.

Cizek, Eugen. 1977. *Structures et Idéologie dans "Les Vies Des Douze Césars" de Suétone.* Paris: Les Belles Lettres.

Clarke, Steve. 2002. "Conspiracy Theories and Conspiracy Theorizing." *Philosophy of the*

Social Sciences 32: 131–150 = 2006. "Conspiracy Theories and Conspiracy Theorizing." In *Conspiracy Theories: The Philosophical Debate*, D. Coady, ed. Hampshire: Ashgate: 77–92.

———. 2006. "Appealing to the Fundamental Attribution Error: Was it All a Big Mistake?" In *Conspiracy Theories: The Philosophical Debate*, D. Coady, ed. Hampshire: Ashgate: 129–132.

Classen, Carl Joachim. 1980. "Verres' Gehilfen in Sizilien: Nach Ciceros Darstellung." *Ciceroniana* 4: 93–114.

Coady, David. 2006a. "An Introduction to the Philosophical Debate About Conspiracy Theories." In *Conspiracy Theories: The Philosophical Debate*, D. Coady, ed. Hampshire: Ashgate: 1–11.

———. 2006b. "Conspiracy Theories and Official Stories." In *Conspiracy Theories: The Philosophical Debate*, D. Coady, ed. Hampshire: Ashgate: 115–127 = 2003. "Conspiracy Theories and Official Stories." *International Journal of Applied Philosophy* 17: 197–209.

———. 2006c. "The Pragmatic Rejection of Conspiracy Theories." In *Conspiracy Theories: The Philosophical Debate*, D. Coady, ed. Hampshire: Ashgate: 167–170.

———. 2007a. "Introduction: Conspiracy Theories." *Episteme: A Journal of Social Epistemology* 4: 131–134.

———. 2007b. "Are Conspiracy Theorists Irrational?" *Episteme: A Journal of Social Epistemology* 4: 193–204.

Coffey, M. 1976. *Roman Satire*. Bristol: Bristol Classical.

Cohen, David. 2005. "Theories of Punishment." In *The Cambridge Companion to Ancient Greek Law*, M. Gagarin and D. Cohen, eds. Cambridge: Cambridge University: 170–190.

Colin, J. 1956. "Les Vendanges Dionysiaques et la légende de Messaline (48 ap. J.-C.): Tacite, *Annales*, XI 25–38." *Les Études Classiques* 24: 25–39.

Comaroff, Jean, and Comaroff, John. 2003. "Transparent Fictions; or, The Conspiracies of a Liberal Imagination: An Afterword." In *Transparency and Conspiracy: Ethnographies of Suspicion in the New World Order*, H. G. West and T. Sanders, eds. Durham, NC: Duke University: 287–299.

Cornell, Tim. 1996. "Hannibal's Legacy: The Effects of the Hannibalic War on Italy." In *The Second Punic War: A Reappraisal*, T. Cornell, B. Rankov, and P. Sabin, eds. London: Institute of Classical Studies: 97–117.

Courtney, Edward. 1980. *A Commentary on the Satires of Juvenal*. London: Athlone.

Cowles, Frank Hewitt. 1917. *Gaius Verres: An Historical Study*. Vol. 20. Cornell Studies in Classical Philology. Ithaca, NY: Cornell University.

———. 1929. "Cicero's Debut as a Prosecutor." *Classical Journal* 24: 429–448.

Crawford, Jane W. 1984. *M. Tullius Cicero: The Lost and Unpublished Orations*. Vol. 80. Hypomnemata. Göttingen: Vandenhoeck and Ruprecht.

Crook, J. A. 1956–1957. "Suetonius 'Ab Epistulis.'" *Proceedings of the Cambridge Philological Society* 4: 18–22.

Dack, Edmond van't. 1963. "A studiis, a bybliothecis." *Historia* 12: 177–184.

Devillers, Olivier. 2003. *Tacite et les Sources des "Annales": Enquêtes sur la méthode historique*. Louvain: Éditions Peeters.

d'Ippolito, Federico. 1969. *Ideologia e Diritto in Gaio Cassio Longino*. Vol. 122. Pubblicazioni della Facoltà giuridica dell'Università di Napoli. Naples: E. Jovene.

Doolen, Andy. 2004. "Reading and Writing Terror: The New York Conspiracy Trials of 1741." *American Literary History* 16: 377–406.

Drexler, Hans. 1976. *Die catilinarische Verschwörung: Ein Quellenheft*. Darmstadt: Wissenschaftliche Buchgesellschaft.

Duckworth, George E. 1952. *The Nature of Roman Comedy: A Study in Popular Entertainment*. Princeton: Princeton University.

Duff, J. D., ed. 1970. *D. Iunii Iuvenalis satvrae XIV: Fourteen Satires of Juvenal*. With a new introduction by M. Coffey. Cambridge: Cambridge University.

Dyck, Andrew R. 1996. *A Commentary on Cicero, "De Officiis."* Ann Arbor: University of Michigan.

Dyson, Stephen L. 1992. *Community and Society in Roman Italy*. Baltimore: The Johns Hopkins University.

Earl, D. C. 1963. "Two Passages of Sallust." *Hermes* 91: 125–127.

———. 1966. "The Early Career of Sallust." *Historia* 15: 302–311.

Edwards, Catharine. 1993. *The Politics of Immorality in Ancient Rome*. Cambridge: Cambridge University.

———. 1997. "Unspeakable Professions: Public Performance and Prostitution in Ancient Rome." In *Roman Sexualities*, J. P. Hallett and M. B. Skinner, eds. Princeton: Princeton University: 66–95.

———. 2000. *Suetonius: Lives of the Caesars*. Oxford World's Classics. Oxford: Oxford University.

Ektor, J. 1980. "L'impassabilité et l'objectivité de Suétone: confrontation avec Tacite." *Les Études Classiques* 48: 317–326.

Everitt, Anthony. 2009. *Hadrian and the Triumph of Rome*. New York: Random House.

Fantham, Elaine. 1991. "*Stuprum*: Public Attitudes and Penalties for Sexual Offenses in Republican Rome." *Echos du Monde Classique* 10: 267–291.

Fenster, Mark. 1999. *Conspiracy Theories: Secrecy and Power in American Culture*. Revised and updated in 2008. Minneapolis: University of Minnesota.

Ferguson, John, ed. 1979. *The Satires: Juvenal*. New York: St. Martin's.

Flower, Harriet I. 2000. "The Tradition of the *Spolia Opima*: M. Claudius Marcellus and Augustus." *Classical Antiquity*: 19: 34–64.

Forehand, Walter E. 1985. *Terence*. Boston: Twayne.

Forrest, W. G. G., Stinton, T. C. W., and Green, Peter. 1962. "The First Sicilian Slave War." *Past and Present* 22: 87–93.

Frazel, Thomas D. 2004. "The Composition and Circulation of Cicero's *In Verrem*." *Classical Quarterly* n.s. 54: 128–142.

Fredericks, S. C. 1971. "Rhetoric and Morality in Juvenal's 8th Satire." *Transactions of the American Philological Association* 102: 111–132.

Fredrick, David. 2003. "Architecture and Surveillance in Flavian Rome." In *Flavian Rome: Culture, Image, Text*, A. J. Boyle and W. J. Dominik, eds., Leiden: Brill: 199–227.

Frisch, Hartvig. 1947. "The First Catilinarian Conspiracy: A Study in Historical Conjecture." *Classica et Mediaevalia* 9: 10–36.

Futrell, Alison. 2001. "Seeing Red: Spartacus as Domestic Economist." In *Imperial Projections: Ancient Rome in Modern Popular Culture*, S. Joshel, M. Malamud, and D. McGuire, eds. Baltimore: The Johns Hopkins University: 77–118.

Gascou, Jacques. 1984. *Suétone Historien*. Rome: École Française de Rome.

Gilula, Dwora. 1979/1980. "Terence's *Hecyra*: A Delicate Balance of Suspense and Dramatic Irony." *Scripta Classica Israelica* 5: 137–157.

———. 1980. "The Concept of the *Bona Meretrix*: A Study of Terence's Courtesans." *Rivista di filologia e di istruzione classica* 108: 142–165.

Ginsburg, Judith. 1993. "*In Maiores Certamina*: Past and Present in the *Annals.*" In *Tacitus and the Tacitean Tradition*, T. J. Luce and A. J. Woodman, eds. Princeton: Princeton University: 86–103.

Girardet, Raoul. 1986. *Mythes et Mythologies Politiques*. Paris: Éditions du Seuil.

Goldberg, Sander. 1986. *Understanding Terence*. Princeton: Princeton University.

Goldman, Alan H. 1982. "Toward a New Theory of Punishment." *Law and Philosophy* 1: 57–76.

———. 1995. "The Paradox of Punishment." In *Punishment: A Philosophy and Public Affairs Reader*, A. J. Simmons, M. Cohen, J. Cohen, and C. R. Beitz, eds. Princeton: Princeton University: 30–46.

Goodnight, G. Thomas, and Poulakos, John. 1981. "Conspiracy Rhetoric: From Pragmatism to Fantasy in Public Discourse." *Western Journal of Speech Communication* 45: 299–316.

Goshorn, Keith. 2000. "Strategies of Deterrence and Frames of Containment: On Critical Paranoia and Anti-Conspiracy Discourse." *Theory and Event* 4.3. Project MUSE. Web. 5 Aug. 2011. ⟨http://muse.jhu.edu/⟩.

Gowers, Emily 1993. *The Loaded Table: Representations of Food in Roman Literature*. Oxford: Clarendon.

Graumann, Carl F. 1987. "Conspiracy: History and Social Psychology—A Synopsis." In *Changing Conceptions of Conspiracy*, C. F. Graumann and S. Moscovici, eds. New York: Springer-Verlag: 246–251.

Graumann, Carl F., and Moscovici, Serge, eds. 1987. *Changing Conceptions of Conspiracy*. Vol. 3. Springer Series in Social Psychology. New York: Springer-Verlag.

Green, Peter. 1961. "The First Sicilian Slave War." *Past and Present* 20: 10–29.

Greenwood, L. H. G., ed. 1978 (reprint). *Cicero: The Verrine Orations*, 2 vols. Cambridge, MA: Loeb Classical Library.

Griffin, Miriam T. 1976. *Seneca: A Philosopher in Politics*. Oxford: Clarendon.

Griffith, J. G. 1981. "Spartacus and the Growth of Historical and Political Legends." In *Spartacus: Symposium Rebus Spartaci Gestis Dedicatum 2050 A*. Sofia: Editions de l'Académie Bulgare des Sciences: 64–70.

Groh, Dieter. 1987. "The Temptation of Conspiracy Theory, Or: Why Do Bad Things Happen to Good People?" In *Changing Conceptions of Conspiracy*, C. F. Graumann and S. Moscovici, eds. New York: Springer-Verlag: 1–37.

Gross, Robert A., ed. 2001. "The Making of a Slave Conspiracy, Part 1." *William and Mary Quarterly* Third Series, 58: 913–976.

———. 2002. "The Making of a Slave Conspiracy, Part 2." *William and Mary Quarterly* Third Series, 59: 135–202.

Grube, G. M. A. 1974. *Plato's "Republic."* Indianapolis, IN: Hackett.

Gruen, Erich S. 1966. "P. Clodius: Instrument or Independent Agent?" *Phoenix* 20: 120–130.

———. 1969. "Notes on the 'First Catilinarian Conspiracy.'" *Classical Philology* 64: 20–24.

———. 1974. *The Last Generation of the Roman Republic*. Berkeley: University of California.

Habicht, Christian. 1990. *Cicero the Politician*. Baltimore: The Johns Hopkins University.

Hardie, Alex. 1997–1998. "Juvenal, Domitian, and the Accession of Hadrian (*Satire* 4)." *Bulletin of the Institute of Classical Studies* 42: 117–144.

———. 1998. "Juvenal, the *Phaedrus*, and the Truth about Rome." *Classical Quarterly* n.s. 48: 234–251.

Hardwick, Lorna. 2003. *Reception Studies*. Oxford: Oxford University.

Hardy, E. G. 1917. "The Catilinarian Conspiracy in its Context: A Re-Study of the Evidence." *Journal of Roman Studies* 7: 153–228.

Harrill, J. Albert. 2008. "Cannibalistic Language in the Fourth Gospel and Greco-Roman Polemics of Factionalism (John 6:52–66)." *Journal of Biblical Literature* 127: 133–158.

Hart, H. L. A. 1968. "Prolegomena to the Principles of Punishment." In *Punishment and Responsibility: Essays in the Philosophy of Law*. Oxford: Clarendon: 1–27.

Henderson, M. I. 1950. "De Commentariolo Petitionis." *Journal of Roman Studies* 40: 8–21.

Highet, Gilbert. 1954. *Juvenal the Satirist: A Study*. Oxford: Clarendon.

Hinds, Stephen. 2007. "Ovid among the Conspiracy Theorists." In *Classical Constructions: Papers in Memory of Don Fowler, Classicist and Epicurean*, S. J. Heyworth, with P. G. Fowler and S. J. Harrison, eds. Oxford: Oxford University: 194–220.

Hofstadter, Richard. 2008. *The Paranoid Style in American Politics and Other Essays*. New York: Vintage Books, Vintage Edition.

Hooley, Daniel M. 2007. *Roman Satire*. Malden, MA: Blackwell.

Hooper, William Davis. 1993 (reprint). *Marcus Porcius Cato: "On Agriculture"; Marcus Terentius Varro: "On Agriculture."* Cambridge, MA: Loeb Classical Library.

Hopkins, Keith. 1978. *Conquerors and Slaves*. Cambridge: Cambridge University.

Horn, Eva, and Rabinbach, Anson. 2008. "Introduction." *New German Critique* 103: 1–8.

Hunter, Richard. 1985. *The New Comedy of Greece and Rome*. Cambridge: Cambridge University.

Hunter, Virginia J. 1994. *Policing Athens: Social Control in the Attic Lawsuits, 420–320 B.C.* Princeton: Princeton University.

Hurley, Donna W. 2001. *Suetonius "Divus Claudius."* Cambridge: Cambridge University.

Husting, Ginna, and Orr, Martin. 2007. "Dangerous Machinery: 'Conspiracy Theorist' as a Transpersonal Strategy of Exclusion." *Symbolic Interaction* 30: 127–150.

Ihm, Maximilian. 1933. *C. Suetoni Tranquilli Opera*. Vol. I: De Vita Caesarum Libri VIII. Leipzig: Teubner.

Ireland, S. 1990. *Terence: The Mother in Law*. Warminster: Aris and Phillips.

Jähne, Armin. 1986. *Spartacus: Kampf der Sklaven*. Berlin: Deutscher Verlag der Wissenschaften.

James, Sharon L. 1998. "From Boys to Men: Rape and Developing Masculinity in Terence's *Hecyra* and *Eunuchus*." *Helios* 25: 31–47.

Jones, A. H. M. 1970. *Augustus*. New York: W. W. Norton and Company.

Jones, Brian W. 1992. *The Emperor Domitian*. London: Routledge.

———. 1996. *Suetonius: Domitian*. Bristol: Bristol Classical.

———. 2000. *Suetonius: Vespasian*. Bristol: Bristol Classical.

Jones, Francis L. 1939. "The First Conspiracy of Catiline." *Classical Journal* 34: 410–422.

Kaplan, Arthur. 1973. "Religious Dictators of the Roman Republic." *Classical World* 67: 172–175.

Katz, Leo. 1987. *Bad Acts and Guilty Minds: Conundrums of the Criminal Law*. Chicago: University of Chicago.

Kauer, Robert, and Lindsay, Wallace M. 1990 (reprint). *P. Terenti Afri Comoediae*. Oxford: Oxford University.

Kavka, Gregory S. 1978. "Some Paradoxes of Deterrence." *The Journal of Philosophy* 75: 285–302.

Keane, Catherine. 2003. "Theatre, Spectacle, and the Satirist in Juvenal." *Phoenix* 57: 257–275.

————. 2012. "Historian and Satirist: Tacitus and Juvenal." In *A Companion to Tacitus*, V. E. Pagán, ed. Malden, MA: Wiley-Blackwell: 403–427.

Keaveney, Arthur. 1992. *Lucullus: A Life*. London: Routledge.

Keeley, Brian L. 1999. "Of Conspiracy Theories." *The Journal of Philosophy* 96: 109–126.

= 2006. "Of Conspiracy Theories." In *Conspiracy Theories: The Philosophical Debate*, D. Coady, ed. Hampshire: Ashgate: 45–60.

————. 2007. "God as the Ultimate Conspiracy Theory." *Episteme: A Journal of Social Epistemology* 4: 135–149.

Ker, James. 2012. "Seneca in Tacitus." In *A Companion to Tacitus*, V. E. Pagán, ed. Malden, MA: Wiley-Blackwell: 305–329.

Knight, Peter. 2000. *Conspiracy Culture: From the Kennedy Assassination to "The X-Files."* London: Routledge.

Koestermann, Erich. 1968. *Cornelius Tacitus "Annalen."* Band IV: Buch 14–16. Heidelberg: Carl Winter.

Konstan, David. 1974. "Terence's *Hecyra*." *Far Western Forum* 1: 23–34.

————. 1983. *Roman Comedy*. Ithaca, NY: Cornell University.

Kruglanski, Arie W. 1987. "Blame-Placing Schemata and Attributional Research." In *Changing Conceptions of Conspiracy*, C. F. Graumann and S. Moscovici, eds. New York: Springer-Verlag: 219–229.

Lamb, W. R. M. 1988 (reprint). *Lysias*. Cambridge, MA: Loeb Classical Library.

Lambrecht, Ulrich. 1984. *Herrscherbild und Principatsidee in Suetons Kaiserbiographien*. Bonn: R. Habelt.

Lanni, Adriaan. 1997. "Spectator Sport or Serious Politics? οἱ περιεστηκότες and the Athenian Lawcourts." *Journal of Hellenic Studies* 117: 183–189.

————. 2004. "Arguing from 'Precedent': Modern Perspectives on Athenian Practice." In *The Law and the Courts in Ancient Greece*, E. M. Harris and L. Rubinstein, eds. London: Duckworth: 159–171.

Last, Hugh. 1948. "Sallust and Caesar in the *Bellum Catilinae*." In *Mélanges de philologie, de littérature et d'histoire anciennes offerts à J. Marouzeau*. Paris: Les Belles Lettres: 355–369.

Lefèvre, Eckard. 1999. *Terenz' und Apollodors Hecyra*. Munich: C. H. Beck.

Lepore, Jill. 2005. *New York Burning: Liberty, Slavery, and Conspiracy in Eighteenth-Century Manhattan*. New York: Alfred A. Knopf.

Levene, David S. 1993. *Religion in Livy*. Leiden: E. J. Brill.

Levens, R. G. C. 1980 (reprint). *Cicero: The Fifth Verrine Oration*. J. H. Betts, ed. Bristol: Bristol Classical Press.

Levick, Barbara. 1976. *Tiberius the Politician*. London: Thames and Hudson.

Levy, Neil. 2007. "Radically Socialized Knowledge and Conspiracy Theories." *Episteme: A Journal of Social Epistemology* 4: 181–192.

Lincoln, Bruce. 1989. *Discourse and the Construction of Society: Comparative Studies of Myth, Ritual, and Classification*. New York: Oxford University.

Lintott, Andrew. 1999. *The Constitution of the Roman Republic*. Oxford: Clarendon.

Littman, Robert J. 1976. "The Meaning of *Polyphagus*." *American Journal of Philology* 97: 369.

Lowrie, Michèle. 2008. "Evidence and Narrative in Mérimée's *Catilinarian Conspiracy*." *New German Critique* 103: 9–25.

Luce, T. J. 1965. "The Dating of Livy's First Decade." *Transactions of the American Philological Association* 96: 209–240.

Luke, Trevor. 2010. "Ideology and Humor in Suetonius' *Life of Vespasian* 8." *Classical World* 103: 511–527.

Lutz, Cora. 1950. "Any Resemblance . . . Is Purely Coincidental." *Classical Journal* 46: 115–120.

Macé, Alcide. 1900. *Essai sur Suétone*. Paris: Bibliothèque des Écoles Françaises d'Athènes et de Rome.

Mackenzie, Mary Margaret. 1981. *Plato on Punishment*. Berkeley: University of California.

MacMullen, Ramsay. 1966. *Enemies of the Roman Order: Treason, Unrest, and Alienation in the Empire*. London: Routledge.

Mandik, Pete. 2007. "Shit Happens." *Episteme: A Journal of Social Epistemology* 4: 205–218.

Marec, Ervan, and Pflaum, Hans-Georg. 1952. "Nouvelle inscription sur la carrière de Suétone, l'historien." *Comptes-rendus des séances de l'Académie des inscriptions et belles-lettres* 96: 76–85.

Marincola, John. 1997. *Authority and Tradition in Ancient Historiography*. Cambridge: Cambridge University.

Maróti, Egon. 1961. "*De Suppliciis*: Zur Frage der sizilianischen Zusammenhänge des Spartacus-Aufstandes." *Acta Antiqua Academiae Scientiarum Hungaricae* 90: 41–70.

Martin, Ronald H. 1990. "Structure and Interpretation in the 'Annals' of Tacitus." *Aufstieg und Niedergang der römischen Welt* 2.33.2: 1500–1581.

Mayor, Adrienne. 2010. *Poison King: The Life and Legend of Mithridates, Rome's Deadliest Enemy*. Princeton: Princeton University.

McDermott, William C. 1949. "Vettius Ille, Ille Noster Index." *Transactions of the American Philological Association* 80: 351–367.

McGee, Jennifer. 2011. "Conspiracy Theory in the Age of the Internet: The Case of the 'Birthers'." Aichi *Shukutoku Daigaku chi no akaibu (ribozutori) [ASKA-R: Aichi Shukutoku Knowledge Archive (repository)]* 1: 53–66. Web. 5 Aug. 2011. ⟨http://hdl.handle .net/10638/1155⟩.

McKeown, Niall. 2007a. *The Invention of Ancient Slavery?* London: Duckworth.

———. 2007b. "The Sound of John Henderson Laughing: Pliny 3.14 and Roman Slave-owners' Fear of Their Slaves." In *Fear of Slaves—Fear of Enslavement in the Ancient Mediterranean*. A. Serghidou, ed. Franche-Comté: Presses universitaires de Franche-Comté: 265–279.

Melley, Timothy. 2000. *Empire of Conspiracy: The Culture of Paranoia in Postwar America*. Ithaca, NY: Cornell University.

Milnor, Kristina. 2005. *Gender, Domesticity, and the Age of Augustus: Inventing Private Life*. Oxford: Oxford University.

Momigliano, Arnaldo. 1971. *The Development of Greek Biography*. Cambridge, MA: Harvard University.

Morford, Mark. 1972. "A Note on Juvenal 6.627–61." *Classical Philology* 67: 198.

———. 1977. "Juvenal's Fifth Satire." *American Journal of Philology* 98: 219–245.

Morgan, Gwyn. 2006. *69 A.D.: The Year of Four Emperors*. Oxford: Oxford University.

Moscovici, Serge. 1987. "The Conspiracy Mentality." In *Changing Conceptions of Conspiracy*, C. F. Graumann and S. Moscovici, eds. New York: Springer-Verlag: 151–169.

Müller, Karl, ed. 1975 (reprint). *Fragmenta Historicorum Graecorum*, 5 vols. Frankfurt am Main: Minerva.

Muse, Kevin. 2007. "Sergestus and Tarchon in the *Aeneid*." *Classical Quarterly* n.s. 57: 586–605.

Nisbet, R. G. M. 1992. "The Orator and the Reader: Manipulation and Response in Cicero's *Fifth Verrine.*" In *Author and Audience in Latin Literature*, A. J. Woodman and J. Powell, eds. Cambridge: Cambridge University: 1–17, 216–218.

Nörr, Dieter. 1983. "C. Cassius Longinus: der Jurist als Rhetor (Bemerkungen zu Tacitus, *Ann.* 14.42–45)." In *Althistorische Studien: Festschrift H. Bengtson*, H. Heinen, K. Stroheker, and G. Walser, eds. Wiesbaden: Franz Steiner: 187–222.

Norwood, Gilbert. 1923. *The Art of Terence.* Oxford: Basil Blackwell.

Nousek, Debra. 2010. "Echoes of Cicero in Livy's Bacchanalian Narrative (39.8–19)." *Classical Quarterly* n.s. 60: 156–166.

Oakley, S. P. 1998. *A Commentary on Livy Books VI–X.* Vol. II: Books VII–VIII. Oxford: Clarendon.

Ogilvie, R. M. 1965. *A Commentary on Livy, Books 1–5.* Oxford: Clarendon.

Owen, David S. 2010. "Othering Obama: How Whiteness is Used to Undermine Authority." *Altre Modernità, Other Modernities* 3: 112–119.

Pagán, Victoria Emma. 2004. *Conspiracy Narratives in Roman History.* Austin: University of Texas.

———. 2006. *Rome and the Literature of Gardens.* London: Duckworth.

———. 2008. "Toward a Model of Conspiracy Theory for Ancient Rome." *New German Critique* 103: 27–49.

———. 2010. "Forestalling Violence in Sallust and Vergil." *Mouseion* 10.1: 23–44.

Parker, Holt N. 1998. "Loyal Slaves and Loyal Wives: The Crisis of the Outsider—Within and Roman *exemplum* Literature." In *Women and Slaves in Greco-Roman Culture: Differential Equations*, S. R. Joshel and S. Murnaghan, eds. London: Routledge: 152–173.

Patterson, Orlando. 1982. *Slavery and Social Death: A Comparative Study.* Cambridge, MA: Harvard University.

Pauw, D. A. 1980. "Impersonal Expressions and Unidentified Spokesmen in Greek and Roman Historiography and Biography." *Acta Classica* 23: 83–95.

Penwill, J. L. 2004. "The Unlovely Lover of Terence's *Hecyra.*" *Ramus* 33: 130–149.

Phillips, John. 2006. "Review of Pagán, *Conspiracy Narratives in Roman History.*" *Southern Humanities Review* 40: 290–293.

Pierce, Karen F. 1997. "The Portrayal of Rape in New Comedy." In *Rape in Antiquity*, S. Deacy and K. F. Pierce, eds. Swansea: Classical Press of Wales: 163–184.

Pigden, Charles. 1995. "Popper Revisited, or What Is Wrong with Conspiracy Theories?" *Philosophy of the Social Sciences* 25: 3–34. = 2006. "Popper Revisited, or What Is Wrong with Conspiracy Theories?" In *Conspiracy Theories: The Philosophical Debate*, David Coady, ed. Hampshire: Ashgate: 17–44.

———. 2006. "Complots of Mischief." In *Conspiracy Theories: The Philosophical Debate*, David Coady, ed. Hampshire: Ashgate: 139–166.

———. 2007. "Conspiracy Theories and Conventional Wisdom." *Episteme: A Journal of Social Epistemology* 4: 219–232.

Pipes, Daniel. 1997. *Conspiracy: How the Paranoid Style Flourishes and Where It Comes From.* New York: Free Press.

Poma, Gabriella. 1978. "Le secessioni e il rito dell'infissione del *clavus.*" *Rivista Storica dell'Antichità* 8: 39–50.

Popper, Karl. 1966. *The Open Society and Its Enemies.* 5th edition revised. Princeton: Princeton University.

Potter, David S. 1991. "The Inscriptions on the Bronze Herakles from Mesene: Vologeses

IV's War with Rome and the Date of Tacitus' *Annales*." *Zeitschrift für Papyrologie und Epigraphik* 88: 277–290.

Power, Tristan J. 2009. "Suetonius *Galba* 1: Beginning or Ending?" *Classical Philology* 104: 216–220.

Reynolds, L. D. 1991. *C. Sallusti Crispi: Catilina, Iugurtha, Historiarum Fragmenta Selecta.* Oxford: Clarendon.

Richlin, Amy. 1984. "Invective against Women in Roman Satire." *Arethusa* 17: 67–80.

———. 1992. *The Garden of Priapus: Sexuality and Aggression in Roman Humor.* Revised edition. New York: Oxford University.

Riggsby, Andrew M. 1999. *Crime and Community in Ciceronian Rome.* Austin: University of Texas.

Roberto, Umberto. 2005. *Ioannis Antiocheni Fragmenta ex Historia Chronica.* Berlin: Walter de Gruyter.

Robinson, O. F. 2007. *Penal Practice and Penal Policy in Ancient Rome.* London: Routledge.

Roisman, Joseph. 2006. *The Rhetoric of Conspiracy in Ancient Athens.* Berkeley: University of California.

Rosivach, Vincent J. 1998. *When a Young Man Falls in Love: The Sexual Exploitation of Women in New Comedy.* London: Routledge.

Rutledge, Steven. 1998. "Trajan and Tacitus' Audience: Reader Reception of *Annals* 1–2." *Ramus* 27: 141–159.

———. 2001. *Imperial Inquisitions: Prosecutors and Informants from Tiberius to Domitian.* London: Routledge.

Sailor, Dylan. 2008. *Writing and Empire in Tacitus.* Cambridge: Cambridge University.

Saller, Richard. 1980. "Anecdotes as Historical Evidence for the Principate." *Greece and Rome* 27: 69–83.

Salmon, E. T. 1935. "Catiline, Crassus, and Caesar." *American Journal of Philology* 56: 302–316.

Scott, Kenneth. 1933. "The Political Propaganda of 44–30 B.C." *Memoirs of the American Academy in Rome* 11: 7–49.

Seager, Robin. 1964. "The First Catilinarian Conspiracy." *Historia* 13: 338–347.

Sharrock, Alison. 2009. *Reading Roman Comedy: Poetics and Playfulness in Plautus and Terence.* Cambridge: Cambridge University.

Shaw, Brent D. 2001. *Spartacus and the Slave Wars: A Brief History with Documents.* Boston: St. Martin's.

Sherwin-White, A. N. 1966. *The Letters of Pliny: A Historical and Social Commentary.* Oxford: Clarendon.

Shumate, Nancy. 2006. *Nation, Empire, Decline: Studies in Rhetorical Continuity from the Romans to the Modern Era.* London: Duckworth.

Slater, Niall W. 1988. "The Fictions of Patriarchy in Terence's *Hecyra*." *Classical World* 81: 249–260.

Smith, Clement Lawrence. 1901. "A Preliminary Study of Certain Manuscripts of Suetonius' *Lives of the Caesars*." *Harvard Studies in Classical Philology* 12: 19–58.

———. 1905. "A Preliminary Study of Certain Manuscripts of Suetonius' *Lives of the Caesars*: Second Paper." *Harvard Studies in Classical Philology* 16: 1–14.

Sørensen, Villy. 1984. *Seneca: The Humanist at the Court of Nero.* Translated by W. G. Jones. Edinburgh and Chicago: Canongate and the University of Chicago.

Soubiran, J. 1964. "Thèmes et rythmes d'épopée dans les *Annales* de Tacite." *Pallas* 12: 55–79.

Spencer, Walter Elliott. 2001. "Conspiracy Narratives in Latin Literature." PhD, Classical Philology, University of Illinois, Urbana-Champaign.

Stanev, Nikola. 1981. "Un Heros Condamne: Configurations a l'appreciation de la posterite." In *Spartacus: Symposium Rebus Spartaci Gestis Dedicatum 2050 A.* Sofia: Editions de l'Académie Bulgare des Sciences: 95–101.

Stangl, Thomas. 1964. *Ciceronis Orationum Scholiastae.* Hildesheim: Georg Olms.

Stevens, C. E. 1963. "The Plotting of B.C. 66/65." *Latomus* 22: 397–435.

Stockton, David. 1971. *Cicero: A Political Biography.* Oxford: Oxford University.

Strauss, Barry. 2009. *The Spartacus War.* New York: Simon and Schuster.

Sukic, Christine. 2006. "'I stand on change and shall dissolve in changing': Une représentation baroque de l'héroïsme." *Etudes Epistémè* 9: 215–233.

Syme, Ronald. 1939. *The Roman Revolution.* Oxford: Oxford University.

———. 1958. *Tacitus,* 2 vols. Oxford: Clarendon.

———. 1964. *Sallust.* Berkeley: University of California.

———. 1971. *Emperors and Biography: Studies in the "Historia Augusta."* Oxford: Clarendon.

———. 1977. "The Enigmatic Sospes." *Journal of Roman Studies* 67: 38–49.

———. 1980a. "Biographers of the Caesars." *Museum Helveticum* 37: 104–128.

———. 1980b. "Guard Prefects of Trajan and Hadrian." *Journal of Roman Studies* 70: 64–80.

———. 1982. "The Marriage of Rubellius Blandus." *American Journal of Philology* 103: 62–85.

Sztompka, Piotr. 1999. *Trust: A Sociological Theory.* Cambridge: Cambridge University.

Tannenbaum, R. F. 2005. "What Caesar Said: Rhetoric and History in Sallust's *Coniuratio Catilinae* 51." In *Roman Crossings: Theory and Practice in the Roman Republic,* K. Welch and T. Hillard, eds. Swansea: Classical Press of Wales: 209–223.

Tatum, W. Jeffrey. 1991. "Review of Bradley, *Slavery and Rebellion in the Roman World, 140 B.C.–70 B.C.*" *Classical Philology* 86: 252–258.

Taylor, C. C. W. 1982. "Plato on Punishment." *Classical Review* 32: 198–200.

Taylor, Lily Ross. 1950. "The Date and the Meaning of the Vettius Affair." *Historia* 1: 45–51.

Tempest, Kathryn. 2007. "Saints and Sinners: Some Thoughts on the Presentation of Character in Attic Oratory and Cicero's Verrines." In *Sicilia Nutrix Plebis Romanae: Rhetoric, Law, and Taxation in Cicero's Verrines,* J. R. W. Prag, ed. London: Institute of Classical Studies: 19–36.

Thompson, Edward Arthur. 1974. "Peasant Revolts in Late Roman Gaul and Spain." In *Studies in Ancient Society,* M. I. Finley, ed. London: Routledge and Kegan Paul: 304–320 = 1952. "Peasant Revolts in Late Roman Gaul and Spain." *Past and Present* 2: 11–23.

Tiffen, Rodney. 2005. "Deep Throat Comes Out: Revisiting Watergate." In *Australian Review of Public Affairs,* Digest 25 July 2005. Web. 5 Aug. 2011. ⟨http://www.austra lianreview.net/digest/2005/07/tiffen.html⟩.

Townend, G. B. 1959. "The Date and Composition of Suetonius' *Caesares.*" *Classical Quarterly* n.s. 9: 285–293.

———. 1961. "The Hippo Inscription and the Career of Suetonius." *Historia* 10: 99–109.

———. 1972. "The Earliest Scholiast on Juvenal." *Classical Quarterly* n.s. 22: 376–387.

———. 1973. "The Literary Substrata to Juvenal's Satires." *Journal of Roman Studies* 63: 148–160.

Toynbee, Arnold J. 1965. *Hannibal's Legacy: The Hannibalic War's Effects on Roman Life,* Volume II. Oxford: Oxford University.

Treggiari, Susan. 1985. "Review of Hopkins, *Death and Renewal*." *American Journal of Philology* 106: 256–262.

Urbainczyk, Theresa. 2004. *Spartacus*. London: Bristol Classical Press.

van den Berg, Christopher S. 2012. "Deliberative Oratory in the *Annals* and the *Dialogus*." In *A Companion to Tacitus*, V. E. Pagán, ed. Malden, MA: Wiley-Blackwell: 189–211.

Vasaly, Ann. 1993. *Representations: Images of the World in Ciceronian Oratory*. Berkeley: University of California.

Venturini, Carlo. 1980. "La conclusione del processo di Verre (osservazioni e problemi)." *Ciceroniana* 4: 155–175.

Verbrugghe, Gerald P. 1972. "Sicily 210–70 B.C.: Livy, Cicero, and Diodorus." *Transactions of the American Philological Association* 103: 535–559.

von Stackelberg, Katharine T. 2009. "Performative Space and Garden Transgressions in Tacitus' Death of Messalina." *American Journal of Philology* 130: 595–624.

Vout, Caroline. 2007. *Power and Eroticism in Imperial Rome*. Cambridge: Cambridge University.

Vretska, Karl. 1976. *C. Sallustius Crispus: "De Catilinae Coniuratione."* Vol. 2. Heidelberg: Carl Winter.

Wallace-Hadrill, Andrew. 1982. "*Civilis Princeps*: Between Citizen and King." *Journal of Roman Studies* 72: 32–48.

———. 1983. *Suetonius: The Scholar and His Caesars*. New Haven: Yale University.

Walsh, P. G. 1994. *Livy Book XXXIX (187–183 B.C.)*. Warminster: Aris and Phillips.

Walters, Jonathan. 1998. "Making a Spectacle: Deviant Men, Invective, and Pleasure." *Arethusa* 31: 355–367.

Wardle, D. 1992. "Cluvius Rufus and Suetonius." *Hermes* 120: 466–482.

Wellesley, Kenneth, ed. 1986. *Cornelii Taciti "Ab Excessu Divi Augusti Libri XI–XVI."* Leipzig: Teubner.

West, Harry G., and Sanders, Todd, eds. 2003. *Transparency and Conspiracy: Ethnographies of Suspicion in the New World Order*. Durham, NC: Duke University.

Westerman, William Linn. 1945. "Slave Maintenance and Slave Revolts." *Classical Philology* 40: 1–10.

White, Hayden. 1973. *Metahistory: The Historical Imagination in Nineteenth-Century Europe*. Baltimore: The Johns Hopkins University.

Williams, Kathryn F. 2006. "Pliny and the Murder of Larcius Macedo." *Classical Journal* 101: 409–424.

Wilson, Marcus. 2003. "After the Silence: Tacitus, Suetonius, Juvenal." In *Flavian Rome: Culture, Image, Text*, A. J. Boyle and W. J. Dominik, eds., Leiden: Brill: 523–542.

Wolf, Joseph Georg. 1988. *Das Senatusconsultum Silanianum und die Senatsrede des C. Cassius Longinus aus dem Jahre 61 n. Chr.* Heidelberg: Carl Winter.

Wolpert, Andrew. 2002. *Remembering Defeat: Civil War and Civic Memory in Ancient Athens*. Baltimore: The Johns Hopkins University.

Woodman, A. J. 2004. *Tacitus: "The Annals."* Indianapolis, IN: Hackett.

Wyke, Maria. 1997. *Projecting the Past: Ancient Rome, Cinema, and History*. New York: Routledge.

Zernike, Kate. 2011. "Conspiracies Are Us." *New York Times*, May 1, 2011: News, p. 1.

Zukier, Henri. 1987. "The Conspiratorial Imperative: Medieval Jewry in Western Europe." In *Changing Conceptions of Conspiracy*, C. F. Graumann and S. Moscovici, eds. New York: Springer-Verlag: 87–103.

BIBLIOGRAPHY

INDEX LOCORUM

2.24–28, 50, 52, 142n25; 2.25, 145n91;
2.29–35, 144n77; 2.47, 140n2; 2.99–
103, 143n65; 2.163–170, 65; 3.13–14,
64; 3.49–54, 51, 63, 142n26; 3.58–125,
64; 3.60–61, 63; 3.63, 63; 3.84–85,
63; 3.93–99, 64; 3.100, 64; 3.112, 64;
3.[113], 146n105; 3.116–118, 141n22,
143n61; 3.122–124, 64; 3.222, 140n4;
3.306–308, 141n16; 4.1–33, 146n99;
4.37–38, 58, 144n71; 4.46–48, 144n74;
4.72–118, 58; 4.102–103, 58; 4.104–
106, 58; 4.110, 144n76; 4.137, 143n56;
4.147, 140n7; 4.153, 47; 4.153–154,
141n22; 5.36–37, 141n22, 143n61; 5.52–
55, 140n7; 5.146–148, 141n22, 143n55;
6.105, 142n30; 6.112, 142n30; 6.114–
132, 56; 6.114–135, 141n22; 6.133–134,
143n55; 6.185–199, 63; 6.190, 63; 6.231–
241, 47, 135n33; 6.272, 140n12; 6.385,
141n22, 144n78; 6.451, 140n12; 6.527–
530, 63; 6.531, 63; 6.532–541, 63; 6.542–
547, 63; 6.548–552, 63; 6.553, 63; 6.558–
559, 143–4n65; 6.[559], 141n22; 6.615,
143n56; 6.615–617, 141n22; 6.620–623,
143n55; 6.620–626, 141n22; 6.634–
640, 139n91; 6.638, 141n22, 143n60;
6.655–661, 29, 135n28; 6.660–661,
143n55; 7, 120; 7.35, 140n12; 7.79, 56,
141n22; 7.91, 141n22, 143n61; 7.199,
142n32; 8.39–40, 54, 142n39; 8.39–70,
59; 8.40, 141n22; 8.72, 143n56; 8.90,
145n82; 8.105–106, 59; 8.105–107, 52,
142n28; 8.[170], 143n56; 8.193, 143n56;
8.211–212, 56, 143n57; 8.212, 59, 141n22;
8.[223], 143n56; 8.231–239, 53, 142n34;
8.231–244, 59; 8.235, 53, 59; 8.259–
268, 58–59, 144–5n79; 9.96, 140n12;
9.145–146, 141n23; 10.1–5, 48, 140n8;
10.4, 57; 10.4–5, 123; 10.15–16, 141n22;
10.15–18, 56, 57, 143n58; 10.19–21, 57,
60, 144n66; 10.20–21, 141n22; 10.58–
64, 55; 10.61–72, 55, 57; 10.65–67, 55,
143n51; 10.69–72, 55, 143n52; 10.71, 55;
10.73, 140n12; 10.122, 52; 10.122–123,
57; 10.123–125, 142n32; 10.286–288, 52;
10.288, 57; 10.308, 143n56; 10.329–336,
56; 10.329–345, 57, 141n22; 11.100, 64;
11.108–109, 64; 11.116, 64; 11.117–118,

64, 146n108; 11.120, 64; 12.129, 141n22;
13.17, 57, 141n22; 13.84, 145n82; 13.162–
165, 140n7; 14, 47; 14.28–29, 140n5;
14.41–42, 52; 14.96–106, 146n107;
14.187, 140n7; 14.252–253, 143n55;
14.328–331, 56; 14.330, 141n22; 15.1–13,
59; 15.26, 59; 15.27, 47, 145n96; 15.37,
140n12; 15.71, 140n12; 15.78–81, 60,
145n82; 15.83, 15.87–88, 60, 145n85;
15.94, 60; 15.110–112, 147n113; 15.120–
131, 60; 15.129–131, 60; 15.142–143, 61,
145n89; 15.146–149, 61, 145n89; 15.159,
61; 15.171, 62; 15.171–174, 61, 145n92;
16.29–30, 141n23

Livy 1.10.7, 142n29; 2.3–6, 59; 4.45.1–2,
43, 139n94; 7.3, 139n93; 7.10.5, 43;
8.6.3, 42; 8.18, 139nn91,93; 8.18.2–3,
42, 138n89; 8.18.4, 42; 8.18.5–9, 42;
8.18.11, 12, 13, 42; 8.18.12, 42, 139n93;
9.18.4, 42; 9.28, 139n93; 10.18.7, 42;
10.25.12, 42; 22.33.1, 139n96; 25.40.2,
64, 146n109; 32.26, 36; 32.26.7, 36;
32.26.10, 37; 33.36, 37; 33.36.3, 37;
34.2.3–4, 134n24; 39.6.7, 146n110;
39.29.8–10, 37; 39.29.9, 37; 39.41.6,
37; 40.19.9–11, 37
Lucan 8.5–8, 57, 144n67
Lysias 12.85, 73, 149n37; 12.88, 73, 149n38;
26.14, 73, 149n39; 27.7, 73, 149n40

Martial 2.34.6, 143n60; 4.43, 6.75, 139n91,
143n60

Pausanias 8.9.7, 146n98
Pliny *Ep.* 1.18, 152n2; *Ep.* 1.20.10, 134n7;
    Ep. 1.24, 152n2; *Ep.* 3.14, 41, 138n83;
    Ep. 3.14.5, 138n82; *Ep.* 3.8, 89; *Ep.* 5.5,
    145n87; *Ep.* 5.8, 145n87; *Ep.* 5.10,
    152n2; *Ep.* 8.12, 145n87; *Ep.* 9.34,
    152n2; *Ep.* 10.94, 152n2; *Pan.* 48–49,
    144n73, 158n120
Pliny *Nat.* 10.74, 155n53; *Nat.* 16.108,
    155n53
Plutarch *Cic.* 28–29, 149n50; *Cic.* 46.2–3,
    150n52; *Galba* 15.2, 143n62; *Luc.* 42.7,
    157n89; *Num.* 4.1–2, 146n107
Polybius 9.10, 146n109

Tacitus *Ag.* 3.3, 159n23; *Ann.* 1.1.3, 49,
141n18; *Ann.* 1.10.2, 97; *Ann.* 2.13, 101;
Ann. 3.23, 142n42; *Ann.* 3.51.1, 142n42;
Ann. 4.1, 143nn48,50; *Ann.* 4.27, 44,
139–140n97; *Ann.* 4.32–33, 141n18;
Ann. 4.33.4, 141n18; *Ann.* 4.34, 155n53;
Ann. 4.57, 143n48; *Ann.* 5.11.1, 55–56;
Ann. 6.27, 54; *Ann.* 6.27.1, 142n41;
Ann. 11.26–38, 56, 143n54; *Ann.* 13.19.3,
54, 143nn43,45; *Ann.* 14.22.1, 54;
Ann. 14.22.3, 54; *Ann.* 14.42, 14.45,
81; *Ann.* 14.42.1, 81, 151nn80,82;
Ann. 14.42.2, 80, 81; *Ann.* 14.43–
44, 20, 67, 80; *Ann.* 14.43.1, 80,
85; *Ann.* 14.43.2, 83; *Ann.* 14.43.3,
82, 84; *Ann.* 14.43.4, 84, 85, 151n81;
Ann. 14.44.1, 83, 151n87; *Ann.* 14.44.3,
41, 84, 138n85; *Ann.* 14.44.4, 82,
83; *Ann.* 14.45.1, 81, 85, 151n92;
Ann. 14.45.2, 85; *Ann.* 14.51.1, 85;
Ann. 14.53–57, 85; *Ann.* 14.53.3, 86,
152n95; *Ann.* 14.59, 55; *Ann.* 15.38.1,
4, 129n12; *Ann.* 15.44.2, 4, 129n13;
Ann. 15.44.4, 4, 53, 130n14, 142n37;
Ann. 15.60.1, 143n59; *Ann.* 15.60.2–
64, 143n59; *Ann.* 15.68.1, 147n10;
Ann. 15.73.1, 156n73; *Ann.* 16.9.1,
143n59; *Ann.* 16.21–35, 56; *Hist.* 1.1.4,
18, 133n78, 159nn21,23; *Hist.* 1.7,
143n63; *Hist.* 1.25.2, 157n108; *Hist.*
2.64.2, 156n75; *Hist.* 2.89.2, 156n75;
Hist. 3.62, 143n63; *Hist.* 3.67.1, 156n75;
Hist. 3.84.4, 144n70; *Hist.* 4.13.1,
143n64

Terence *Hec.* 72–73, 35; *Hec.* 76–197, 30;
Hec. 120–122, 35; *Hec.* 161–170, 35;
Hec. 179–181, 136n46; *Hec.* 187–188,
136n47; *Hec.* 198–204, 30, 135n35; *Hec.*
274–280, 34; *Hec.* 299, 136n50; *Hec.*
316–317, 30; *Hec.* 323, 136n51; *Hec.*
357, 34; *Hec.* 361–414, 30; *Hec.* 400,
30; *Hec.* 451–515, 31; *Hec.* 466–467,
136n48; *Hec.* 477–481, 136n52; *Hec.*
516–576, 31; *Hec.* 577–622, 31; *Hec.*
600, 136n55; *Hec.* 623–726, 31; *Hec.*
654, 136n49; *Hec.* 816–840, 31; *Hec.*
830, 31; *Hec.* 862, 35; *Hec.* 865–868, 31,
32, 135n37

Valerius Maximus 9.2.1, 157n95
Varro *Rust.* 1.17.5, 41, 138n84
Velleius 2.61.4, 155n50
Vergil *Aen.* 5.121, 52

GENERAL INDEX

Acilius Glabrio, Manius, 37, 114
Aelius Lamia, 58, 114, 144n78
Aelius Spartianus, 120
agency, 3, 20, 64–65, 84; divine, 44
agency imperative, 33, 82
agency panic, 10
Agrippa, 86, 97, 111
Agrippina the Elder, 54, 99
Agrippina the Younger, 54, 56, 143n55
Alföldy, Géza, 40
"all and only," 71, 83
Allen, Danielle, 71, 72
allusion, 20, 23, 29, 45, 48–59, 67, 79, 91, 120–123
anagnoresis, 30, 32, 36
Anderson, William, 30, 36
anger, 18, 47–49, 60–61, 69, 78–79, 120
Antony, 76, 97
Aquilius, Gaius, 24, 25, 39
Aquilius Niger, 98, 100
Asinius Epicadus, 116
Attianus, 119
Augustus, 54, 86, 90, 97–99, 100, 102, 106, 109–112, 116
Aurelia, 107
Avidius Cassius, 116

Bacchanalian Conspiracy, 14, 37
Bacchis, 30–36, 92
Baldwin, Barry, 60
Basham, Lee, 9, 12, 14
Baurmann, Michael, 91–92
belief, 3–4, 10–11, 63, 83–84, 122

Berenice, 105
Berry, D. H., 78
"birther" movement, 122
blame, 1, 4, 5, 8, 15, 31–36, 43, 47–66 *passim*, 84, 120, 123
Bona Dea, 76, 107
boomerang effect, 93, 114
Bradley, Keith, 40, 117
Braund, Susanna, 47, 48, 51, 62, 64, 70
Burrus, 85

Caecilius of Caleacte, 37
Caecina, Aulus, 113
Caesar. *See* Julius Caesar
Caligula, 14, 99–103, 112, 116
Calpurnius Piso, Gnaeus, 99
cannibalism, 38, 59–60, 62
Carney, T. F., 90
Carter, John, 110
Cassius Longinus, Gaius, 20, 41, 67–68, 80–87, 123
Catilinarian Conspiracy, 3, 14, 16, 27, 52–54, 57, 59, 67, 76, 106; conspirators, 19, 20, 53, 67, 76, 78, 93, 123; first, 95–96
Catiline, 7, 28, 45, 50–55, 61–62, 65, 73, 76–79, 95–96
Cato the Elder, 1, 28, 139n91
Cato the Younger (Marcus Porcius Cato), 19, 20, 67, 68, 76–79, 84–87, 95, 109, 123
Celsus, 120
Christians, 4, 53, 54, 59, 65

www.ingramcontent.com/pod-product-compliance
Ingram Content Group UK Ltd.
Pitfield, Milton Keynes, MK11 3LW, UK
UKHW042139050325
455862UK00005B/375